TESTIMONIALS

Global Witness is part of a global Machiavellian plot.

MPLA government, Angola

Global Witness is just a bunch of well-intentioned hooligans.

Diamond-industry official quoted in *Poisoned Wells*, by Nick Shaxson

Global Witness is an enemy of the state.

General Salim Saleh, brother of Uganda's President Yoweri Museveni

Global Witness are worse than the Khmer Rouge.

Prime Minister Hun Sen of Cambodia

I will hit them until their heads are broken.

Hun Neng, former governor of Cambodia's Kampong Cham
Province and brother of Prime Minister Hun Sen

British Espionage Teams on Mission to Discredit Zimbabwe.

Story about Global Witness investigation, the *Herald*, 14 May 2001

Global Witness? I call them blind witness.

President Paul Kagame of Rwanda

Is Global Witness above the law?

Spokesman for Beny Steinmetz Group Resources, shortly before
losing a legal case they had brought against Global Witness

*It was very naughty of them...using their big power to blacken my
name. They're trying to frame people like me.*

Taib Mahmud, chief minister of Sarawak

Global Witness, Global Deceitful, Global Lies.

Catholic priest Miguel Piovesan, after Global Witness uncovered his links to illegal logging in Peru's last reserve for uncontactable tribes

Global Witness are amateurish to the point of bogus.

Mining billionaire Dan Gertler's Fleurette Group

Should I decide who are my friends because of the threat of investigation, pressure from Global Witness or public relations?' *Gertler said, rising from his chair to stride the room. 'Never!'*

Dan Gertler, shortly before being sanctioned by the US for corruption in DRC

[Global Witness] are a group of economic vandals who do not care about the lives they destroy.

Ivan Lu, executive director of Malaysian logging company Rimbunan Hijau (PNG) Ltd

Very Bad People

Very Bad People

The Inside Story of the Fight Against the World's Network of Corruption

Patrick Alley

monoray

First published in Great Britain in 2022 by Monoray, an imprint of
Octopus Publishing Group Ltd
Carmelite House
50 Victoria Embankment
London EC4Y 0DZ

www.octopusbooks.co.uk
An Hachette UK Company
www.hachette.co.uk

Distributed in the US by
Hachette Book Group
1290 Avenue of the Americas
4th and 5th Floors
New York, NY 10104

Distributed in Canada by
Canadian Manda Group
664 Annette St.
Toronto, Ontario, Canada M6S 2C8

ISBN 978-1-91318-348-6 (Hardback)
ISBN 978-1-91318-349-3 (Trade paperback)

A CIP catalogue record for this book is available from the British Library.

Printed and bound in the UK

10 9 8 7 6 5 4 3 2 1

This FSC® label means that materials used for the product have been
responsibly sourced

This **monoray** book was crafted and published by Jake Lingwood,
Alex Stetter, Monica Hope, Juliette Norsworthy, David Eldridge,
Ed Pickford and Serena Savisi.

This book is dedicated to those people around the world who daily risk their freedom, and sometimes their lives, standing up to the Very Bad People this book is about – I am humbled by what you do. I hope this book contributes something to the cause, even if that's only giving people some idea of what you're up against.

AUTHOR'S NOTE

Every story in this book is true. Global Witness's work can be dangerous and I have changed some names and anonymized the identities of many of our sources for their security, or because their jobs meant they shouldn't have talked to us in the first place. Some events I describe have been conflated to make the vast amounts of information we have, and their complexity, more manageable.

CONTENTS

The Prince of Darkness is a gentleman.

William Shakespeare, *King Lear*, Act 3, Scene 4

FOREWORD

By George Soros

My foundation has long been involved in promoting transparency and fighting corruption. Global Witness is one of the most effective and innovative groups working in this area. Global Witness first came to my attention in the early 2000s. More or less uniquely at the time, Global Witness focused on the nexus between human-rights abuses and environmental destruction, paying particular attention to the links between natural-resource exploitation, conflict and corruption.

I first met Global Witness's three young founders at my home in London. We were introduced by the then president of the Open Society Foundations, Aryeh Neier. The trio presented a business plan in the hope of receiving funding from OSF. They set out ambitious plans for an anti-corruption movement, based on some early successes in Cambodia and Angola. The business plan, like most such documents, was long and didn't say that much of interest. But one idea leaped off the page.

Frustrated by the theft of Angolan oil revenues by the country's own government, Global Witness developed a concept for a campaign that was eventually to be known as 'Publish What You Pay' (PWYP). The idea was to get oil and mining companies to disclose the payments they make to various governments. The amounts could then be added up and the governments could be held accountable by their people for the monies they received.

Global Witness as an organization was somewhat anarchic and had very little money, but I greatly admired the passion, ambition, leanness and anger of the founders. I wanted to see them develop their concept and challenge the status quo that allows such abuses in our system. I decided supporting them was a risk worth taking; my instinct was that Global Witness would find further success. It was a good instinct.

I used my influence and convening power to socialize the Publish What You Pay campaign idea with senior policymakers around the world, and I provided extra funding for Global Witness's work. In 2002, the campaign was formally launched. The British government soon took up the cause and formed the Extractive Industries Transparency Initiative (EITI), which has become the most important anti-corruption mechanism for the extractives sector. This was a significant step forward in the battle against corruption.

Global Witness's investigations around the world have gone on to unearth and expose many corrupt deals. Deals that deprived some of the world's poorest but resource-rich countries of billions of dollars that could otherwise have been spent on the health, education and other needs of their populations. Deals such as the US$1.1 billion paid by oil companies Shell and Eni to obtain one of Nigeria's richest oil blocks; the bribery behind an Israeli billionaire's initially successful attempt to take control of the world's richest untapped deposit of iron ore in Guinea for a pittance; and the timber-for-arms trade that propped up Liberian dictator Charles Taylor's brutal regime.

The purpose of Global Witness's exposés is always to use the evidence to create or reform governmental and intergovernmental policies and legislation, and to shift the norms of the way companies do business. I have always been very happy to apply whatever influence I have to help amplify Global Witness's advocacy efforts.

Twenty years have passed since our first meeting, numerous new laws have been passed to tackle corruption and my Open Society Foundations have been supporting Global Witness ever since.

I was delighted when Patrick told me he was writing a book about Global Witness's work. It is a story that needs to be heard. Patrick exposes an alarming shadow world of corrupt businesspeople and politicians, and the network of enablers and organized criminals behind them. Stories such as those you will read here are more usually found in the pages of thrillers, but these stories are frighteningly and unfortunately true. Corruption is one of the greatest enemies of democracy; to win the fight we need champions like Global Witness.

INTRODUCTION

HOTEL EUROPA, CINISELLO BALSAMO, MILAN, 4 AUGUST 2000

Leonid Minin opened a bleary eye as one of the prostitutes got up from the bed, grabbed her handbag and made her way to the bathroom, locking the door behind her. Her hands shaking, she fumbled around in her bag, found her phone and dialled her friend who was working the streets nearby. Unaware of this call and the danger it posed to him, Minin let his gaze move on around the room, taking in the evidence of what had been a pretty good party. Bottles of booze scattered everywhere, the floor littered with hurriedly discarded clothing, and one of the girls kneeling by the coffee table, busy preparing some of the best-quality cocaine you could buy. Leonid Minin liked sex and cocaine. Then he lay back and closed his eyes as the other two girls got back to work. And then suddenly the room was full of police.

What had started as a routine response to a call from a prostitute scared of an increasingly violent client had become a drugs bust. Minin was arrested, told to get dressed and carted away to the police station at nearby Monza. Then the detectives arrived and began to turn over the room. It turned out that the cocaine was one of the least interesting things they found.

The eyes of the preliminary judge assigned to the case widened as she examined the US$150,000 worth of cash in various currencies and the half a million dollars' worth of Russian diamonds the police had seized. Then she turned her attention to Minin's bulging briefcase, which was sitting on her desk, and began leafing through the fifteen hundred documents it contained. And her eyes widened some more.

The documents told the story of Minin's oil and diamond deals and his burgeoning trade in tropical timber. But what really caught her eye were the brochures extolling the virtues of missile systems and various other deadly weapons. And there were the emails between Minin and some of his customers. One of these was Charles 'Chucky' Taylor, namesake son of the warlord president of Liberia. And she scanned what looked like shopping lists for enough small arms to fight a war, which is exactly what they were.

Multilingual and with passports from as many countries as the languages he spoke, Leonid Minin was a senior figure in the Ukrainian Mafia until he had to flee a turf war and expanded his horizons. The routine police raid just north of Milan had opened a rare window into an organized-crime and arms-trafficking network intimately involved in the resource-fuelled conflicts that were then ripping numerous West African countries apart.

As she realized the significance of the contents of room 341, the preliminary judge knew that this was going to be no ordinary Saturday. She picked up the phone and dialled a colleague of hers. 'Walter, you'd better get over here.'

When, bored out of my mind, I quit my job in the construction industry in 1989, not in a million years did I think I'd end up tracking criminals like Leonid Minin. It all started with a rather crazy idea born over numerous lagers in north London pubs.

In the early 1990s, a shared interest in the decades-long civil war in faraway Cambodia led me and two friends to ponder how to bring it to an end. The achievement of peace had defied countless people and numerous governments, so I assume it was the beer that led us to think we had something else to bring to the table. Wars need money, we thought. If we could find out how the war was being paid for, then maybe we could cut off the money supply? This turned out to be one of the founding principles of Global Witness, the investigative campaigning organization we created. You can sort out most things if you follow the money. The other founding principle was anger. We didn't like seeing bad guys get away with it. 'Fuck 'em,' we said as we clinked our glasses. It has been our motto ever since.

We were not the most obvious candidates for the job. We knew little about Cambodia and we were not trained investigators or peacemakers; in fact, we weren't trained in anything at all. It didn't look too promising.

My brief career as a middle manager in the construction industry hadn't prepared me for going undercover and probing the finances of a ruthless guerrilla army in a war zone, so there was no option but to learn fast. Our first undercover investigation, in early 1995, took us into the wild no-man's land of the Thai–Cambodian border and began to open our eyes onto a world we thought existed only in fiction.

We had stumbled upon a network. We called it the 'shadow network', because every time we investigated a case, there it was again, lurking in the dark corners. For us, this shadow network was a world within a world that commits or enables some of the greatest crimes ever perpetrated. Like a spider's web, this network is intricately constructed, alive to the faintest tremors of opportunity or risk, alerting the predators at its centre. The network is virtually invisible, but if it is stirred by the breeze – and if you know what you're looking for – the gossamer shimmers; an anomaly against the clear sky. If you can spot these anomalies, then you can find your way into the network and, if you are lucky, discover the dark secrets it hides. But it is not a job for the faint-hearted.

Almost 30 years have passed since our first foray into the workings of this toxic shadow network and the initial discoveries we made. We had inadvertently discovered a niche. This world contains its fair share of 'conventional' crime bosses like Leonid Minin, but its most senior crime lords are often hiding in plain sight. They include heads of state and captains of industry – the very pillars of society. Very Bad People. Their rank and privilege allow them to act with impunity and obtain unimaginable power. And all power corrupts.

We began to specialize in uncovering the looting of valuable natural resources like timber, diamonds, oil and minerals from some of the poorest countries on Earth. This plunder was carried out not only by arch crooks like Minin but also by corporations that are household names, whose operations far from the public eye were, as we discovered, often no less criminal than those of the Mafia.

From our first investigation, we realized we had walked into the intersection between human rights and environmental abuse, a nexus that no other organization worked on. This was the world of grand corruption – a concept known but little understood when we started out. Corruption is often dismissed as something that happens only 'over there', in some poor, hot and dusty country overseas. It is also often depicted as a victimless crime. It is far from either of these things.

Corruption kills millions of people 'over there' every year, as they die in resource-funded wars, or from lack of food or basic healthcare because their political leaders have looted their nations' coffers. But the corruptors – the criminals and corporations that pay the bribes, and the enablers who help park the proceeds in luxury real estate in London, New York, Paris and beyond, or in offshore bank accounts where their spoils are safe from prying eyes – are very much 'over here'. The perpetrators might well live next door to you.

Corruption is a cancer that eats away at societies. It chews the innards out of the rule of law; it favours the rich and powerful at the expense of the world's most vulnerable people; it undermines international efforts to protect the environment and it gnaws away at the foundations of democracy itself. In fact, to a greater or lesser extent, we are all victims of corruption. The trouble is that most of us don't know it.

To nail Very Bad People like these, you need to ask how someone like Minin gets away with their crimes. How did he end up owning a hotel in one of Europe's top cities instead of skulking away in some hideout in fear of the law knocking on his door? How did he manage to ship the countless millions of dollars he stole in Ukraine or earned from his arms sales to Spain and then Italy?

To make and then hide the billions of dollars of countries' wealth stolen every year, you need a whole service industry behind you. Happily for the criminals, it already exists. Most of us use parts of it ourselves, comfortably unaware that some of our fellow customers are crooks who use the same lawyers, banks and accountancy firms we do. Most of us have heard of those tax havens based on palm-fringed islands in the Caribbean or the Pacific, but we are perhaps less aware that most of them are also 'secrecy jurisdictions' whose business is to register companies that mask the real owner's identity. And we are probably less aware again that the US and the UK and its dependent territories are the biggest secrecy jurisdictions of them all. The multinational corporations and super-rich who use the brass-plate companies these countries provide share the facilities with organized-crime gangs, terrorist organizations, narco-smuggling rings, sex traffickers and buccaneer entrepreneurs who need a safe and secret place to base their operations. Organized crime is just like any other business, except that its entrepreneurs exploit opportunities on the other side of what society determines is an acceptable line of legality, and it's a very thin and wobbly line. The shadow network services them all.

Global Witness's ambition is to change the heart of the system that allows this to happen. My colleagues and friends over the years have been made up of campaigners, journalists, lawyers, academics frustrated by academia, fundraisers, activists, accountants, students and bored refugees from commerce who, together with our allies and partners across the world, have achieved some unlikely successes against seemingly hopeless and sometimes dangerous odds. We have also missed tricks and made terrible mistakes.

On the one hand, this book tells the story of how we came together and the crimes that we started to suspect and take on. But on the other it also charts the growth of our understanding and often our confusion about the economic system that we used to accept at face value.

Each chapter documents a case from our casebook. You can learn, as we did, about the existence of the shadow network, and you can witness us occasionally give it a black eye. What we came up against was a breathtaking catalogue of super-crimes. We will take you into some of the most dangerous places in the world and introduce you to warlords, arms traffickers and Mafia bosses. You'll sit in the boardrooms of multinational companies where top executives make criminal decisions that impact entire nations. You'll travel with our sometimes quirky, sometimes maverick investigators as they try to unravel the labyrinthine complexity of crooked deals, and you'll see what it's like to tread the corridors of power – feeling rather like trespassers, amazed that anyone let a bunch of hooligans like us through the door. You may even get an inside view of how we helped topple a president and thus brought the odd war to an end.

The nineties were good to the diamond cartel De Beers. Its famous slogan, 'A Diamond is Forever', seemed to be borne out as hundreds of millions of dollars' worth of gems flooded into Europe, Israel and elsewhere despite the uncomfortable fact that they came from the diamond fields of war-torn countries in West Africa. No questions were asked as De Beers' vaults in London's Charterhouse Street filled up with these stones. Not until we came along anyway, and the term 'blood diamonds' was born.

When Israeli billionaire Beny Steinmetz laid his hands on the world's biggest untapped deposit of iron ore, for nothing, he was lauded in the press for landing 'The Deal of the Century'. But how exactly did he get that deal, and what was the cost to the owners of that deposit, an impoverished West African nation struggling to rebuild after years of dictatorship?

The owners of some of London's most valuable real estate didn't blink an eye as they sold a £150 million property empire to a series of companies whose real owners were masked by layer upon layer of secretly owned companies, put together as skilfully as a Russian doll. No one else seemed to care who ultimately owned those companies or where the money had come from. But we did.

We probe the inner workings of two of the world's top oil companies, following their proud announcement that they'd snapped up Nigeria's richest offshore oil block. But was the deal above board, as they claimed, or was it as dirty as the billions of barrels of oil they hoped to extract?

Perhaps the family members of the president of Kazakhstan or the son of the brutal dictator of an oil-rich African nation really are successful businesspeople in their own right, as some UK High Court judges seem to believe. How else to explain their vast wealth, their mansions, superyachts and private jets?

And how was it that cargo ships stuffed to the gunwales with tropical logs from an African war zone arrived every month in European and Chinese ports as humanitarian aid flowed the other way? Quick to dump their camouflage fatigues, victorious warlords donned suits crafted in Paris or London, bought the obligatory gold Rolex and became respectable. The unfortunate citizens they inherited, traumatized by years of war, remained mired in indescribable poverty, suffocating under the malevolent smog of dictatorship.

These are just some of the stories I cover in this book. Except they're not stories. These are real-life cases documenting some of the biggest crimes ever pulled off. Forget the $10 million in gold that some conventional thugs nicked in a heist on a security van that makes the national headlines; that's small fry. Some of the crimes we're talking about here were almost limitless in scale. For example, where did the son of a dictator find the US$600–800 million he spent on his luxury lifestyle in just four years?

As for me and my colleagues at Global Witness, after an amateurish start we became more adept at probing into the darkest, most rotten corners of the global economy, where crime and legitimate business meet, merge and become so indistinguishable from each other that even the key players don't know what side they're on. We discovered how a whole service industry – a pinstripe army of accountants, lawyers, PR companies, company formation agents and real estate agents among others – helps to keep the lid on some of the greatest and most secretive crimes ever committed.

Well, we took a different point of view, and I hope to show you that, as we went along, we felt increasingly sure about what we were doing, and began to really understand our mission: to frustrate and even close down the bad guys – the Very Bad People of this book's title.

And, more than anything, I hope what you will glean is that the only limits to achieving change are self-imposed. Our friend and mentor Anita Roddick, the co-founder of the Body Shop, said, 'If you think you're too small to have an impact, try going to bed with a mosquito in the room.' As one of our earliest and most important supporters, she recognized the mosquito in us.

PROLOGUE

In the 1940s Saloth Sar, the son of a well-to-do farmer from northern Cambodia, was sent to Paris to finish his education. Uninspired by his studies in electrical engineering, this mild-mannered student became fired up by radical left-wing politics and joined the French Communist party. He returned to Cambodia in the 1950s, changed his name to Pol Pot and went on to found the Communist Party of Kampuchea. It would evolve into one of the most infamous movements of all time, responsible for committing the greatest genocide since Nazi Germany.

It became better known as the Khmer Rouge.

THAI–CAMBODIAN BORDER, JANUARY 1995

At the hamlet of Nuan Sung, we turned right off the main road onto a red dirt track, heading west through the scrub towards the border that lay just on the other side of the hills ahead. This is the kind of territory that scares me most. Remote and silent. No habitation of any kind. No people. Just the road, scattered trees and undergrowth. We wanted to probe as close to the border as we could get, and borders can be dangerous places. You never know what you'll find: you might meet border guards who think you're a spy, or stumble on a smuggling route, or maybe mistakenly cross the unmarked border into Khmer Rouge territory – and then it's curtains for sure. Over all of this hung the fact that the Thai timber Mafia and their allies in the army held sway over the whole border area. If something happened to us here, no one would talk. We would simply disappear.

What on earth had brought us to do a stupid thing like this?

*

Just six years earlier, I'd been approaching the end of an eight-year skirmish with the world of commerce. Slowly but steadily rising through the ranks in a large company that supplied construction equipment, I was sent on an expensive course at Ashridge Management College together with a group of other aspiring young executives. There in the Hertfordshire countryside we learned how to motivate our staff, inspired by real-life examples of how to increase sales of Trebor mints, the fascinating world of archival storage and the birth of the Post-it Note. My main takeaway from the experience was that I was bored shitless. But then fate took a hand.

My long-term relationship broke up and, beating the 1989 property crash by a whisker, my girlfriend and I divided the spoils from selling our house and went our separate ways. With some half-baked idea about wanting to discover myself, I bought a rucksack, bade farewell to my friends and, aged 31, set off on the backpacker trail to Asia and Australia. I had enough money to fund an itinerant lifestyle for a couple of years.

The first of those years went by amazingly fast. I came back to the UK for a few weeks to see family and friends and, having so far failed to discover myself, planned to disappear once more. But on a blisteringly hot summer's day in 1990, I climbed a narrow staircase that took me to the first floor of a small and shabby office overlooking Upper Street in Islington, north London. It was a day that changed my life.

Over the weekend I had read a long article in *The Sunday Times Magazine* describing the exploits of a small group of environmental detectives who had gone undercover to infiltrate the ivory trade – a branch of organized crime that threatened the African elephant with extinction. The article described how these freelance investigators located a secret ivory factory in Dubai. Blagging their way into the adjoining warehouse, they'd got inside a large cardboard box with a small hole cut in the side, had themselves raised above the partition wall by a forklift truck and from this vantage point filmed the factory next door, where a Hong Kong Chinese smuggling gang was in action. I was hooked.

The Environmental Investigation Agency (EIA), co-founded by Allan Thornton, Jennifer Lonsdale and Dave Currey, had just seven staff, an equal number of volunteers and virtually no money at all, with campaigns and investigations funded by credit-card debt. One of my first jobs was to open the hundreds of letters of support from fellow readers of that *Sunday Times* article. Sitting on the floor – there were no spare desks – I read offers to raise funds through street collections and sponsored walks. I had found a niche and helped start to build a fundraising team.

A couple of weeks later, two campaigners returned from an investigation into the killing of pilot whales in the Faroe Islands. One of them was a slim woman whose delicate looks belied an amazing inner strength, exemplified by the way she warded off the unwelcome attentions of a leering man off the Holloway Road, after which she became known as 'Back Off Buster'. Charmian Gooch had been brought up to question authority.

Already captivated by the headline-hitting campaigns of Greenpeace, Friends of the Earth and Amnesty International, she'd heard about EIA via a BBC documentary and volunteered but found herself hired instead.

Some months later we were joined by another volunteer. Simon Taylor had always been a rebel, an unwilling product of the English public-school system. Emblematic of his overall attitude to authority was his cheerful admission that he would be completely unemployable in any conventional job. And now we were three.

We played hard and spent long hours in the pubs of Islington celebrating our friendship, talking about the work we did and railing at the whalers, ivory smugglers and all the others who were screwing up the world. And during the course of these conversations, on a sunny afternoon in 1992, we found that each of us was fascinated with events unfolding on the other side of the world: in Cambodia.

Supported by China and North Vietnam, Pol Pot's Khmer Rouge guerrillas launched a civil war to overthrow Cambodia's dictator, Lon Nol. This domestic conflict had been subsumed into the maelstrom of the Vietnam War that was raging along Cambodia's eastern borders in the 1960s and 1970s, and the country was torn apart. The Vietcong had invaded northeast Cambodia in 1970, both to support the Khmer Rouge and to protect their secret supply line – the Ho Chi Minh Trail. In response, wave after wave of US B-52 bombers had illegally carpet-bombed this neutral country and Cambodia descended into further chaos. But the worst was yet to come.

Well supplied with weapons by China, the Khmer Rouge swept to power in 1975. Year Zero had begun.

Pol Pot's agrarian revolution demanded the torture and extermination of the country's intellectuals, which included anyone who wore glasses. Great swathes of the population were marched across the country to vast labour camps, where they were forced into slavery, digging dykes for irrigation systems that would never work. Paintings by one of the few survivors of the notorious Tuol Sleng prison, where 18,000 people died, captured the almost unimaginable tortures inflicted to force prisoners to confess to outrageous and imaginary crimes against the state. These pictures rival the gory medieval depictions of Dante's *Inferno*. No one really knows how many died, but between 1975 and 1979, when the Khmer Rouge were overthrown by neighbouring Vietnam, between one and three million people were killed or died of malnutrition or disease; somewhere over a third of the population of this small country. To this day it remains the biggest genocide since the Nazi Holocaust.

These terrible events, carried out in almost total secrecy behind Cambodia's closed borders, were made famous by the 1984 Hollywood movie *The Killing Fields*, while public concern was stoked up by the evocative books of John Pilger and the films he made with British film director David Munro. We had all seen *Year Zero*.

Following the Vietnamese invasion in 1979, the Khmer Rouge had fled into Thailand and invisibly integrated into the vast refugee camps that had sprung up along the Thai–Cambodian border. From there, they made incursions into Cambodia to strike at the new regime; but with the end of the Cold War, their support from China had dried up and they needed to develop a new strategy. From the camps in Thailand, they began to build networks with Thai businesses and the military.

By the early 1990s, Cambodia was in the news again, but for more positive reasons. In the United Nations' biggest-ever peacekeeping intervention until that time, 20,000 UN troops were deployed across Cambodia to implement the Paris Peace Agreements, which had been signed in 1991. Elections took place in 1992 and were narrowly won by the Royalist Funcinpec Party led by Prince Ranariddh, the vain and, as we shall see, corrupt son of the much-loved and wily King Sihanouk. The incumbent Hun Sen's communist Cambodian People's Party, which had ruled since the Vietnamese invasion in 1979, came a close second, but this former Khmer Rouge cadre refused to step down. Bowing to Hun Sen's demands, the UN caved and – even now you can hardly believe this – Cambodia ended up with two prime ministers: the Royalist Prime Minister No. 1 and the Communist Prime Minister No. 2. But this wasn't the only problem.

Initially a party to the peace negotiations, the Khmer Rouge did an about-face, boycotted the elections and, from the dense rainforests of northern and western Cambodia, they re-embarked on an unceasing war of attrition against the government. What was odd was how they could afford to fight on such a scale. The money had to be coming from somewhere.

Meeting, in our own time, in the light-filled flat Simon shared with his partner, Lara, in a run-down cavernous old house in Lancaster Gate that had been split into bedsits and small offices, we scoured news articles covering events in Cambodia and we began to notice a sideshow. We read in the press that from their remote logging camps dotted along Thailand's border with Cambodia, Thai companies were importing timber, presumably felled in Cambodia's dense western rainforests – the same forests that sheltered the die-hard cadres of the Khmer Rouge. Was this how the Khmer Rouge were funding their war?

What was certain was that Cambodia's newfound and fragile peace and the multibillion-dollar international effort that led to it were being put at risk, perhaps even fatally undermined.

Tough, brutal and entirely ruthless, the Khmer Rouge were seasoned jungle fighters. The wars in Vietnam and Afghanistan are testament to the fact that even the well-resourced and highly mechanized military forces of superpowers can't win a guerrilla war. This seemed self-evident, and yet no one in the world seemed to be doing anything about it. But if that timber trade was indeed the guerrillas' economic lifeline, might cutting it bring an end to the war?

The signatory governments of the Paris Peace Agreements, including Thailand itself, were doing little or nothing to close down the Khmer Rouge timber trade. Perhaps some of these governments had taken their eye off the ball, but others – we thought – had more sinister intent. There is always money to be made in a war zone. Was it possible that the Thai government was actually complicit?

And if governments weren't acting, who could? Was this an environmental problem because they were cutting down the rain-forest? Or was it a human-rights problem because the timber trade was funding the war? The answer was, of course, both. But back then – and this is still largely true now – there were environmental groups like Greenpeace and Friends of the Earth, and there were human-rights groups like Amnesty International and Human Rights Watch, but none of them strayed outside their areas of focus. While Cambodia's continuing civil war was an international concern, shutting off the finance to it did not seem to be on anyone's agenda.

Nursing our lagers in the bars of the Betsey Trotwood and the Horseshoe, two pubs just around the corner from EIA's offices in Clerkenwell, we pondered this conundrum. The strategy could be staggeringly simple. If we surmised correctly, then closing the Thai–Cambodian border to the timber trade would cut off the Khmer Rouge's funding. Without that, they couldn't fight. We were no experts in international peacebuilding, but it seemed obvious to us. 'Why doesn't someone do something about this?' we asked ourselves. We mused for a while longer and then someone said, 'Why don't we?'

We sketched out a plan. Mimicking EIA's methodology, we would create a false identity as European timber buyers. Then, armed with secret-camera equipment, we would travel along the Thai–Cambodian border visiting the timber companies that we had read were based there, and ask them how much timber they were importing, who they were importing it from, how much they paid for it and who they were selling it to. With solid evidence, if we could get it, then maybe, just maybe, we could convince the governments who had signed the Paris Peace Agreements to put pressure on Thailand to close down this bloody trade.

And that was it. The three of us – Simon aged 30, Charmian at 29 and me a venerable 35 – would take down the Khmer Rouge. Naïve beyond belief. Unrealistic, idealistic and very likely impossible. The craziest idea we could have had. But it was utterly compelling, and we couldn't get it out of our heads. We ordered another round of lagers in order to ponder the next question, which was...

'How the fuck...?'

*

The number-one challenge was that we didn't have any money. Challenges two to ten included that beyond what was said in a few press articles we had read we knew very little about what was actually happening in Cambodia and Thailand. None of us had ever been to these countries, other than me during my short sojourn to Thailand as a backpacker. We didn't know anything about the timber industry or forests. We had no contacts who could give us the vital insights we needed. Charmian and Simon had some campaign experience at EIA, while I was still a fledgling fundraiser with some commercial management experience. There weren't many parallels with that and what we wanted to achieve. Charmian and I both had low-paying day jobs, me with EIA while she had left to join Media Natura, a PR company working to publicize worthy ventures such as Fairtrade coffee. Simon had just finished a short consultancy with Greenpeace and was now being supported by his partner Lara's Ph.D grant.

To round all this off, we had no organization and barely any network from which to mobilize support. We needed an entity we could raise funds for, and a bank account to put the money in. And we needed a name. A name that would stick, that would give some idea of what we did, one that would last the test of time.

With an early-afternoon appointment looming with a lawyer that Charmian knew, who had agreed to set up the company for us, we sat in the café at the Africa Centre in Covent Garden to grab a quick lunch and settle on a name. We arrived at Global Witness. It sounded good. It rolled off the tongue. We were worried that we might get confused with Jehovah's Witnesses, but once you had met us that thought would probably be dashed. We went from the café into the grey cold of a wet autumn day and made for Peter Hooper's nearby office. On 15 November 1993, Global Witness was born. It had no office, no money and no logo. But it had life.

Through her work, Charmian knew a leading graphic designer called Pierre Vermeir. He had designed a new logo for the medical charity Médecins Sans Frontières and he offered us the choice of one of the rejects, for free. We opted for a series of white arrows depicting a dynamic running figure set inside a deep-red circle, somehow it seemed to fit. But the next challenge was the major one. Money.

We started out by shaking charity collection tins outside London Tube stations. Joined by several of my volunteers from EIA, we would get up at 5am and stand in the grey chilly dawn to tap the rush-hour passengers streaming out of Bank and other Tube stations in the City of London, but Global Witness was totally unknown and hadn't done anything. Why would anyone give us money?

We put together amateurish placards with photos of tigers, forests and the Khmer Rouge to try to convey our complex message about the nexus of natural-resource exploitation, conflict and environmental and human-rights abuses. I think that the tigers were probably the only things that a bleary-eyed City worker noticed and by the time we packed up to go to our day jobs, the maximum take was less than ten pounds between us. But we persisted because it was all that we had.

Then a few of our friends clubbed together to pool some money. This and the loose change from our Underground collections came to a grand total of around £1,000. It was something, but we knew that we weren't going to save the world this way.

In parallel, we had begun to do the research we needed to do. Being unemployed, Simon was the only one of us who could devote his weekdays to this. Reading avidly and using our meagre funds to make calls to contacts in the US and elsewhere, he began to build new relationships. We met with the then head of Friends of the Earth and asked for £6,000 to carry out our first investigation, but they turned us down. We wrote to Oxfam and were invited to meet a senior official there. Ushered into his office and waiting nervously for him to join us, we saw our proposal on his desk. Scrawled across it were the words 'Will they survive?' They obviously didn't think so and turned us down too.

The months were passing and it was becoming clear that if we didn't get some serious money, this thing was not going to get off the ground. I talked with my wife, Breda. I had met her within a week of volunteering at EIA in 1990 and we had always encouraged each other in our nascent careers. She led the fundraising team at a London success story, the Almeida Theatre, a regular job with a modest salary. Should I give up my job at EIA and launch into an uncertain future with Global Witness? She was unequivocal. 'You must do it,' she said. 'I'll do all I can to support you.'

Charmian suggested that we talk to Allan Thornton, EIA's founder and my boss, and tell him about our plans. For me this was a high-risk strategy. Allan, a tall, softly spoken Canadian, was an iconic figure in the environmental movement. He had founded Greenpeace in the UK and had purchased and sailed in the first *Rainbow Warrior* ship. But he could also be an irascible boss. I got on well with him, but it wasn't uncommon for one of my colleagues to step over some unseen line and find themselves instantly sacked. So, with some trepidation, Charmian, Simon and I met him for a drink on a warm summer evening in our old haunt, the Betsey Trotwood, and told him of our plans. He listened intently, put down his glass, reached into his pocket and took out his wallet. He extracted all the notes that were in there and handed them across the table. 'I think it's a brilliant idea,' he said. 'I'll do all I can to help you.' He had given us £100, a lot of money in those days. More than that, it was an incredibly meaningful vote of confidence.

Allan offered me redundancy from EIA, which meant three months' salary tax free. Even more generously, I could still use the office, the phones and the fax machine. On top of that, he commissioned us to write a report outlining the situation in Cambodia – a report we knew he didn't really need – for which he would pay us £200.

When I had been seeking escape routes from my construction job, I'd been given one piece of advice that I have never forgotten. In life you'll probably get three or four potentially life-changing opportunities. The first trick is to recognize them when they come along, and the second is to make the right choice. Leaving my old career had been the first such opportunity that I remembered. Marrying Breda had been the second. This was the third. I was in.

Charmian's financial commitments meant that she couldn't change course immediately, but with her moral and intellectual support Simon and I took the plunge. We could pay Simon £60 a week.

For another £60 per week, we rented a tiny one-room office above Frank Lord's junk shop on the corner of St John Street in Clerkenwell, most of which was taken up by a huge and immoveable Victorian safe. On one rainy Sunday in September 1994, assisted by Breda and Lara, we moved in our meagre possessions: a melamine trestle table liberated from EIA, two chairs, a telephone we had salvaged from somewhere, a battered blue filing cabinet that had been dumped in one of the corridors of the building Simon and Lara lived in, and Simon's ancient Amstrad computer. As we stood there toasting the future with a bottle of champagne, looking out of the two large sash windows that opened onto a grey, rainswept St John Street, we watched as workmen clearing out an office across the road dumped two shiny black filing cabinets into a skip. Without a word we rushed down and humped them up the two flights of narrow stairs. Inside one of them, hidden among a number of hanging files, was a laptop computer. This was sophistication beyond our dreams, and although we toyed for a while with the idea of trying to locate the company and returning it, in the end we felt it would be insulting providence and so we kept it.

The next day Simon and I went to *our* office. We had enough money to pay the rent for a month, but fate took a hand just a few weeks after we'd moved in when a letter arrived at our PO Box. We were trepidatious as we broke the seal, because we could see it was from Novib, the Dutch arm of Oxfam, to whom Simon had sent a proposal some weeks before. Our hearts leaped as we read the letter: it said that they would grant us £18,000 to investigate the Thai–Khmer Rouge timber trade. 'Fuck me, we're on,' I said.

The downside was that now we had to do what we said we'd do.

We hadn't wasted the 18 months since we had first dreamed up the idea of Global Witness. We had been contacting people who could help us and we now had a network of names in the US, Thailand and Cambodia. Our first job was to meet some of these people in person. Allan had advised us that to make any serious changes in the world, you needed to go to Washington, DC. Like it or not, the US was the most powerful country on the planet and the tentacles of its influence spread far, and so in November 1994 Simon and I landed at Dulles Airport to meet the political influencers, diplomats, spies, schemers and other experts on almost any subject under the sun who might be able to help us. We stayed with an old friend from EIA days. Pete Knight, known affectionately as 'Pet Shop Pete' for his work trying to stop the illegal trade in exotic birds, was our first guide to Washington and how it worked, and it was great to put faces to what up to now had just been distant names.

Burma activist Faith Doherty, a party-loving, highly knowledgeable force of nature, gave us invaluable insights into the inner workings of the Thai government and military, learned from her time spent with the rebels on the Burma border. Likewise Katie Redford, a young American environmental lawyer who had recently founded a small NGO called EarthRights International, gave us valuable insights into the region. We also talked to staff at Human Rights Watch, who represented the grown-ups in this movement we were now part of, and who gave us sound advice. In the dimly lit smoky basement bar of the Childe Harold near Dupont Circle, we listened avidly to the experiences of a bona fide spy, who had been stationed on the Thai–Cambodian border with the UN in the early 1990s. And Craig Etcheson, an eccentric academic expert on the Khmer Rouge, proved an enthusiastic ally whose skill on The Hill – the home of the US Congress and its hundreds of congressional offices packed with staffers beavering away on every topic under the sun – would later be crucial to our campaign.

We had just returned to London when, in a surprise move, the Thai government announced that their border with Cambodia would be closed immediately to the timber trade. They were quickly followed by the Cambodians, who announced that the border would be closed from their side on 1 January 1995, with an 'amnesty' allowing the export of 'abandoned' logs until 30 April. Had our job been done for us before we'd even begun?

Noticeable by its absence was any recent information as to what was actually going on along the Thai–Cambodian border. If it was closed, then great. But would the Cambodian amnesty really be limited to 'abandoned' logs, or was this a euphemism that would allow continued logging? Cynical about both governments' sudden changes of heart, we still needed to check it out for ourselves.

One of our first conundrums was how we were going to get the information we needed, beyond the historical background information we were already getting, and the conjecture and rumour that seemed to surround everything to do with Cambodia. We couldn't enter Khmer Rouge territory; it was a war zone and as far as we were concerned it was stuffed full of Westerner-hating fanatic guerrilla fighters, the IS of its day. This left Thailand and the logging companies based along the border – but even if we could find them, what incentive did they have to tell us anything? Doing the right thing didn't seem to be their obvious motivation, but making money was. They had to think there was something in it for them.

If we were going to infiltrate the Thai timber industry, we could hardly do it as Global Witness, so we decided to create false identities and pose as European timber buyers, something we had never done before. We had a lot to learn and no teachers. In his James Bond books, Ian Fleming gave MI6 the cover name of Universal Export. This had a nice ring to it, we thought, and if it was good enough for James Bond it was good enough for us.

So we printed up four sets of Universal Export business cards with a logo of the globe on them. Two of them bore Simon's and my real names, to match our passports: we needed these if we were talking to the authorities, because lying about your name could lead to an espionage charge. Two bore false names: mine was Chris Manners (the surname borrowed from old friends of the family) and Simon's was Richard Sutton.

If anyone phoned the number on the card, their call would be answered 'Universal Export' by Charmian in London. If they faxed us, nothing would happen because we didn't have a fax machine. The cover was pretty thin, but it would serve. In those pre-internet days, there was no easy way for anyone to check our bona fides.

We visited one of the only two spy shops we knew of in London – the cheaper one, which slumbered gently in seedy squalor in Kilburn, behind those blacked-out windows that you'd more likely associate with a massage parlour.

The owner, a pallid and perspiring man with large, black-framed spectacles, guided us through various ingenious items of equipment beloved of private detectives whose main business was catching out unfaithful husbands and wives. Although the spy gear was good, the experience lacked the romanticism of James Bond's 'Q' branch. But it was the right place to come: mobile-phone scanners, mobile-phone bugs, 'ordinary' bugs, secret cameras, telephone-recording devices and, of course, bug detectors that would tell you if one of his other customers was spying on you.

To us, the cameras were state-of-the-art cool. A lens the size of a pinhead set into a black plastic disc about the size of a penny. The black disc was, in turn, mounted on a green rectangular printed circuit board measuring around 10 x 5cm. The snag was that this was just a lens; it could not record film or sound and needed an external power source. So in addition to the lens, which cost a hefty £400, we needed a battery pack that took eight AA batteries; this would power the lens for about an hour. For sound we needed an amplifier. This came in a black plastic casing the size of a cigarette packet, with a tiny external microphone like the ones you see people on TV wearing on their lapels.

To record the film taken through the lens we bought a Sony Hi8 camcorder from a cluttered electronics emporium on Tottenham Court Road, and a black Lowe camera bag to put it in. These were the last preparations for an undercover investigation that would take us to one of the most exciting – and arguably one of the most dangerous – places in the world.

We planned this first investigation to last around five weeks. The main objective was to locate and infiltrate the Thai timber companies we had monitored in the press, to find out for ourselves how strong their links were with the Khmer Rouge, and to see if our working theory was correct – that the trade in Cambodian timber was funding the Khmer Rouge's war effort.

We weren't naïve enough not to be scared because we knew we were going to bandit country. The area was remote – way off the tourist track – and we were not pleased to learn that the rebel group had just issued a US$5,000 reward, a huge sum for the average Cambodian or Thai, for the capture of any Westerner. Around the time we had moved into our office, three Western tourists who had been kidnapped during a Khmer Rouge raid on a train in southern Cambodia in July were found buried in a shallow grave. They had been shot. We thought back to the question scrawled on our proposal by the man from Oxfam. 'Will they survive?'

With this knowledge hovering on the periphery of our thoughts, the time finally came to go. On 11 January 1995, Breda and I crammed ourselves into Simon and Lara's ancient blue 2CV and we drove together through the cold quiet streets of north London and the bleak suburbs along the Westway to Heathrow Airport for the start of Global Witness's first-ever investigation. In the cold light of that January dawn, this didn't seem like such a terribly good idea after all.

Simon and I were paranoid. Would we be spied on at every turn? Would our phone calls be monitored and our plans intercepted? Would undercover agents be dogging our footsteps? We didn't know, but we would have to watch what we said and who we said it to. Our hearts were in our mouths as we hugged Breda and Lara goodbye.

Simon and I arrived at dawn the next day at Bangkok's Don Mueang Airport to catch our connecting flight to Phnom Penh. As we walked along long yellow-hued corridors that smelled faintly of wet dog, the odour that air-conditioning units exude in the tropics, we imagined that the immigration officials, customs officers and the police, squeezed into their skin-tight chocolate-brown uniforms, were expecting us and about to pounce. Weighed down by our seven pieces of hand luggage each, including the secret camera and fake business cards, we elicited no attention from anyone.

Then, safely aboard, we strained our necks for our first view of Cambodia, and watched as the flat agricultural plains of Thailand suddenly ended in a clean line as they met the dense rainforests on the other side of Cambodia's western border. It looked like Thailand had been shaved. We watched the deep-green jungle unfurl beneath us, a solid canopy for mile after mile. And under that canopy, underneath our plane, perhaps looking up at us, were the Khmer Rouge. Then the plane went into a steep descent to Phnom Penh's Pochentong Airport to avoid potential rocket attack.

All our hopes and fears had geared up towards this moment; we were on our own and I was scared shitless.

1

THE BORDER

Phnom Penh was a revelation from the moment the plane door opened and the tropical heat flooded in. As we stood at the top of the steps, we looked out over the runway quivering under the heat haze, towards the sugar palms that soared to immense heights over the fields that surrounded the airport. The air was filled with unidentifiable tropical smells and the ring of the flat-sounding bells of distant Buddhist monasteries.

Cambodia had an electric atmosphere that seeped into every crevice, corner and pothole of this beautiful, seedy and decaying French colonial city. An atmosphere you only get to experience in a country coming out of a war, a country trying to leave the years of horror behind but shocked by the sudden influx of the 20,000 UN peacekeeping troops. Shocked, too, by the deluge of foreigners from all over the world who had ended its 20 years of isolation. Many of these could populate some of the stranger works of fiction. Some came to help rebuild the country – development organizations like Oxfam, Médecins Sans Frontières and Save the Children. Many more came to report on it, this almost mythical land and the momentous peace treaty that promised to bring an end to years of civil war. They were followed by the wheeler-dealers who came in to profit from the massive contracts on offer to rebuild an entire country, and those who would run the hotels and clubs to entertain these interlopers. Some came to exploit opportunities for crime, to make corrupt deals, run brothels, traffic children and smuggle drugs. And some came just for adventure. All of these people and institutions were dumped unannounced on a population reeling from decades of chaos and trauma.

After the UN left, the big news was over and the international journalistic elite had gone off in search of more fertile pastures.

They left behind them an enthusiastic and passionate press pack of mainly young reporters who could make their career in the febrile atmosphere of what was otherwise regarded as a news backwater. Now they covered the difficult birth of democracy in Cambodia, which was already afflicted with a congenital and potentially fatal disease: corruption.

It was into this melee that we landed on 12 January 1995.

This was a nation at war. The dense rainforests of the north and west of the country still contained the jungle strongholds of the Khmer Rouge, like Samlot, Pailin and Anlong Veng. But the rebels' influence was not confined to these bases. Government control was limited to the big towns; the rest of the country depended on a scattering of poorly armed and ill-disciplined flip-flop-wearing soldiers. At dusk this control evaporated, replaced by the Khmer Rouge across much of the west and north. For foreigners, travel outside of the main towns after 4pm was highly dangerous and only the foolhardy risked it.

There was no fighting in Phnom Penh but there was no mistaking that a war was going on. We couldn't hear it, we couldn't see it, but the sheer fact of it – the presence of it – pervaded everything; it governed the whole atmosphere of the place.

We booked into the overwhelmingly bleak China Nanjing Hotel, with its view over a large crossroads filled with a seething mass of pushbikes, 'motos' (mopeds) and rickshaws; it was like looking down into a termite nest. And then we made our first call.

'Is that Johnny Miller?' Simon asked.

'Yeah, who's that?' a curious voice answered.

'Er, we can't tell you right now, but we'd like to meet you.' We were even more paranoid now that we were in Phnom Penh. Johnny, a foreign correspondent for the BBC, probably thought we were simple.

'Okay, well, what do you do?' he asked.

'Hmm, we can't tell you that either. But we're happy to explain everything when we meet,' Simon answered. There was a pause.

'Okay. Let's meet at the Foreign Correspondents' Club.' Johnny probably thought it would be wise to meet in a crowded space where he could call for help if we turned out to be as mad as we seemed.

But before we went to meet him, we had another task. We had delayed assembling the secret-camera gear until now, to minimize any unwanted interest at airport security. We laid the constituent parts on the bed. I unpicked the stitching at one end of the camera bag with a scalpel and then cut a hole in the padding and inserted the circuit board and lens. I glued this to the inside of the outer skin of the bag with just the pin head of the lens visible through a tiny hole we'd cut for the purpose. Simon ran the two wires from the circuit board into the main body of the bag, where they were connected to the camcorder and the battery pack. The amplifier fitted snugly into a little equipment pocket on the inside lid of the bag, with one wire connecting it to the camcorder. The microphone cable ran from the amplifier through the lining of the bag and the mic itself was sown into the top seam, protruding a tiny bit below the lid. Simon finished the job by making all the connections safe with a hot-glue gun.

It was an afternoon's work and we were pleased with it. Slung over the shoulder, the bag rested at waist height. Unless you knew the lens was there, it was as good as invisible. Of course, the camera bag itself was very visible but we decided to employ reverse psychology. Most people we were likely to meet would not know of the existence of secret cameras, so a bag with a camera in it didn't pose a threat because the camera was safely and obviously stowed away. Or so we hoped anyway. The psychology was all.

Around 8pm, we took a couple of the ubiquitous moto taxis from outside the hotel, asked for the FCC and disappeared into the warm tropical night. The heaving bicycle traffic around the hotel soon gave way to quiet side streets.

'Where you from?' my driver asked in broken English.

'Ireland,' I replied.

'Ah, *póg mo thóin*,' he laughed. One of the few pieces of Gaelic I understood, 'Kiss my arse.' The Irish UN peacekeepers had a lot to answer for.

We climbed the wide stone stairs of the FCC and discovered the best bar in the world, occupying the top floor of a faded ochre French Colonial-era house on the banks of the Tonle Sap River. Sheltering under a high, red-tiled roof supported by tall stone pillars, its balconies looked across the road to the wide, silt-filled Tonle Sap carrying clumps of tropical vegetation on its way to the Mekong; the bar's rear windows gazed over the vast pagoda'd roof of the National Museum. The fairy-tale Royal Palace, home to the arch survivor and father of the Cambodia people, the wily King Sihanouk, was just a few yards down the road.

Ceiling fans cut through the heavy tropical air as hordes of geckos, motionless and seemingly glued to the walls and rafters, looked down on nests of armchairs and tables containing small groups of people hatching plots, fomenting or dispelling rumours, trying to find romance in what was a pretty incestuous environment and, above all, getting drunk. It was bliss.

Johnny was everything we imagined a foreign correspondent to be. Eloquent and handsome, he drove around the dusty potholed streets in a Vietnam War-era American Army jeep. He had a host of great stories and a wicked sense of humour, and was an integral part of Phnom Penh's vibrant journalist community. Fearless in his work, he took great personal risks to get the best stories. The story of the moment was an army offensive against the Khmer Rouge unit that had kidnapped and executed the three Western backpackers the year before.

Sitting on a high wooden bar stool drinking ice-cold cans of Tiger Beer, we explained why we were there. He was enthusiastic, which was like an adrenalin shot for us. Brought up by missionary parents in Sarawak, Malaysia, he loved forests and was passionately concerned about their destruction. We learned that although many journalists were aware that something bad was happening in Cambodia's jungles, no one really knew exactly what.

'I've heard rumours that the wife of General Chavalit, the Thai defence minister, controls a lot of the cross-border trade,' he told us, which would be big news if we could prove it. His information added some snippets to what we already knew, but his grasp of context was invaluable. He also opened his address book to us, introducing us to most of the local press pack. They in turn put us in touch with others and we began to piece together the political context and the reality of working in Cambodia.

We worked hard in Phnom Penh. We needed to glean as much information as we could, and we found that in this reborn country there was almost no one that you couldn't meet.

From other journalists we picked up snippets of information, including some hard facts and observations combined with large doses of rumour and conjecture with some second-hand titbits thrown in. There were, apparently, many sawmills north of Aranyaprathet in Thailand, opposite Thma Puok in Cambodia's Banteay Meanchey Province, which was solid Khmer Rouge territory. Sitting at a small round table in the garden of the English-language *Phnom Penh Post*, Matthew Grainger, a bespectacled and earnest Kiwi who was passionate about the subject, told us about the handfuls of Khmer Rouge scattered throughout the mountains to the south and offered all he could to help.

We also found it surprisingly easy to meet senior government ministers and other officials; they were new to their roles in a new government and perhaps hadn't yet learned to be aloof. We met with the Royalist Funcinpec Party's minister of national defence, Tea Chamrath, and the ministers of environment and tourism. In another meeting, General Toan Chay enlightened us with information on the Thai–Khmer Rouge timber trade between 1993 and 1994, and told us that the Thais had closed the border to the north but added, 'In the south, we don't know...' Indeed, we had heard that in the south 300 timber trucks a day were crossing into Thailand from Koh Kong and Battambang provinces.

At the end of each day, we'd return exhausted to our hotel room to write up our notes and discuss the next steps. The end result was an emerging picture of chaos but with few hard facts to go on. Every evening was spent at the FCC. It was fun for sure, but we were listening. Always listening.

One of the revelations for us was discovering the invidious impacts of corruption – not something we had ever considered working on when we began Global Witness. When we arrived in Cambodia, we had thought the issue was pretty simple: the bad-guy Khmer Rouge were threatening to undo the work of the new good-guy democratically elected government. Instead what we found was a political leadership seizing as much money and power as it could, regardless of ideology or the impacts on the people. An almost lone political voice warning against the corruption and political rot was the former finance minister and sitting MP Sam Rainsy. One morning we turned up outside his house on the back of our motos and asked for a meeting. It took a few tries – he was a busy man – but after a few days he eventually agreed. He was a diminutive, smartly dressed man with outsize spectacles, and he and his elegant wife, Saumura, were part of Cambodia's social and political elite. Exiled to France during the Khmer Rouge years, they had returned to help rebuild their country. She was deputy governor of the Cambodian Central Bank, and he a banker, and they had much to offer a country where the intelligentsia had been exterminated as a matter of Khmer Rouge policy.

Like Johnny and our reporter friends, they were enthusiastic and offered their support. While in government, Rainsy had tried to curb corruption in the forest sector but had failed; but he evidently thought that we might be able to contribute something. He invited us to join him on a visit to his constituency, Siem Reap, best known as the iconic site of Cambodia's glorious past, the ancient temples of Angkor Wat. His invitation was not to see the temples, however, but to talk to villagers in his constituency, to hear what life was like for a typical Cambodian. It was an offer we couldn't refuse.

Two days later we took the short flight to Siem Reap – travelling by river was far too dangerous for a foreigner then – and touched down to be met by Rainsy's official car complete with two body-guards, one armed with the de rigueur AK47, the other with a B40 rocket launcher.

We learned a little of what it is to be a VIP as we travelled out into the Cambodian countryside. Large stickers on the windscreen advertised the fact that the car belonged to an MP, with the result that the barriers at the numerous military checkpoints were raised as we approached and something between a wave and a salute was thrown in our direction, no questions asked. It was a small exercise in experiencing power and it was dangerously addictive.

The myriad problems this war-scarred country faced were belied by its beauty: seemingly endless emerald-green rice paddies – vast expanses of flat, low-level land – pierced by lines of the ubiquitous sugar palms, which rose slender and very, very tall, their fronds swaying gently in silhouette against the big Cambodian sky. Occasionally we passed red signboards emblazoned with a white skull and crossbones bearing a stark message in English and Khmer – 'Danger! Mines!'

We finally arrived at Sad Dai commune. The village comprised around 60 families living in weathered wooden huts raised from the ground on precarious-looking stilts, roughly congregated around a dusty centre. A few scrawny chickens pecked about through a litter of scraps. It was achingly poor.

Everyone turned out to see Rainsy and Saumura. The fact that he had turned up with a couple of white guys was an added bonus. We were objects of fascination – especially to the kids, who reached out nervously to touch our skin to see if white people felt different to them, and then backed off laughing with pleasure at having got away with it.

But we were here to work, to hear the story the villagers had to tell; and it was a story of famine. We were no aid workers, we had never been to a village like this in our lives, but what we saw shocked us. Despite the vast and costly international intervention in Cambodia, villages like this had been marooned in a sea of neglect, invisible to a government that was far more interested in personal enrichment and power than the wellbeing of their people. Without exception the kids had reddish hair, a symptom of protein malnutrition; some had the distended stomachs infamous from every famine story you see on TV; and, although not yet the bags of bone in those same images, they were alarmingly thin. They were on the verge of famine.

Their parents and grandparents told us what they thought was the cause of their plight – the gradual destruction of the forests on which they had depended for food and medicine for generations, and in which lived the spirits they worshipped. They told us about the resulting changing climate: the dry season, which used to last only six months, was getting longer and their crops were being strangled by drought. They had to travel further to get water for everyday use. It is one thing to read about poverty and malnutrition, or to see it on TV, but when you meet people who struggle every day just to eat while their leaders routinely rob the country blind, you get angry. The villagers pleaded for help, for some kind of assistance, believing or maybe just hoping that we could do something to alleviate their suffering. But Simon and I were no saviours. We were starting out on the long road to try to tackle some of the root causes of their plight, but there was nothing we could do that would change their lives one jot in the short term, and this was a depressing and humbling realization. But the anger drove us on.

We returned to Siem Reap that evening in reflective mood. In contrast to the experiences of the day, we had a simple dinner with Rainsy and Saumara, sitting under the sloping roof of a wide veranda in a wooden restaurant on the banks of the Mekong. Then Rainsy had a bright idea: 'Let's go and see Angkor Wat by moonlight!' This was an amazing opportunity. Angkor Wat, the world's largest religious building, is the main temple of a vast complex covering an area of over 400km^2.

There were no tourists in Cambodia in 1995. Although Angkor was just a few kilometres north of Siem Reap, it was considered unsafe at night due to Khmer Rouge presence, while some of the outlying temples were lethal at any time. Our enthusiasm to see the place coupled with our reluctance to appear nervous in front of Rainsy and Saumura overrode our common sense and most of the security protocols we had agreed with Charmian before we left.

We piled into Rainsy's Toyota Corolla together with the two bodyguards and drove into the ink-black night. We soon left the town behind, and the car was cocooned in darkness. We could dimly see that the deserted road was flanked by high trees, but little else was visible. After around half an hour we arrived at the majestic flagged causeway that leads across the moat to the main temple itself. Or it would have been majestic if we had been able to see it. The flaw in Rainsy's plan was that there was no moon.

Undeterred, we picked our way over the causeway's rough flag-stones and nosed forward towards the temple, which we couldn't actually see until we virtually bumped into it. The atmosphere was amazing; at least to begin with, the night sounds of the surrounding forest were all we could hear. But then, as our ears became accustomed, we began to sense unexplained sounds emanating from the darkness. The guards became nervous, staring into the blackness at the crack of a twig or the rustling of grass or at what could have been a distant whisper. Our nerves began to be on edge. One of the guards cocked his AK47 while the other raised his RPG and their eyes tried to pierce the night. They were nervous and told us that we should leave.

Then a distant whisper became a definite voice. The spell was shattered, and we made for the car. With headlights stabbing the night, illuminating the deserted single-track roads and highlighting the encroaching jungle, we made it back to the bright lights of the town. It was a stark demonstration that the Khmer Rouge did indeed instil fear throughout the country by night.

We returned to Phnom Penh humbled by what we had seen: the human cost of the greed perpetuated by the country's leaders. It was what we had set up Global Witness to tackle and it reinforced our determination to succeed on the next leg of our journey. We were heading for Thailand in three days.

In a grotty, nicotine-stained room in a backpacker hostel off Bangkok's Khao San Road, Simon and I planned the border trip. We spread large-scale Vietnam War-era US military maps on the bed and it was guesswork that led us to our initial focus. My finger traced the line of the border south of the town of Trat, in southeast Thailand, where Thai territory gradually narrowed until it was just a long narrow sliver of land sandwiched between the Cambodian border and the sea.

'Look, Simon,' I said. 'The land's really thin here, not much room for a timber company to hide in. Maybe we should start there?' I asked, smiling; half question, half joke. 'Why not?' he said.

It was a mad notion of course, but it seemed like a good idea at the time. From there we would travel north and then follow the border east after Aranyaprathet until we reached the border with Laos. Around 700km in all.

We needed a translator who could gauge the moods of the people we met and to act as an early-warning system if any situation became hostile. This could be the difference between life and death. One of the many people whose brains we'd picked in London introduced us to Dtee (pronounced 'Dee'), a petite and ballsy Thai activist who combined passion and enthusiasm and emanated a quiet strength. She was perfect.

We also needed to be as inconspicuous as possible; this was not easy for two tall Western guys, but was helped by the hiring of a white Toyota Hilux pick-up truck with tinted windows, ubiquitous in rural Thailand. Inside it, we were as good as invisible.

On the afternoon of 23 January, we left Bangkok and headed southeast. The modern motorways, crowded with garishly painted honking trucks piloted by crazy, seemingly amphetamine-fuelled drivers, gradually gave way to quieter routes and, around six hours later, to the virtually deserted roads close to Thailand's eastern border. Shortly after dark we rolled into the tiny settlement of Nuan Sung, which boasted a military checkpoint controlling the only road going south into that narrow sliver of land we had identified before. The only other things it boasted were the Sexy Lady restaurant and a small brothel close by. Hotels in rural Thailand are usually brothels, and it was this one that we booked; Dtee in one room, and me and Simon sharing the adjoining one.

There was only one place to get dinner. Except for Dtee, the Sexy Lady restaurant was completely devoid of any women as far as we could see, but it gave us a (sort of) innocuous vantage point from which we could observe all the road traffic and hang out with the soldiers and a few workers who seemed to frequent the place.

Trying to talk over the truly terrible Thai disco music thudding in our ears, we ate a really good meal and discussed our plan of action for the next day. Then, tired after the long drive, Simon and I collapsed onto the double bed in our seedy room and gazed with consternation at the ceiling, which was entirely covered by a giant mirror. I fell asleep wondering what ghastly sights it had reflected in its dismal career.

The next day, efficient-looking black-uniformed Marines carrying American M16 automatic rifles asked us a few cursory questions and waved us through our first military checkpoint. Here, close to the sea, we could still be thought of as tourists, even though we were the only foreigners we saw.

After just a few kilometres, to our amazement, our mad theory proved correct. There, on the left, was a vast field the size of three or four football pitches, neatly stacked with row upon row of massive rainforest logs. It simply wasn't possible to hide a log-storage area this size along this narrow wedge of land. A wooded hillside rose behind the field, which marked the Cambodian border. The other side of that, just a few kilometres away, was Khmer Rouge territory.

Although the log-storage area seemed deserted, we could take no chances, especially with the military just up the road, so we connected the battery cables in the secret-camera bag and pressed 'record'. I slung the bag over my shoulder, and we climbed out of the

Hilux and walked among the massive trunks, most of which were as thick as we were high, and which lay in neat rows on the dusty red soil, filling the space between the road and the hillside.

We realized the yard was temporarily deserted so Simon took out his SLR and the motor-wind purred as he took shot after shot. We began to sweat under the searing tropical sun and flies buzzed our faces. We counted the logs and then, as there was nothing else to glean here, we left. This had turned out to be an easy introduction to the Khmer Rouge timber trade, and the first major conclusions we drew were that the trade did indeed exist, and that there was no attempt to hide it; both important points. Would the investigation all be this easy?

We drove fast down the straight, deserted road. The flat-calm sea glistened to the right, and that menacing hillside, never more than a kilometre away, rose to the left. After an hour, we drew into the small port of Kalapandha. This was the end of the road; beyond was Cambodia.

A few single-storey houses and the odd warehouse clustered alongside the small harbour. Around ten gaily painted wooden fishing boats with precarious superstructures were tied up to the quays, loaded with stacks of thick, rough-sawn planks. To the uninitiated this scene would have looked more picturesque than dangerous, but that timber could only have come from one place, Cambodia, and we knew that we had stumbled onto a timber-smuggling operation. The question was, how big?

We walked along the jetty and got into conversation with the fishermen – or, more correctly, the smugglers. Very casually I asked, 'Hi, nice-looking timber – where's it from?'

'Koh Kong,' a fisherman replied, pointing towards the neighbouring Cambodian province.

'Wow,' Simon said. 'We thought that was Khmer Rouge-controlled territory.'

'It is, but they're okay. We go every day up the waterways. My company runs three boats a week, around ninety cubic metres of timber each time.'

This conversation was repeated with a number of the fishermen, and we gleaned that there were around 25 companies operating out of Kalapandha, each bringing in around 3 shipments per week. We did some rough calculations and worked out that this 'picturesque' operation was generating around US$270,000 per week for the Khmer Rouge. This was the first intimation of the scale of the trade we had come here to investigate. If this little port was earning them over US$1 million per month, what the hell was the total?

Pleased with our first day's work, we stayed another night in the brothel. But now we felt far more uneasy than before. Now we had something to hide. We were in possession of film and photographs that would be hard to explain away as a tourist. If we were questioned now, we would have to lie. We had so easily crossed a line and we neither felt nor could afford to be at our ease.

Nuan Sung disappeared behind us as we headed northwest. We cranked up Pink Floyd's 'Shine On You Crazy Diamond' on the car cassette player to calm our nerves (our equivalent of Robert Duvall playing 'Ride of the Valkyries' in *Apocalypse Now*) and got ourselves into a positive frame of mind: that it was quite okay and normal for us to be here, even though it patently wasn't. It's what conmen must do.

We turned off the road onto a track that ran straight towards the hills, taking us ever further from the relative security of the main road. The truck threw up clouds of red dust behind us, unhelpfully advertising our presence to anyone who might be watching. As we skirted a bend at speed, a Thai Marine base loomed up on the left, perhaps an indication that this was an insecure area?

After another five minutes, we came to a massive fenced-off compound, stuffed to the gunwales with rows of logs. On the far side, nestling under the hill, a series of low wooden huts, bristling with radio aerials, comprised the logging company's offices. Beyond them the dirt track snaked up into the forest and into Khmer Rouge territory.

The bluster that had helped us drive so confidently into the wilderness vanished. We were nervous as hell and stopped outside the barbed-wire gates of the log yard, summoning up the courage to go in. Every second's delay aroused yet more curiosity and we could see some people on the veranda of the office, perhaps 100m away, looking in our direction, talking to each other, and pointing. 'Sod it,' I said. I gunned the engine and we drove right into the centre of the place while Simon pressed the battery connectors onto the secret camera's power pack. He and Dtee climbed out of the truck. She started talking to some of the workers that began to gather near us; Simon came around to the driver's window, with the camera lens pointing towards the door.

'I'm really nervous,' he said.

'Well, can you turn around and be nervous pointing the other way, and film those trucks?' I answered helpfully. Simon gave me a withering look.

Two massive articulated log trucks emerged from the track that came through the trees from the Cambodian side, each laden with three or four huge tree trunks. Simon swung round and held the bag steady as the trucks powered into the compound amid a cloud of dust. There was no doubt about this. They could only have come from Khmer Rouge territory, and if the filming worked then we had the first concrete proof that they were currently exporting timber into Thailand in breach of both governments' stated border closure. Moreover, they were doing it within sight of the Marine base that we passed on the way in, so the collusion between the Thai military and the timber Mafia was also beyond question. The trouble was that we were in the middle of this nest of vipers; the Marines behind us, the Khmer Rouge in front, and the Thai logging Mafia all around us.

We stayed for what seemed like an age but which was probably only 20 minutes. This was our first attempt at filming people undercover and our psychology was all wrong. We hadn't acted like people who had a legitimate reason to be there. Instead, we had acted like the trespassers we were, and like a dog sensing fear the company workers were on their guard. We blustered through our cover story without much conviction, but if we kept talking then hopefully our interlocutors wouldn't have time to think.

Finally we made our excuses and left, just desperate to get the 4km of dirt track behind us and regain the relative security of the main road. Feeling more relaxed as we rejoined the highway, we began to talk ten to the dozen.

'The company is called Suan Pha Siam,' said Dtee, sounding a lot calmer than I felt. 'And they told me they're dealing directly with the Khmer Rouge.'

'And the film's great,' Simon responded as he peered into the Hi8's viewfinder. 'And it shows the guy telling Dtee that they're buying the timber from the KR – we've got them.'

The experience of our first sting was sobering. It had been dramatically successful on one level. Our plan to explore even the most unlikely-looking side roads had paid dividends. Going undercover and using a secret camera, we had captured hard evidence, and we had been lucky that those two log trucks arrived when they did. But we had come close to blowing it, through our own stupidity. We had got away with it and we learned from the experience.

We drove north and visited another log yard. The guard at Chao Praya Akanay told us that they had a permit to import 30,000 cubic metres of timber, and to prove it he pulled a bundle of papers from a filing cabinet. He rifled through them and laid a two-page document on the rough wooden table. Standing under the wooden veranda of the company's office, Dtee translated it. It was an import permit granted to the company and was signed by Sanan Kachornprasart, the Thai interior minister. I breathed in sharply. This proved that the much-rumoured collaboration between the Thai government and the Khmer Rouge was not only real, but went to the highest reaches of the Thai government. Dtee read the permit, holding it in front of the secret camera's lens.

We left, astonished at how freely the Thai timber workers talked. Evidently the trade was so widely accepted here that they felt they had nothing to hide.

In order to convince the governments of Thailand and Cambodia and the international community to act on whatever it was we found, the evidence we gathered would have to be 100 per cent credible. We decided upon an evidentiary standard similar to that used by UN investigators. If three entirely separate sources gave us the same information, then we could be pretty sure we were on the right track. We figured out that some of the best sources of intelligence could be the drivers of the trucks that hauled the logs from the forests and across the border into Thailand. They knew where they had been, where they were going, how often they did it and how much they carried. Perhaps best of all, they were so far down the food chain they had nothing to hide; they had no vested interests and they were bored.

We put this to the test when we stopped next to three trucks parked up at a cluster of rough wooden buildings that marked a roadside café. One of the drivers lay in a semi-stupor in the hammock he'd hung from the logs he was carrying. We ducked under the logs and offered him a cigarette, the ubiquitous passport to conversation. Relaxed in his sarong and a much-weathered T-shirt, with a scarf wrapped around his head, he was friendly, bored, curious about these *farang* (foreigners) and happy to talk. He worked for Suan Pha, the company near the Marine base.

The driver, who was delivering the logs to a sawmill in the historic city of Ayutthaya, told us that 100 trucks a day made the 60-km journey from the forests in Cambodia, across the border and into that same yard we had just visited. Each one carried between 1 and 5 trees. At around 5 cubic metres per tree, Suan Pha was importing 2,500 cubic metres per day. We had been told that the Khmer Rouge take was US$35 per cubic metre, so from Suan Pha alone they were making just under US$90,000 per day during the dry season. The numbers were racking up.

He also told us that the Khmer Rouge issued laminated photo IDs to the drivers, which permitted them to pass their checkpoints. It hadn't occurred to us that a rebel army holed up in the forests would be so organized. But now we knew, we really wanted one of those passes, or at least get sight of one. A Khmer Rouge document could be a game changer. We asked to see his pass, but he said he'd surrendered it to his boss after he entered Thailand. Damn.

Seventy-five kilometres north of Trat on Highway 317 lies the town of Pong Nam Ron. According to the map, a road ran east from there to the Cambodian border, and then continued for another 15km to Pailin, the Khmer Rouge capital and frontline military stronghold. Pailin had an almost mythical fascination for any Khmer Rouge watcher. It was hidden in dense jungle, surrounded by landmines, inaccessible and deadly. Was this east–west road another timber smuggling route?

As we drew into town we stopped for a Coke and took stock. Pong Nam Ron consisted of an unprepossessing collection of a few concrete municipal buildings and a shanty-like covered market, but we didn't have time to take much else in. We needed to use every daylight hour, so we climbed back into the truck, with Simon at the wheel, and headed for the border. And then we came across a sight that haunts me still. On the left of the road there was another log-storage area; big, but not as big as the ones we'd seen before.

What set this one apart was that just behind a sign mounted on two wooden posts that read 'Display Tech (Thailand) Co. Ltd', part of the trunk of a truly gigantic tree was lying alongside the road. At its base it measured around 3.5m in diameter. Behind it, against the treeline, were the ubiquitous rows of logs, but this tree was the mother of them all. The base of the trunk was adorned with garlands of flowers.

We got the camera going and sauntered in. We had learned our lesson and acted as though we owned the place. In fact, the rest of the area was deserted except for a solitary caretaker, who, happily, was bored and wanted some conversation. We proffered our Universal Export business cards and a cigarette, and expressed interest in buying the tree.

'So old, so old...' he mused.

'How old is it?' I asked. 'It looks amazing.'

'It's 1,300 years old. The villagers hung garlands on it to respect its spirit. It came from the Ol Sa Reo forest near Pailin.'

Even though we were lying about wanting to buy the tree, this made us feel a little sick. The locals venerated it, and it had been cut to fuel a killing machine.

'Who is Display Tech?' Simon asked, pointing at the white-painted sign.

'American company, the owner stays in Pattaya.'

Americans buying timber from the Khmer Rouge? That surprised us. If it was true there would be plenty of scope for embarrassment there, and for some leverage to stop this trade.

'We'd really like to buy this tree – you don't have this guy's phone number, do you?' Simon pressed.

The guard did have his phone number. The American's name was Larry Bridges and he was in business with the guard's cousin, a Thai businessman named Pairath Charoenphol. The guard was scant on detail but told us something extraordinary – that Pairath had a timber concession from the official Cambodian government but that he also paid the Khmer Rouge for the logs.

'So Pairath pays *both* sides?' Simon asked.

'Yes,' the guard replied. Simon and I glanced at each other.

'That sounds crazy,' Simon said.

'It's not crazy, the Khmer Rouge control the forest, the trees belong to them.'

If we'd got this right, the enormity of the situation was beginning to dawn on us. Could the Cambodian government actually be cooperating with their battlefield enemy in a trade that raised money so *both sides could fight each other*?

It seemed utterly insane.

'This is like Milo Minderbinder,' I said to Simon, referring to the arch wheeler-dealer in *Catch-22*, who sold bombs to the US Air Force and anti-aircraft ammunition to the Germans, so it didn't matter much to him who won the war – he would profit either way. We could scarcely believe the sheer cynicism of the situation. If our discovery was correct, then this trade was fuelling a war that was killing and maiming thousands of people, undermining an embryonic peace process *and* destroying the rainforest. With *both* Cambodian sides *plus the Thai government and military* complicit, the world was far, far madder than we had ever thought.

And now it seemed there were Americans involved too.

We knew right away that we needed to 'get' Larry Bridges and Pairath. A core part of Global Witness's ethos from day one was to get the bad guys. We needed to meet them, secretly film them, and then take them down. We didn't quite know how to take them down, but we were learning our trade as we went along and hoped we'd figure it out.

'Oh, can we see your Khmer Rouge pass?' Simon took the plunge.

'Only the drivers have those,' the man responded without batting an eye.

With much to think about, we climbed back into the truck and carried on towards the border, but we'd covered only a few kilometres before we were met by a roadblock, two concrete sentry boxes with a red-and-white pole slung between them, manned by five or six Thai Marines. They were definitely suspicious of us, and after a futile conversation we headed back the way we came.

We called in on another timber company. The manager told us they had just signed a two-year concession with the Khmer Rouge, for which they had paid 50 million baht up front to cut the trees and would have to pay another 50 million to bring the timber out. At the time, 100 million baht equated to US$4 million. He added that there was fighting just across the border. The war was very close by.

That evening, we booked into a hotel in Chanthaburi, the largest town along the whole border. By contrast with virtually every other town in the region, Chantaburi was modern and clean; and, as far as we could tell, the hotel was not a brothel, which was a plus. We felt less conspicuous and more relaxed than anywhere else we'd stayed thus far.

Our first job was to call Larry Bridges. We were nervous about this, even at the end of a phone line. A muffled voice answered, sounding a long way off. Larry said he wasn't in Thailand but would be in May. He'd heard we'd visited his log yard and was keen to do business. Would we come and meet him in May at the hotel where he always stayed, the Royal Cliff Beach Hotel in Pattaya? One foot in the door of the lion's den. We promised we would be there.

The next day we embarked on the long drive from Chanthaburi to Aranyaprathet, a Thai border town with a Wild West reputation. We took the scenic route, exploring the networks of small roads close to the border. It was around 5pm, not that long before the tropical night falls like a curtain, that we found ourselves on a dusty track, stopping occasionally to talk to locals, to see if there were any log-smuggling routes. The usual welcoming Thai smile was absent. People weren't communicating, their faces sullen, and answered us in single syllables. The atmosphere was almost unbearably heavy.

Coming up on our right we could see a track heading east and we slowed right down to take a look. The track ran straight down a gentle hill and after around 300m we could see a checkpoint. Closer to hand, a guy in a pea-green military jacket and a white canvas sun hat was just coming off the track and onto the road we were on. As he got closer, we asked him what was down the track. His face was shaded by the brim of his hat but as he looked up his eyes became visible, like searchlights from hell. They were so full of menace and hate it took our breath away. Without a word, he turned and headed down the road we had just come from. Although nothing tangible had happened, it was a bowel-wrench-ingly terrifying moment – I literally shivered. Then it dawned on us we were just across the border from the major Khmer Rouge base of Phnom Malai, and that was a Khmer Rouge checkpoint. Jesus, we could so easily have turned down that track without realizing it. And the guy we'd just seen? We had no doubt he was a Khmer Rouge soldier.

Places have different sell-by dates and we had just passed ours at Phnom Malai. I put my foot down and we left our Khmer Rouge friend as a diminishing silhouette in the rear-view mirror.

Back in London, Simon, Charmian and I sat in our office going over the evidence we had gathered, weirdly soothed by the familiar roar of London traffic rising from the junction below us.

The Thai and Cambodian governments' much-publicized closure of the border was now provably a lie. We reckoned the Khmer Rouge were generating US$10–20 million per month from their timber trade with Thailand. Far from being a spent force, they were arguably one of the richest rebel groups in the world. The incredible international effort to bring an end to the Cambodian Civil War was being seriously undermined, while the Cambodian people were paying the price.

We compiled the evidence into Global Witness's first report. We knew that it would need to be readable, credible and accessible. We worked with Dan Brown, a former colleague at EIA who had taught himself graphic design. As we sat long into the night in his small flat in Islington, the light from his Apple Mac screen illuminated our tired faces and the coffee mugs strewn about the room. Sometimes laughing, sometimes bickering over small points, we made edit after edit, sometimes slicing away entire sentences, and slowly the report took shape. *Forests, Famine & War – the Key to Cambodia's Future* was a rather thin document, but it was to the point and we were proud of it. Its 13 pages were sandwiched between covers that bore the photograph of the much-mourned 1,300-year-old tree we had seen down the road from Pailin. In the early hours of the morning, Dan pressed the button and the PDF emailed its way to the printers, and we stumbled home to our respective beds.

The first target of our report was the upcoming meeting of the International Committee on the Reconstruction of Cambodia (ICORC), due to be held in Paris in March 1995. This meeting would bring together the Cambodian government, the countries providing it foreign aid and the lending institutions like the World Bank and the International Monetary Fund (IMF), to assess Cambodia's progress. Together the aid they provided comprised around 50 per cent of the country's national budget. The meeting would be strained. Journalist Nate Thayer, a veteran Cambodia watcher, wrote in the *Phnom Penh Post* just ahead of the meeting: 'Many diplomats are convinced that the veneer of democracy is crumbling and the political thuggery that has kept Cambodia one of the last running sores of Southeast Asia is on the ascendancy.'

We wanted to add to the Cambodian and Thai governments' strain. We possessed fantastic information, probably more even than any intelligence service except Thailand's, who were unlikely to help, but we were still an unknown organization with no track record. Ahead of the Paris meeting, we wanted to brief the UK Foreign & Commonwealth Office (FCO), but just getting a meeting with them was a feat in itself. Who were we, and why should they meet with us? But we persisted and, somewhat awed, we were finally led along the stately corridors and up the grand staircases built at the height of the Empire, ending up in a small room on an upper floor trying to get the attention of a rather hostile, bored woman who evidently didn't believe what we were telling her. We had no idea if anything we had said or done would find its way into the papers the government ministers and officials would bring with them to Paris, but we were sure as hell going to go.

Simon and I checked into a small hotel near the conference centre and then made our way to our first appointment at the Quai D'Orsay, the majestic building that houses the Ministry for Europe and Foreign Affairs on the Left Bank of the Seine. As in London, we had a struggle to get the meeting in the first place, but when we arrived, we were escorted to an ornate office where we met an extraordinarily well-groomed civil servant. Elegant and urbane, he listened as we poured out the findings of our border investigation, the information we had sweated blood to obtain.

'Why are you working on Cambodia?' he asked. 'Such a small country of no strategic value.'

'Pompous shit,' Simon said as we regained the street.

With our noses flattened by another governmental brick wall, we decided to organize our first-ever press conference instead. We sent invitations to all the main press agencies and hired a small room in the hotel. We arrived early and set up the room, placing a copy of the report and press release on each chair, and paced nervously as the 11am start time approached. And went. At 5 past 11, we thought that journalists were probably always late. At 10 past, we were becoming uneasy; by 20 past we knew that no one would come. At half past, we thought how humiliating and awkward it would be if just one solitary journalist showed up in the empty room. 'Fuck this,' I said, and in silent agreement we bundled up the reports and press releases and scuttled out. We were chastened, but even then rather amused.

We joined the press scrum outside the conference centre as the dignitaries arrived, including the two Cambodian prime ministers in separate cars. I moved through the crowd and as Hun Sen emerged from his limousine, I thrust our report towards him and he instinctively took it. Simon did the same with Ranariddh. I doubt either one read it, but it made us feel better.

For us, Paris was a washout, but it was a salutary lesson that even the best information is useless if you can't get people to look at it.

In May we returned to the border. The Cambodian government's amnesty to remove abandoned logs had expired and the Thai border closure remained in force, on paper at least. If any logs were crossing the border now, then there were no excuses. We knew the loggers were racing against time: the onset of the rainy season would reduce the laterite logging roads to mires, and that would close down the trade more effectively than any half-arsed government edict. This meant a re-run of the whole trip: 3,500km of hard driving that would take us down every border track we could find. We also had an appointment to keep. We had not forgotten the American logger Larry Bridges and the 1,300-year-old tree.

Slightly surer of our ground now, we were accompanied by another translator, this one nicknamed 'A', an accomplished journalist. Yet things didn't always go our way. We returned down that remote 4-km road past the Thai Marine base at Trat and into the log yard of Suan Pha Siam. Although we had learned one lesson from our previous trip, which was to waltz right in and present our cards as though we owned the place, something had changed.

This time around, the atmosphere was hostile, and we had to drag answers out of people. We felt uneasy. The yard contained slightly fewer logs than before, and we wanted to get filming them. As we drove out, we paused by the gate and Simon's motor wind took shot after shot. As he was photographing, I saw that the guys on the office veranda were running towards their vehicle. I shouted to Simon and 'A' to get in, and they didn't need to be told twice. They piled into the back and in classic car-chase style, Simon was still closing the door as I revved the engine and skidded a full circle around a pile of logs and sped out of the compound as fast as I could. I just hoped the Marines were keeping inside their base as I saw the dust being thrown up by the loggers' vehicle a few hundred metres behind.

I put my foot down while Simon reached for the mobile phone. We had security protocols in place and he was going to phone Charmian in the UK to let her know what was happening and to give our GPS position. Then if we didn't make contact at an agreed time, she'd start raising hell with the authorities and the British Embassy. That was, if we had had a phone signal – but we didn't. The only choice we had now was to lose our tail.

We began to thank the fact that the track was deserted and we screamed through those 4km in record time. After what seemed like a lifetime, we swerved onto the main road and headed towards Trat. We weren't going to lose our friends on this single straight road, but maybe we could in the town.

I overtook the few cars and lorries ahead and we began to put more distance between us and the loggers' vehicle. After around 15 minutes, we drove with relief between the low white buildings that marked the outskirts of the town. We turned off a side street into another, and yet another, and pulled up in the shade of a tall warehouse, concealed from view and with an exit route already planned, our hearts thumping. We still had no phone signal, so we just waited there for another 15 minutes until we felt the coast was clear, and then edged out of town and headed north. We apologized to our translator and said it wasn't usually like this, although we didn't necessarily believe that ourselves.

But sometimes things did go our way. Sipping cold water on the shady veranda of the Chanthaburi Romphoroow company, we asked the manager what was by now a routine question, tinged with hidden desperation. 'Is it true what we've heard, that the Khmer Rouge issue ID cards to the truck drivers?'

'Yes, this is true, I can show you.' He got up and went into the darkness of the office and we heard a desk drawer being opened and various objects being shifted around. He came out a minute later and there in his hand was a thick stack of laminated light-blue cards held together by a rubber band. He handed one to Simon and one to me. They were just bigger than a playing card, with the back of the card bearing the company name, while the front was headlined with beautifully ornate Khmer script, with space below for the worker's name and the validity period of the card. The worker's passport-style photo occupied the top left-hand corner and had been rubber-stamped with a circular device with more Khmer script and the numbers 909 below them.

Khmer Rouge Division 909.

It felt brilliant to hold that card in my hand. We tried not to look too excited as I held it in front of the secret camera, as inconspicuously as I could.

'That's amazing, I've never seen one of these before. I had no idea the Khmer Rouge were so sophisticated,' Simon said.

'The Red Khmer are very well organized. They control who comes into their territory, and they take a cut of every cubic metre of timber, so they need to be well organized. But they are good to deal with, they honour their deals.' A message we'd heard repeatedly.

'I don't suppose we could have a copy of this card, could we?' I asked.

'Take them,' the man said and smiled. 'I have hundreds of them.'

Scarcely believing our good fortune, we drove fast towards Highway 317. Tucked away in our luggage we now had documentary proof of the timber trade from the Khmer Rouge themselves.

We were heading for the Khukhan Aroonsawat Company in Thailand's Sisaket Province. It was rumoured to be owned by the Khmer Rouge military leader and Pol Pot's most senior, loyal and ruthless general, the one-legged Ta Mok, known as 'the Butcher'. Both he and Pol Pot were based in the regime's main stronghold of Anlong Veng, situated around 16km south of the border pass at Chong Sa-ngam.

Whether because of fear or the meal of the night before, my guts were in a state of revolution. Field investigations like these leave no room for privacy and every few kilometres we had to stop so I could rush out and squat by the side of the road. Outwardly funny, but losing fluids in this heat could be a serious thing, and I drank copious quantities of water, but felt weak and not really in the mood to do what we had to do.

At the small town of Khukhan, we took the road heading south, which gradually narrowed and became increasingly remote. The road was bordered by low scrub, blocking our views to left and right, and we gingerly drove on, ignorant of what we would find. A checkpoint, a village or maybe the border itself?

On the left-hand side of the road was a solitary building, an office of the Thai Royal Forest Department (RFD). Given that the forests on the Thai side of the border had been shaved, as one of our spook friends had put it a year before, the only timber the office was likely to regulate had to come from Cambodia.

We parked in the shade of the white concrete building, switched on the secret camera and, presenting our Universal Export cards, were able to meet with the director. We sat around his desk and probed him for information as to whether any timber was crossing the border, and the role of the Khukhan Aroonsawat Company. He and the two staff members with him were friendly and unsuspecting, but our questions were careful – we were a long way from any kind of safety and, as far as we could judge, only a few kilometres from the border. All the while I felt the stomach cramps that heralded the next run to the loo. Nothing for it but to ask where it was, and I was none too pleased to find that it was in a roofless concrete cubicle in the middle of the large room. To fear and discomfort I added humiliation to my woes, as my trumpeting farts resounded in this tiny cell and must have been audible to everyone in the room outside. Even I could see the funny side, but thankfully for the remains of my dignity nothing was said as I returned to my chair and rejoined the conversation. Maybe my performance was helpful – diarrhoea is a great leveller.

The director's job was to enforce the strict Thai forestry regulations. Imported logs, he told us, had to meet strict requirements as to their dimensions. He was undoubtedly a stickler for the rules and proudly pointed to his record of bringing 52 cases against 36 people this year, including one for the illegal possession of 1,500kg of charcoal. But it was evidently not his job to question the status of the border.

He went on to tell us that Khukhan Aroonsawat had subcontracted two other timber companies that had received an import quota from the RFD. But in this area, unlike on Thailand's eastern border with Cambodia, Thais were not allowed to cut trees in

Cambodia. That was done by the Khmer Rouge themselves. They still held the border and the manager spoke highly of them. 'I was there a year ago,' he said. 'They cooked for me and were gracious, not like the Thai military, who get drunk and shoot in the air.' His only complaint was that the area was hard to inspect because of landmines.

Due to his diligence, Thailand could be assured that only trees that met their strict technical standards would enter the country. The fact that they had been felled illegally, that the border was technically closed and that Thailand was in contravention of its commitments under the Paris Peace Agreements was of no concern to the director of this remote outpost.

Thanking him, we got back into the Hilux and followed his directions as we drove further south towards the border, where Khukhan Aroonsawat's log yard lay. It was a small wooden house with a few empty log trucks parked outside. The manager confirmed what the forestry director had told us a few minutes before. The Khmer Rouge had felled the trees and were waiting for the rubber stamp from the Thai Interior Ministry to import the logs, 20,000 cubic metres of them. It seemed relations between the Thai Army and the Khmer Rouge were totally relaxed. It was as if there was no border between them. They were simply players in the same business.

Simon took the wheel and we headed south. Towards the border. After around ten minutes, we could see the ubiquitous red-and-white pole of a military checkpoint slung across the road. Dressed in full combat gear, these were elite troops: Thai Rangers. Steel helmets pulled low over their eyes, their webbing belts heavy with magazine pouches for the M16 rifles they gripped in readiness, these soldiers were in no mood for conversation. Uneasy with our presence, they barked questions at us. What were we doing here? Where did we think we were going? All we could elicit, which was valuable in itself, was that the Chong S'ak Nam border crossing lay 10km further down the narrow road snaking away from the checkpoint.

We maintained an outward calm we didn't feel as 'A' heard one of them ask a colleague to radio their officer. We had heard enough. It may as well have been Khmer Rouge territory. It struck me that Anlong Veng, the last outpost of Pol Pot himself and his 'Brother Number Four', Ta Mok, 'the Butcher', had far too much in common with mad Colonel Kurtz's gruesome jungle empire as depicted in *Apocalypse Now*: a deranged old man with the power of life and death commanding a death cult from an ancient Khmer temple hidden away in the depths of the forests.

Before the net closed, we made our apologies, said we were lost and before they could stop us we were back in the Hilux heading north before taking the highway back to Bangkok.

PATTAYA, THAILAND, MAY 1995

Despite stiff competition, Pattaya holds its own as Thailand's sleaziest and tackiest tourist resort. Its mass of concrete hotels crowd what once must have been the shore of a beautiful bay on the Gulf of Thailand.

It was dark when Simon and I drove up to the Royal Cliff Beach Hotel, where we had arranged to meet Larry Bridges. The hotel's ugly nine-storey sandstone-coloured blocks were reminiscent of a large bunker, separated from the seashore by a pool and sunbathing deck. I reversed the Hilux into the nearest available parking space to the hotel entrance. The truck's coating of thick red dust was testament to the thousands of kilometres we had travelled over dirt roads in a world removed from the bling-filled glitz of Pattaya. But these worlds were connected. The money made through the funding of a war was paying for a luxury hotel suite somewhere in these faceless blocks.

Mustering up our courage, we entered the cavernous reception area and asked the receptionist to call Larry's room, and after a short while we were ushered up. The door was opened by an urbane man in his late forties or early fifties; neatly groomed, bearded and carefully dressed in a pale-blue short-sleeved safari suit (horrid).

'Hey, you must be Chris…Richard…C'mon in. Welcome.' This was Larry. 'This here is Tom, he's the guy who exports the timber, and this is my partner, Pairath.'

Thomas D Haylett was a shortish, heavily built and affable man, also bearded, and dressed in jeans and a check shirt. Pairath was a different kettle of fish. Doing the business he did, operating along the Thai–Cambodian border, smuggling timber and dealing with the Khmer Rouge, means needing to be well connected and corrupt, and he looked it. His cold, unblinking eyes stared straight through us, his face pockmarked and scarred. He was outwardly friendly enough, but it felt like it was skin deep at the most. Pairath was a scary man.

We sat on a corner sofa in the dimly lit room, our backs to the wall. Larry sat at a table opposite us with Pairath. Tom plonked himself to our left. I was in the middle of the sofa with Simon to my right. I took my notebook out of the camera bag – partly a deceptive move to provide a reason for having the bag – and set the bag behind me on a shelf above the sofa.

If you're inexperienced in undercover filming, as we were then, you're forever scared of discovery. Every time anyone's eye passed over the camera bag, we thought they'd spotted the lens. On top of that, we had found that the battery pack with its eight AA batteries got incredibly hot – too hot to touch – and we were forever in fear of the thing catching fire. Despite myself, I couldn't help but keep turning around to look towards the bag with a worried look on my face.

But we plunged right in, introduced Universal Export and made our pitch to buy timber. We started by questioning how on earth they could export timber from Khmer Rouge territory.

'I pay both sides,' Pairath said bluntly. 'The Khmer Rouge – the wood belongs to the Khmer Rouge – they are in the forest.'

I tried to suppress the surge of excitement I felt at Pairath's admission of his Khmer Rouge links. 'If you don't pay them, you are in trouble, I guess?' I asked.

'Just like the people who got killed in November,' Larry answered.

'Twenty-seven people got killed in November,' said Pairath, without emotion.

They were referring to the murder of workers for Thai logging company BLP that had taken place just four months before. We were digesting these unpleasant facts when time came to a grinding halt as Thomas Haylett began to talk. In a southern drawl not a million miles away from that of Western star Slim Pickens, he began to drone on about the quantity and quality of wood they could procure.

'Well, I reckon we could get you anything you want. Why, just the other day we exported 27,000 board feet of lumber to the States. I got a company you see, Lumber World, based out of West Palm

Beach, Florida. We import thousands and thousands of board feet into the States every year...'

He went on and on and on. So much so that we began to lose some of our fear and started being lulled to sleep, but among the boredom were some gems.

'So we'll be here as long as we can get the wood, you know; they could close everything down tomorrow,' Larry interrupted.

'We thought they had,' Simon said. 'As I said to you on the phone, I thought they had.'

'They have, they have – he's the only one who can get this stuff.' Thomas gestured towards Pairath, who tipped his head and allowed a thin smile.

'That must have taken some skilled negotiation,' I said.

'Skilled negotiation,' Larry confirmed. 'He was able to get in with the right people, you know.'

'Hey, you know what impressed me?' asked Thomas. We said we didn't, but we felt pretty sure we'd find out whether we wanted to or not. 'Did you check through Customs when you entered the country?' We said we had.

'We didn't. He...' Thomas nodded towards Pairath, 'just escorts us right in. You know, his connections...' This suggested that the collusion between the Khmer Rouge and the Thai authorities didn't stop with the military on the border but permeated a long way into authorities in Bangkok. We started to wonder just how high up the food chain this went.

Then Larry went into the next room and came back with an ornamental ship's wheel, about 50cm in diameter, newly turned from rosewood and set off with a large quartz clock at its hub. It was one of the tackiest things I had ever seen and a tragic waste of a majestic old tree.

'We can sell you stuff like this too,' said Larry. He couldn't have sold it to me.

'Wow, that's really nice,' Simon and I said, biting our tongues and beginning to think we'd been here long enough. Any longer and either we would give the game away or the camera bag might catch fire.

We bid fond farewells and promised to be in touch.

*

Before returning to London, and by now exhausted, we held press conferences in both Phnom Penh and Bangkok. We scheduled them as close as possible to our planes' departure times so we would be out of there before the news broke, thus establishing a habit that has served Global Witness ever since when we have bad news to deliver in countries ruled by dodgy governments.

We sat at the table at the front of the press room at the Foreign Correspondents' Club in Phnom Penh, waiting nervously for the journalists to arrive. The humiliation of Paris was still fresh in our minds. But people here had been incredibly generous with their time over the past few months, and amazingly supportive to two guys and the crazy idea they were pursuing. Now it was the acid test: would our story be enough for them to file news reports? Gradually the journalists began to drift in and the room became alive with different conversations as they exchanged news and gossip. Above them the whirring of the ceiling fans cut through the humid air, with little effect beyond stirring the thick fug of cigarette smoke into eddies that floated lethargically under the roof beams.

Simon and I took it in turns to present our findings. We kept to the facts, exposing the contrast between what the Thai and Cambodian governments had told the world they were doing – keeping the border closed to timber exports in order to deprive the Khmer Rouge of material support – and what was actually happening on the ground: the free flow of timber trucks earning the Khmer Rouge millions of dollars a month, *with the complicity of both governments*. The 'amnesty' granted by the Cambodian government to export 'abandoned' logs was a myth, a thin lie that gave the loggers carte blanche to cut and export as many logs as they could.

None of the journalists had been to the border and the few scraps of intelligence on this trade were well out of date, so they were hungry for these revelations. Now we would have to wait and see what resulted from the news going down the wires.

Our translator 'A' helped organize a second conference the next day, in Bangkok, where we delivered the same story to another crowded room. The earliest flight we could take was the following morning and when we arrived at the airport we went straight to the nearest news stand. The banner headlines of the English-language *Bangkok Post* shouted 'Chuan dismisses Global Witness report'. Chuan Leekpai was the Thai prime minster. Shit, we had pressed buttons right at the top. The news had spread far as reports from the BBC, Reuters, Associated Press and others winged their way across the world. This was a key part of our strategy. If the policymakers we needed to convince felt there was public concern, then they might act; and press interest was synonymous with public concern.

We were exultant on the one hand, but on the other now felt like someone was shining a spotlight on us as we made our way through Customs to our flight home. We desperately tried to look invisible – not easy when you're loaded down with secret filming equipment, notebooks stuffed full of your findings, hours of secretly filmed interviews on tape, military-grade maps of the border marked with the locations of timber companies and smuggling routes, and rolls of film packed with hundreds of photographs. And, to top it all, Khmer Rouge-issued photo IDs.

WASHINGTON, DC, JULY 1995

Allan Thornton's advice was still ringing in our ears: if you really want to change anything in this world, start with Washington, the epicentre of global influence and power. Through one of our friends at Novib, we were introduced to Oxfam America and they agreed to fund our first post-investigation foray – and better than that they lent us their secret weapon.

Kathy Knight, in late middle age and looking for all the world like the archetypal American-as-apple-pie grandmother, was a veteran anti-Vietnam War activist who recounted tales of the mass demonstrations and sit-ins she had taken part in on the steps of the Capitol in the 1960s and 1970s. All this meant that she knew her way around Washington, which was just as well because it was a maze. We needed to convince key politicians to take up our case, to enact legislation and to exert pressure on the US government to act. We needed the State Department, the equivalent to the UK Foreign Office, to put diplomatic pressure on Thailand to stop trading with the Khmer Rouge.

The offices of these politicians are dotted around the elegant dome of the Capitol in massive buildings named after luminaries and dead forebears like Longworth, Dirksen and Rayburn. We met Kathy in a café close by one of these and she began our education in how Washington works and how we could work it. The US Congress comprises the Senate and the House of Representatives, both of which house specialist committees, by theme or geography for example, which mirror their counterparts in the other house. Kathy told us we would be homing in on the committees focusing on international relations, and in particular the Subcommittee on Asian & Pacific Affairs.

In a refreshing example of democracy, these buildings are open to the public. We left the café and walked a short way under a clear scorching July sky and were almost blinded by the dazzling white walls of the Hart Senate Office Building. We navigated the X-ray machines and body scanners and entered the cavernous air-conditioned cool inside. We entered a vast atrium where towering 15m above us was *Mountains and Clouds* – a massive black steel and aluminium sculpture rather than the real thing. Rather like at the Foreign & Commonwealth Office in London, someone was making a point. The Stars and Stripes and the official state flags mounted on poles in the corridor marked out the offices of the senators.

We were keeping an appointment with a man who was to play a key role in this campaign. In the scruffy backroom, countless photographs of the occupant in the company of everyone from villagers to activists and senior politicians taken in some of the world's hotspots, ranging from Latin America to the Balkans and Southeast Asia, jostled for space with a hoard of souvenirs, defused munitions and posters calling for landmine bans. Somehow squeezed into this space were a small, shabby sofa, a coffee table and a desk piled high with bundles of documents. At this desk sat a wiry dark-haired man in faded Levi's and an un-ironed open-necked white shirt. He held a phone to one ear and had another sandwiched between his shoulder and his other ear and was engaged in two near simultaneous but completely separate conversations. Meanwhile, a single finger of his free hand jabbed sporadically into the keyboard of his computer. Tim Rieser is the most influential man you've never heard of.

Described by prominent Washington news website *The Hill* as one of 'the most powerful staffers in Congress presiding over US foreign policy and US foreign assistance', Tim worked for the Democratic senator Patrick Leahy, a key member of the Department of State and Foreign Operations Subcommittee of the Appropriations Committee. We didn't have a clue what the committee's name even meant, let alone what the committee did, but it turned out to be very simple. Every year, together with its counterpart in the House, it

produces the Foreign Operations Act, which directs how every cent
of US foreign spending is deployed: in its own words, it 'strengthens
diplomacy and development, promotes democracy abroad, provides
critical assistance to allies, and continues lifesaving global health
and humanitarian assistance programs for the world's most vulnerable populations.'

The act was potentially a significant tool for good but also
provided an influential lever if you knew how to pull it. Along with
the Yale academic Craig Etcheson, who we'd met on our first visit
to Washington, Tim had crafted a law that turned out to be one of
our most powerful cards. It required the US president to 'terminate
assistance to any country or organization that he determines is
cooperating, tactically or strategically with the Khmer Rouge in
their military operations'.

Surely, we thought, our evidence of Thailand's role in trading
timber with the Khmer Rouge must count as 'cooperation'. If we
were right, then the US could sanction aid to Thailand. In Thailand's
case the bill applied to only a relatively small amount of military
support, but the diplomatic ramifications of cutting aid to a key ally
were obvious even to us.

We managed to snatch a conversation with Tim, who had
sacrificed one of his phones and answered the other one only
occasionally – sometimes perfunctorily dismissing the caller
or entering into short, businesslike conversations. As hurriedly
as we could, we told him who we were and what we had found
along the Thai–Cambodian border. Unlike the civil servant in the
Foreign Office, he listened intently. Tim was a lawyer and told us
that the crucial clause was unlikely to work because it referred to
military cooperation, not trade. What we needed to do was craft
new language to make the clause fit for purpose. Tim asked us to
go away and come up with some language of our own, which he
would then convert into suitable legalese and include when next
year's bill went to the subcommittee. He really cared. He was an
activist in a position of power.

We left the meeting floating on air. Allan had been right –
Washington really was a place where you could get things done.
In our two weeks there, we met a whole host of staffers in the
House and Senate's subcommittees on Foreign Relations and Asian
& Pacific Affairs.

The State Department was another kettle of fish. We would queue at the reception desk to get our passes and would then be escorted to whichever office we were due to meet, under the watchful gaze of armed security. Walking down seemingly endless corridors we would be conveyed to offices whose reception areas were dominated by photos of President Bill Clinton and Secretary of State Warren Christopher. So labyrinthine was the place that had our various escorts left us, we would never have found our own way out.

Some of the officials we met were hard to convince. They believed or wanted to believe what they had been told by their counterparts in Thailand and Cambodia: that the border was closed, and that our information therefore had to be wrong. And here we began to realize the power of our methodology. We had been there. We could talk with authority about what we had seen. We produced photographs of the lines of log trucks on the Thai side of the border. We showed them the Khmer Rouge ID cards and the log import permit. In short, we knew we were right. We left them with video cassettes of some of the secret film we had taken.

We met with David Harwood, the special adviser to the Undersecretary of State for Global Affairs, and numerous other State Department officials responsible for Thai–Burma Affairs and Vietnam, Laos and Cambodia Affairs, various analysts and, critically, someone from the Political Section of the US Embassy in Bangkok. The man on the ground.

Simon and I were both struck by what we nicknamed the 'Hoover effect'. Sitting across the table from congressional staffers and civil servants, we expounded our adventures along the border and in Phnom Penh. We stuck to the facts, but we were passionate about what we were doing; emphasizing key points, thrusting documents and photos across the table, willing them to take action. But on the other side of the table, as our information was sucked in, we were often met with impassive faces and silence. Talking for 10 or 20 minutes across the table from our stone-faced interlocutors, we struggled to keep our confidence up. We had no idea what they thought or what, if anything, they were taking in.

One of these people was Richard Houghton, legislative assistant to a Republican senator from Wyoming, Craig Thomas, chair of the Senate Foreign Relations Subcommittee on East Asian and Pacific Affairs. Richard was tall, blond and square-jawed like only

Americans can be and was built like a US Marine. We could read nothing from his reaction to our information, but as it turned out this meeting proved to be one of the key ones.

On 21 July his boss, Senator Thomas, issued a three-page statement to the US Senate expressing his concerns about continued links between Thailand and the Khmer Rouge and detailed specific instances of Thai involvement with the timber trade. Our information. In his conclusion, he said:

> *I have made my concerns about this issue clear to both of our ambassadors-designate [to Thailand and Cambodia] and to the State Department. I hope this statement makes it clear to the Thai government. If a significant effort is not made as promised by the Thai government to fully investigate and stem the cross border trade and their dealings with the Khmer Rouge, then I would find myself placed in the position of calling on our government to abide by that provision of Pub.L. No. 103-306 requiring that the President shall 'terminate assistance to any country or organization that he determines is cooperating, tactically or strategically with the Khmer Rouge in their military operations'.*

Tim Rieser's law.

'They took us seriously!' Simon exclaimed in disbelief as we sat in the dimly lit bar of the Childe Harold. 'Us?' I responded. 'A couple of gobshites from London.' Our information had made it onto the record of the US Senate; and, although we were no experts at diplomacy, we could imagine the flurry of cables between the Thai Embassy and their masters in Bangkok. We could scarcely believe that we had been taken seriously at this level because we still didn't take ourselves very seriously.

We began to learn the dark arts of manipulation as we continued our advocacy. The only congressman we actually met was Dana Rohrabacher. We passed the Bear Flag of California and entered an office scene that could have been taken straight out of a *Far Side* cartoon: the staffers were a collection of enormously vast men perching on chairs that were too small for them, all beavering away on work for this notoriously right-wing politician. In the inner sanctum we were met by a man in a fawn tropical suit sitting under a large-framed photograph of his bearded self, clutching a surfboard in the waves off California.

He gestured for us to take two chairs in front of his desk and sat impassively as we gave him the same briefing we'd by now given to so many others. When we finished, he sat back in his chair. 'I ain't known as an environmentalist.'

Simon leaned forward and said, 'But this is about a trade that's generating millions for the *communist* Khmer Rouge.' Like a Pavlovian reaction, Rohrabacher propelled himself forward in his chair. '*Communist* Kaymair Rouge? Well, we better goddamned do something about that...'

We never discovered what it was that he did, but we presume his voice was added to the growing concern about what was happening in Thailand and Cambodia.

It had been a whirlwind seven months. We had proved that the Khmer Rouge's continuing war was funded by timber and that the border closure between Cambodia and Thailand was a fallacy; the international community had begun to wake up to these facts. We had demonstrated that the timber trade wasn't something that could be written off as an environmental issue but was in fact the main fuel of a deadly civil war. A war where corruption had overtaken any sense of idealism and patriotism – on both sides – and that now posed a mortal threat to Cambodia's fledgling democracy.

And we had shown that a few determined people could begin to shift international policy. We hadn't yet won. This kind of challenge can take years, even decades. But we had made a start.

POSTSCRIPT

What we didn't know back in 1995 was that Thai prime minister Chuan Leekpai had closed the Thai border on 27 May, the day after our press conference in Bangkok. Before we went to Washington. In any case we had already learned that Thai promises of border closures weren't worth the paper they were written on.

In April 1996, while on a visit to Phnom Penh, we were leaked an explosive set of documents. They exposed that on 8 January 1996 there was a secret high-level meeting in Bangkok. Thailand's deputy prime minister and minister of defence, General Chavalit, met with

Cambodia's ambassador to Thailand, Roland Eng, and the minister of agriculture, Tao Seng Huor, to discuss the problem of 'old logs' abandoned along the Thai–Cambodian border.

At 3pm on the same day, the bosses of 13 Thai logging companies went to the Cambodian Embassy and also met with Roland Eng and Tao Seng Huor.

After these meetings, the Cambodian co-prime ministers signed three letters addressed to the Thai prime minister. They made a deal. These letters were requests for 18 Thai timber companies to export almost 1.1 million cubic metres of old logs through various specific border points. These letters, officially opening the border to the Thai–Khmer Rouge timber trade on a massive scale, effectively undid everything we had achieved so far.

We estimated that the Khmer Rouge take from the deal was US$95 million; in addition to this, the letters detailed that the Cambodian government would be paid US$35 per cubic metre of timber. The IMF, with sight of the government's books, saw no mention of an expected influx of the US$35 million this amounted to – it was totally off budget. No one knew where that money would have gone. Except, perhaps, Cambodia's two prime ministers. This was an unpleasant indication of the gross corruption that was already pervading Cambodia's new government and, as a direct result, the IMF withdrew from the country, saying that the destruction of Cambodia's forests 'was the most important issue facing Cambodia'. This was an almost unprecedented move anywhere. We had exposed that the political leadership of both countries was rotten to the core and diplomatic pressure reached boiling point. Ironically for a communist group, it was the money that got them.

This time the border was closed for good. Starved of funds, the Khmer Rouge began to fall apart, with mass defections taking place. Finally, in the ruins of the temple at Preah Vihear, senior Khmer Rouge officers and the Cambodian military brokered the final defection. On 4 December 1998, 23 years after the Khmer Rouge had brought a living hell to Cambodia, the war ended. It should have ended years before.

2

ANGOLA – BLOOD ON THE ROCKS

The diamond business is imbued with a sense of mystery and glamour. Hard-bitten prospectors and adventurers desperate for the lucky strike that would buy them out of poverty have long been the stuff of stories and legends. The priceless stones they risk their lives to obtain have found their way into the crown jewels of royal families all over the world, and bedeck film stars and supermodels alike. Names like Tiffany, Cartier and Graff evoke the star-studded parties of the 1930s and the legends of Hollywood. But are diamonds priceless?

By the mid-1990s, 80 per cent of all the diamonds being dug out of the ground globally were purchased by one company – De Beers. But it was more than just a company. It was a hugely powerful cartel, enabling De Beers to set the global market price of diamonds.

To maintain their monopoly and keep diamond prices high, De Beers had to buy every diamond they could lay their hands on, regardless of who was selling it, where it came from or at what human cost.

Sitting in his office in Luanda, Aidan McQuade answered the phone. It was no routine call. The leader of his drilling team told him they had safely arrived in the small village of Cangandala, but another truck that had followed them along the same narrow, pitted and remote road from the besieged city of Malange had struck a mine, killing the occupants. These were not the only people who would die as a result of this explosion.

A big man from County Armagh, Northern Ireland, Aidan was the country director for Oxfam in Angola during the 1990s, at the height of the third civil war to subsume the country. His team of engineers had gone to Cangandala, a small village swelled by thousands of people displaced by war, to drill for water.

The problem now was that although the team had arrived safely, they would have to return the 20km along the same road to get back to Malange, and they had no idea whether any other mines had been laid. If the National Union for the Total Independence of Angola (UNITA) unit that laid the mine had breached the government enclave around the city, then the guerrillas could still be there.

The call that finally came to say that his team had made it back okay was a huge relief, but during the hours of anxious waiting, Aidan had made one of the most difficult decisions of his life. His instructions to his programme manager in Malange were succinct: 'You are to shut down operations immediately in Cangandala and shift them to a less exposed part of the enclave.' The programme engineer protested because he hadn't finished his work. No clean water meant that people would die, with children being the most vulnerable.

But Aidan was adamant. He knew that if his staff were killed or injured, it would threaten Oxfam's entire-country operation. It was a decision that haunted him. 'Simply because I can make rational claim to have acted morally and to have managed the security of the situation wisely does little to assuage the thought that I condemned to death women as old as my mother and children who, when I saw them playing in the Cangandala camps, reminded me of my nieces and nephew,' he wrote.

Aidan's experience underlined the horror of war and the personal tragedies of the victims. This is true of all wars, so how is it that someone keeps paying for them?

In 1996, buoyed by our progress but still totally immersed in our work on Cambodia, we were approached by our old boss at EIA, Allan Thornton, with a tantalizing proposition. He asked us to do something that no organization had done before: investigate the role of diamonds in funding war.

It had all started with elephants.

For the past decade, EIA had been investigating the global ivory trade, which was responsible for the slaughter of 70,000 elephants a year in Africa and was the first issue Charmian worked on when she joined EIA in 1987. The daring undercover investigations that had inspired EIA's work took their teams from Africa to the United Arab Emirates and Hong Kong, unearthing the dangerous criminal networks behind the trade. EIA's campaign for an international ban on the ivory trade came to fruition in 1989, when the Convention on International Trade in Endangered Species (CITES) placed elephants on Appendix I and the trade in ivory became illegal under international law.

'South Africa opposed the ban,' Allan told Simon, Charmian and me, as we sat in his office in Clerkenwell. He spoke with quiet authority, his eyes fixing each of us in turn. 'Its military played a role in trading arms for ivory with the rebels fighting civil wars in Mozambique and Angola.'

EIA had signed agreements with the governments of Angola and Mozambique to help them set up national parks to protect elephants and to create jobs. In Mozambique they had some early successes. 'But in Angola the situation has just not stabilized, because of the UNITA militia,' Allan said.

Other than the odd news article about the war there, we knew nothing of Angola; but Allan had become something of an expert on the subject. 'I've been reading about how UNITA is a key player in the diamond trade,' he continued. 'Atrocities are going on, elephants are being poached and landmines are being planted. UNITA are the driving force.'

Allan had sent a friend to Belgium, a major diamond-trading centre, to look into the trade there. He spent a week talking to the different diamond sellers and they told him that Angolan diamonds were making their way onto the market through Belgium, and that De Beers were playing a major role. Allan told us: 'I thought, it's horrifying that the global diamond trade is causing this slaughter of people in Angola. And then I thought I should come talk to you.'

He proposed that we should join with EIA in a campaign to tackle the scourge of conflict diamonds. The proposition was simple enough, but the answer was far from straightforward. This was a completely new issue. Public awareness of the role diamonds played in conflict was zero. Angola was a country we had never been to, diamonds a resource that we knew nothing about, and this was an industry in which we had no contacts. Added to all that, although we'd recently ensconced ourselves in a proper office, Global Witness still consisted of just five people: Simon, Charmian, me and two volunteers, Jon Buckrell and Isobel Gore. Of course, we thought it was a great idea.

*

When we started Global Witness, we knew that we didn't want to be a single-issue organization but had no idea what our second campaign would be. Now, there was something about Allan's proposition that hooked us.

Cambodia had exemplified for us the linkages between environmental destruction and human-rights abuses, but a few years into that work we had learned that the situation was far more complex. That the war was funded by available natural resources – timber in Cambodia – was not just a matter of convenience; it had become a causal factor. The strategic aims of both sides rested on control of the forests and the timber they contained. We had also begun to learn that corruption and natural-resource exploitation were almost inevitable bedfellows, as political and military leaders treated their countries as personal bank accounts and got fat on the national riches.

With our heads down in Cambodia we hadn't been observing the wider world as we should have done. What Allan told us about Angola set our minds racing. Resource-funded wars were not a one-off, but just how big a phenomenon was this?

We met with Allan and EIA's co-founders, Dave Currey and Jennifer Lonsdale, several times to discuss a joint campaign. It wasn't an easy decision. On a personal level it would mean that one of us three would need to stop work on Cambodia. No small thing, given that Cambodia was the reason we had started Global Witness in the first place. We had all fallen in love with the country and its people.

In the comfort of our first proper offices, in Hammersmith, provided for free by Anita and Gordon Roddick's Body Shop Foundation, Simon, Charmian and I spent long hours discussing the pros and cons of Allan's idea, but the global campaign to end the scourge of blood diamonds was finally born in the shabby, atmospheric bar of the Almeida Theatre in Islington. At a time when Ralph Fiennes and Diana Rigg were winning major awards for the Almeida's daring productions of *Hamlet* and *Who's Afraid of Virginia Woolf?*, Global Witness and EIA were cooking up a production of our own.

We talked about a campaign focusing on what we thought De Beers were doing – buying diamonds from ruthless UNITA rebels. We would need to get more evidence and for that we would have to go to Angola. As the evening went on, we all became aware of how dangerous this campaign would likely be. 'We're all going to get killed, aren't we?' I said. 'Yeah,' was Allan's laconic response.

And so the decision was made, but not without some misgivings: our newness as an organization; a fear of the unknown; and something else rather more serious. The wars that had been ripping Angola apart for almost 40 years had killed around 700,000 people. We had taken risks in Cambodia, but would we be chancing our luck tackling yet another civil war? Could we actually make a difference?

The still-unasked question was which one of us would take it on. Eventually, and bravely, Charmian volunteered to take this leap into the dark. 'You guys know Cambodia better than I do,' she said. 'The Khmer Rouge work is scaling down, so maybe this is the time for me to take the diamond issue on.' The three of us had worked amazingly well together on Cambodia and there was comfort in working in a close team, but now Charmian was taking on the responsibility of working on a new issue in a country engulfed in a very nasty war. And she was taking on an extremely powerful adversary: De Beers.

A Portuguese colony since the 16th century, Angola had been at war since the independence struggle began in 1961. Victory for the rebels came in 1975, when Portugal finally threw in the towel and evacuated almost half a million people in one of the largest airlifts in history, but this did not bring peace. Two of the pro-independence groups, the Marxist People's Movement for the Liberation of Angola (MPLA) and the Maoist, anti-Marxist National Union for the Total Independence of Angola (UNITA), led by Jonas Savimbi, began to fight each other for control of the country. Cold War politics intervened, and the two sides became proxies of the opposing superpowers, with the MPLA garnering the support of the Soviet Union while the unlikely bedfellows of the US and China backed UNITA.

This War of Independence morphed into a second war, the Guerra do Mato – the War of the Bush. By the time the 1991 Bicesse

Accords brought hopes of peace, between 150,000 and 300,000 people had been killed. This second war also saw a global event that was to change the face of the conflict and with it the fortunes of the main combatants. The Cold War came to an end and the weapons and money provided by the powers of the East and West dried up.

The MPLA and UNITA needed to find alternative sources of revenue.

Lying off the MPLA government-controlled Atlantic coast, Angola's rich oilfields made it Africa's second-largest oil producer and among the global top 20. Being offshore, oil production was relatively secure from the ravages of the conflict. The government had a fat and secure war chest.

Diamonds, the result of the transformation of carbon through heat and pressure in the Earth's mantle, were brought to the surface via volcanic 'kimberlite' pipes over 40 million years ago. The diamonds contained in these pipes can be mined industrially only by companies with large amounts of capital, specialized machinery and an organized workforce. But in many regions, not least in West Africa and southwest Africa, millions of years of erosion of these kimberlite pipes had washed countless diamonds into riverbeds. To mine them, all you need is a shovel, a bucket and a sieve. These alluvial diamonds were spread over vast areas in Angola. Areas controlled by UNITA. Between 1992 and 1997, the rebels had generated a staggering US$3.7 billion from the sale of diamonds – money enough to fight one of Africa's most brutal and protracted civil wars.

The third war, the Guerra das Cidades – the War of the Cities – saw escalating levels of brutality and intensity of fighting, killing 1,000 people a day between May and October 1993 alone. The country was devastated, with the cities of the central high plains particularly hard hit – including Malange, where Aidan's Oxfam team were urgently trying to provide the beleaguered population with fresh water. By this time Angola's infrastructure, roads, railways and bridges were almost totally destroyed.

The Lusaka Protocol, signed in 1994, offered another stab at peace. While negotiations continued, both sides violated the ceasefire, vying for territory. Not least because of what lay underneath it. The diamond fields were vital to UNITA's existence.

*

Charmian dived headlong into researching the diamond trade, reading everything she could get her hands on. She called up Africa experts and geologists, and she spoke to journalists who were covering the wars in the continent. It wasn't long before she reached what seemed to me a rather surprising conclusion.

'Diamonds are commonly occurring pieces of carbon,' she told us. 'The only way you give them value is by restricting the supply and thereby controlling the price.' And this was the centre of De Beers' business model. This British–South African family-owned company had been in the diamond business for over a century; and by the mid-1990s it sorted, valued and sold around 80 per cent of global diamond production. 'And if you have to buy as many diamonds as possible in order to control the price, then you can't be too fussy about who you're buying from,' Charmian said.

That UNITA funded itself through trading diamonds was well known in the diamond industry, but it was a fact brushed as far as possible under the carpet. Diamond-funded wars were also ripping apart Liberia and Sierra Leone. But the average customer making that portentous trip to the jeweller's to buy their engagement ring had no idea that the symbol of their love might have paid for the bullets or landmines that had maimed or killed men, women and children on the African continent. It was about time someone told them.

When Charmian and Isobel touched down in Luanda in 1997, the Angolan capital was the second-most expensive city in the world after Tokyo. Not because it was an economic powerhouse or a jet-set haven, but because it had been smashed by a quarter of a century of civil wars and was virtually cut off from the bulk of the country, which was under UNITA control. Luanda was totally dependent on international imports of almost everything. This meant that visitors had to bring in large amounts of cash just in order to survive.

Angolan regulations required the completion of a currency declaration form, but Charmian had been told by journalists she'd talked to that Angolan Customs used these forms as a handy guide to how much money people were carrying and simply stole the declared amount when you arrived in the country. There was little choice but to smuggle money in.

Before she left London, Charmian went to the bank and withdrew US$6,000 in cash, a huge amount of money at the time. In the cramped aeroplane loo, Charmian rolled up wads of notes and stuffed some of them into her shoes and her bra. She rolled up yet more notes and inserted them into cardboard tampon containers, which she scattered throughout her luggage.

'I can't tell you how uncomfortable it was to walk on folded dollars,' she told us. 'But the tampon packs worked like a dream, the Customs officers were horrified and backed right off.' And on this note so began Global Witness's first foray into Africa.

Luanda came as a shock. If you had the money, you could go to the Elf (French oil company) supermarket and buy blue cheese, French wine and other luxuries that were flown in every week, or you could afford the US$30 it cost to buy a pizza and wash it down with a US$5 can of Coke. In stark contrast, Angola's population suffered one of the highest infant mortality rates in the world and most people couldn't access clean water. The inflation rate was crippling. 'Luanda is a schizophrenic city,' Charmian told us on one of the rare calls she was able to make.

She and Isobel were deeply affected by what they saw. Once-beautiful colonial buildings lay in ruins, their walls pockmarked by bullets. There were tower blocks with no walls that people lived in. 'I met someone from Médecins Sans Frontières who was crying because of the children that died that day because the Ministry of Health had stolen their medicines to sell on the black market,' Charmian told us.

These two women arriving in a dysfunctional city during a brief interlude in a civil war did not lack guts. They noticed that if they sat in a café, someone would come and sit close to them, and contacts there warned them that taxi drivers would report their movements back to the intelligence services. 'Luanda feels like East Germany must have done,' Charmian said.

The fact that the locks of their hotel room didn't work did nothing to ease their nerves, and they leaped at the offer from someone at the UN who invited them to stay in her flat in a rather decrepit apartment block. Charmian and Isobel climbed several flights of stairs to look for the flat and found themselves in a shabby and deserted corridor. 'Two guys appeared,' Charmian said. 'One reached into my breast pocket to grab the money I had put there. I pulled his hand away.' A myriad thoughts came rushing into her head: 'We had several thousand dollars on us. I had this heavy backpack and if I fell over...'

Charmian continued, 'All the guy had was a tattered pair of running shorts, no knife. I gave him a push and he happened to be standing at the top of the stairs. He fell down and they ran off. Then I started shouting. Criminals can be killed by a mob, so I was shouting, "He's not a thief!" I know he tried to mug me, but I didn't want him to be killed.'

Then, as if nothing had happened, and rather amazingly given their rough introduction to this city, Charmian and Isobel dumped their bags in the flat and hurried off for an appointment with the Israeli ambassador.

They had gone to Angola to look at the role of diamonds funding conflict, but then Charmian had a meeting that raised serious concerns that we were on the wrong track. They needed a fixer and were introduced to an Angolan journalist called Rafael Marques. His father had died in the war and his family had almost starved. The result was that Rafael was an angry man, a fearless critic of the MPLA government and an opponent of the war. In answer to Charmian's questions about diamonds, Rafael told her that the really important issue in Angola was not diamonds at all. It was oil. Rafael's message was mirrored by all the NGOs and diplomats she talked to.

What they were saying was that the greater concern was the MPLA government's total capture of the oil sector. It was opaque. No one outside of a closed circle in the government and the state oil company, Sonangol, knew how much money it generated or what it was spent on. What was clear was that it wasn't being spent on the country's infrastructure. Moreover, peace negotiations had reached a critical stage and diamonds had become a bargaining counter. Everyone told Charmian, 'Don't work on diamonds now.' The message hit home.

'Who am I to fuck up a peace process? I've spent all my time looking at this issue, wasting my time,' Charmian told us when she and Isobel got back to London. 'I know I've been getting sidetracked – something we said we'd never do.'

We met with Allan, Dave and Jenny at their offices to break the news that we shouldn't work on diamonds. But Allan was adamant, passionately telling us that the diamonds were the problem and they needed to be dealt with. In the end we agreed that we would work on oil while EIA would take on diamonds. But then events took another turn. It became clear that Allan was right: the war wasn't ending at all.

We first got to know Philippe Le Billon when he came to visit us at our Hammersmith office. After a stint working for the French government in the war-torn Balkans, he went to study at Oxford University's department of forestry – 'I went from wearing a flak jacket to a tweed jacket,' he joked – and a colleague there introduced him to us. We hired him to run an intel-gathering operation for us in Cambodia and found that he was very good at it. I suspected he was an agent of the DGSE, the French secret service, which always prompted an enigmatic smile. It was with Philippe that Charmian returned to Angola in 1997.

The peace process wasn't going well, and it felt like the country was under the shadow of war. On this trip, during which Charmian renewed previous acquaintances and was making new ones together with Philippe, they met with Aidan McQuade. When he learned what they were up to, he did all he could to help, opening up his contact book and providing all the advice he could as a pretty expert insider.

The course of the campaign was finally set after they attended a workshop held by a leading international NGO. Its head, who knew Angola well and asked us not to reveal his name, confirmed that the most important issue was oil. The corruption in the sector was staggering, he told Charmian and Philippe. Moreover, the oil price was so low that the oil-backed loans the government had entered into were really damaging the country.

'However, he told us that we should not start with oil,' Philippe said after the workshop. 'He said that if we start with oil the government will bar us from coming here. He said we would do better to start with diamonds. The government will use a report on diamonds because it would damage UNITA. Tactically it would be much better to tackle diamonds first.' It seemed that Allan's early hunch had been right.

Back in London, we asked Allan if EIA had started to work on diamonds. They hadn't and he gave us their blessing to take over the campaign, which after all had been his brainchild.

*

Unlike the sparkling gems it traded in, the diamond business in the 1990s was almost completely opaque. Presiding over thousands of trading houses, the industry was dominated by De Beers. In its publicity material, the company portrayed itself as providing an essential service to the rest of the industry. A less charitable view was that it was conducting a massive protection racket – albeit a legal one – like a benevolent Mafia godfather. Its Central Selling Organization (CSO) was, in its own words, established 'in the 1930s to create a reliable and enduring system to balance supply and demand, and prevent wild fluctuations in the market for diamonds. This single-channel marketing system remains fundamental to the stability and prosperity of the entire diamond industry today'.

Which is why De Beers continued filling the vaults below their offices in London's Charterhouse Street with the world's best gems: so that they could control the market and thus control the prices. The diamonds were sold in up to 10 sales per year to their 'Sightholders'. These comprised less than 200 companies authorized by De Beers to buy diamonds in bulk. The Sightholders were obliged to hand over their money for a box of diamonds, with no control over the quantity they received or the price they paid. Take it or leave it. Laurence Graff, the chairman of top-end jeweller Graff, told the *Financial Times* in 2015, 'If you want to be successful with diamonds, you have to get as close to [De Beers] as possible.'

The world's key diamond trading centre was the Belgian city of Antwerp. Its thousands of brokers and traders occupied the diamond district, the streets of which were protected by automatic steel bollards that would only be lowered to admit essential deliveries. On their first visit, Charmian and Isobel entered into the closed world of the diamond business, and began to meet a few of the thousands of brokers and traders that operated there.

Charmian discovered very quickly that the kind of investigations we carried out in Cambodia were completely useless in the context of diamonds. This was an industry characterized by closed-off backroom deals sealed by the shake of a hand rather than reams of paperwork; an industry where everyone knew everyone else and knew what was going on, but with few exceptions wouldn't breathe a word to outsiders.

And even if you were willing to risk your life going into the diamond fields in Africa, there would be very little to see. Whereas it's impossible to hide a timber trade that trucks massive rainforest trees in convoys across a border, you can conceal millions of dollars' worth of diamonds in your pocket. In West Africa, artisanal miners panned for alluvial diamonds in distant riverbeds in war zones, while the buyers operated in fortified compounds in remote villages purchasing stones from smuggling networks and then 'legalizing' them by bribing officials to obtain the correct paperwork. So, whereas we and many others knew that 'conflict diamonds' were making it onto the international market, proving it was very hard indeed. And then we needed to differentiate between the official and the unofficial supply.

'The Angolan Army generals control mines on one side of the river,' Charmian explained. 'That's the "official" supply. UNITA mine on the other; that's the "unofficial" supply. UNITA's goods are going out through Namibia, Zambia and the big one – the DRC.'

Buyers Charmian talked to described how small villages grew into diamond towns, beset by all the evils of the gold rush, like drink and prostitution, with people risking their lives to make a buck. 'It's a right of manhood to go into Angola, get diamonds and provide for your family,' Charmian said.

Isobel, by now a mother, left Global Witness and we transferred one of our first staff members, Alex Yearsley, to work with Charmian. Inspired by the iconic Chico Mendes, who was assassinated for his work trying to save the Amazon, Alex had answered an ad we had placed in the *Guardian* looking for volunteers. 'I want to do field work, to get my hands dirty,' he told us, and got the job.

It was this two-person team that took on the global diamond industry amid rising international concern about the role played by Angola's diamonds in funding conflict. In 1998, the UN Security Council passed Resolution 1173, banning countries from importing Angolan stones other than the official supply. But, as we were to find out, 1173 was notoriously ineffective. Charmian's next investigation took her from Angola to Zambia, a country whose diamond exports far exceeded its virtually non-existent domestic production. Evidently something was not quite right.

Travelling in a beaten-up VW Combi van, and in league with Portuguese investigative journalist Pedro Rosa Mendes, Charmian probed into this anomaly, visiting trading companies, the Zambian Ministry of Mines and the country's Geological Survey. Piece by piece, they built up a picture of how the system of corruption worked in Zambia.

Buyers first had to buy a gemstone sales certificate, obtainable from the Ministry of Mines for 200,000 Zambian kwacha – about US$100 – which authorized them to purchase precious and semi-precious stones. This was easy, unlike the second stage. This required the buyer or a hired guide to enter Angola and make their way to the UNITA-held mine sites, such as Mavinga in Cuando Cubango province, to buy the diamonds. This hazardous trip could take up to two weeks. Prices varied, but buying the diamonds in Angola was cheaper, with UNITA charging around US$100 per carat, or sometimes bartering them for cattle and fish.

The third stage was less risky but just as crucial: laundering the diamonds so that they could be exported in breach of the UN Security Council sanctions. The buyers needed to obtain paperwork that would convince the authorities of the importing countries, like the US, Britain, the Netherlands, Belgium, South Africa and Israel, that these quantities of high-value diamonds really came from Zambia, despite the fact that the country possessed virtually no diamonds of its own. This is where Zambia's Geological Survey came in.

They would provide a valuation certificate detailing the stones' grade, quantity, colour and value in US dollars. Once in possession of this, the relevant department in the Ministry of Mines issued the 'Authorization to export rough gemstones', which was stamped both by them and Customs. 'And voila!' Charmian said. 'The buyer can export completely legal sanctions-busting diamonds to all the major world markets, and nobody knows where the diamonds have really come from!'

These investigations provided us with a wealth of useful background and a growing understanding of the diamond trade. Charmian and Alex gathered testimonies, hearsay and circumstantial evidence, but because this industry was so opaque and much of its business took place in a war zone, we hadn't yet been able to obtain the specific evidence of the standard we would need to convince policymakers of our case. The fact that diamonds were funding the war was widely known, albeit to a relatively small circle – UNSC Resolution 1173 was proof of that – but no one had nailed who exactly was responsible or could prove how these diamonds were entering the market. It turned out that the crucial evidence was contained in an unexpected place: De Beers' own annual reports.

The team scrutinized every line of them, and a window opened and light began to flood in. As they compiled information for our first report on conflict diamonds, they summarized the impacts of the Angolan Civil War for each year between 1991 and 1998. This information was juxtaposed against statements in De Beers' annual reports for those same years. The conclusions were stark. For example, a briefing by the authoritative Catholic Institute for International Relations (CIIR) in London stated that:

> *The extremely destructive conflict was notable for the systematic violation of the laws of war by both government and the UNITA rebels. Indiscriminate shelling of starving besieged cities by UNITA resulted in massive destruction, and the loss of untold numbers of civilian lives [...] It is estimated that 300,000 Angolans – 3 per cent of the population – died as the result of the fighting between October 1992 and late 1994.*

De Beers' annual report for the same year referred to reduced demand for rough diamonds from their CSO but noted: 'That we should have been able to buy some two-thirds of the increased supply from Angola is testimony not just to our financial strength but to the infrastructure and experienced personnel we have in place.'

In 1993, the CIIR documented that 'The United Nations reported that between May and October 1993 as many as 1,000 people were dying every day in Angola – more than any other conflict in the world at the time.' More upbeat, De Beers bragged of 'the substantially increased production of Angolan diamonds – mainly in the higher-value gem qualities – coming on the outside market, of which the CSO successfully bought up about two-thirds.' So, given that UNITA controlled around 80 per cent of Angola's diamond fields, De Beers had done a chunk of our work for us by freely admitting they were likely buying conflict diamonds.

'I can't believe this laissez-faire attitude of the diamond industry,' Charmian said, shocked by what she had read. 'It's obvious that De Beers must be buying conflict diamonds from UNITA, but it just seems to be an unquestioned aspect of how the industry works.'

It was around this time that our free run at the Body Shop Foundation's offices in Hammersmith came to an end and we moved into our third office, halfway up the hill that is Bickerton Road in Archway, north London. On the top floor of a three-storey, red-brick former spectacle factory, the office consisted of one very large room, perhaps 15 x 8m. The original 1920s metal-framed windows that occupied three of the four walls filled the room with light and had fantastic views to the south, all the way across London and to the hills beyond.

The feeling of space and light was paradise in the summer but gave way to a freezing hell in winter. Despite their best efforts, the old cast-iron radiators never got much beyond tepid. This antiquated and inefficient heating system was further compromised by the fact that the somewhat eccentric Cypriot landlord didn't like turning it on. Working in scarves and fingerless gloves and dizzy from the fumes of portable gas heaters, we would periodically go down to his office to complain, with the result that this small balding man would storm up to the office and explode into paroxysms of apoplectic fury, scream obscenities and then disappear again. We remained cold but kept on complaining, mainly for the amusement.

The St John's Tavern at the bottom of the road was one of London's first gastropubs, and many of our best meetings were held there, in front of the fire in a large bar lined with art.

It was in Archway that we started to put our report together, which we hoped would draw attention to what De Beers were up to. The information we'd gathered in our investigations plus the circumstantial evidence in De Beers' own reports made for a powerful cocktail. Putting together a campaign report is always a monumental task, but none is so tough as the debut publication of a completely new campaign, especially when it's only the second campaign of a new organization. There was also the discomforting knowledge that the primary target was a multibillion-dollar company that could drown us in lawyers with one phone call.

Charmian and Alex embarked on a crazy schedule to distil the thousands of pages of documents and interviews down to the core substance – the nucleus that could perhaps herald the beginning of the end of conflict diamonds. The report launch was set for early December 1998, but the sheer weight of work led to delays and the pressure on Charmian and Alex grew and grew as they worked. Charmian listened to Massive Attack to get through working 15 to 20 hours a day, 'getting tireder and tireder, and trying to make the report shorter and shorter'. And the clock was ticking. News from Angola wasn't good, and it seemed likely that the country would go back to war. In addition, there was one crucial piece of the jigsaw puzzle still missing.

De Beers maintained that you couldn't identify the origin of rough diamonds, especially when a parcel contained mixed diamonds from different countries. But we had talked to a number of specialist geologists who told a different story. They had told Charmian about the 'run of mine'.

'There is a profile of production and people become experts in different countries' supply,' she told Simon and me. 'For example, over millennia alluvial diamonds are washed from their source by rivers…and the further from the source they are, the more they are eroded and the smaller they become. So where you find them matters. For example, if diamonds are a certain [larger] size, then they can't have come from that point in the river, but must have come from further upstream.'

These factors were exacerbated by the scale of the illegal exports from Angola. So great were the volumes of stones being smuggled out of Angola to DRC, whose diamonds were generally of a lesser quality, that to mix a parcel up sufficiently to significantly outnumber the Angolan stones to avoid identification posed a problem for the sellers. 'Is it really credible that De Beers' and other major companies' buying offices could get the identification so wrong over such long periods of time?' Charmian asked.

She thought not. Charmian contacted the director of a South African diamond-trading school to double-check our thinking, and he told her that you could identify a mixed parcel by the shape of the stones. Other dealers told her even more – that you could pin a parcel of unmixed diamonds to the exact mine they came from.

But even if we could get a handle on whether or not you could tell where a diamond came from, there was another hurdle to jump: the question of where the paperwork said it came from. Here a combination of misinformation and deliberately weak laws coupled with unfit for purpose international trading regulations played into the diamond smugglers' hands.

The weakest point was Belgium. 'The law is designed to encourage diamonds to come in with no paperwork,' one dealer told us. 'As long as you declare them at the airport then the diamonds become legal tender. You can declare any country of origin, they never query it...it doesn't matter if you've actually flown in from that country. You declare the diamonds, you declare the diamond-buying office of somebody – there are lots of them in Antwerp – that the diamonds are going to be delivered to. But no one checks. So, the Belgian government has a sort of statistical control but there's no import duty, and so diamonds probably poured into Belgium.'

It was not for nothing that Antwerp was the world's leading diamond-trading centre, and that one of the biggest buyers was De Beers. Its head of outside buying was Andrew Coxon, sent to Antwerp by De Beers to pick up the Angolan diamonds that were pouring in, and he could buy a lot. 'There are very few buyers who can buy US$20 million one week and another US$20 million the following week,' he told me.

Whereas many individual traders told us they knew that diamonds were funding war, and they knew that conflict diamonds were entering the market, they simply weren't worried about it. Or not worried enough, anyway. I accompanied Charmian on one of her trips to Antwerp in 1998. Sitting in a small, cluttered diamond-trading office that belied the multimillion trade that was carried on from there, the owner said, 'I know that diamonds are killing people, but I have to earn my money. I know it's wrong because when I hear of the death of a single Israeli soldier my heart bleeds.'

As the drafting of our report was drawing to a close, Charmian and Alex decided to make a last-ditch attempt to see whether we could nail the issue of a diamond's origin. They left our freezing offices on the morning of 1 December and made their way to the more salubrious head office of De Beers' CSO in Charterhouse Street, where they had arranged to meet two senior staff members. 'We wanted to press them once again as to whether it was possible to identify the origin of rough diamonds,' Charmian said.

After the usual pleasantries, one of the men told Charmian and Alex, 'If you are sitting in Tel Aviv or Moscow or New York, whatever the potential for positive identification you have not a clue where they came from...if the [diamond seller] says they are Scottish diamonds, you take his word for it...they could be diamonds from the moon.'

Although Charmian and Alex had interviewed De Beers as themselves, they had brought in a hidden camera, which turned out to be a good call. Later, as they viewed the film, they were in no doubt that this man's comment was untrue. 'We've got them,' Charmian thought. Charmian had been told by numerous geologists that it was possible to identify where rough diamonds originated from. De Beers had buyers in Africa who knew the conditions on the ground and the existence of smuggling networks. Our short investigation in Zambia had exposed how easy it was to bribe officials to falsify a diamond's origin, and Antwerp accepted diamonds from anywhere a seller said they came from.

But more importantly than all that, what those two senior De Beers staff had told Charmian and Alex was that whatever the difficulties – or not – of identifying a diamond's origin, and whatever the truth – or otherwise – of De Beers' claims, the main point was that they didn't care where their diamonds came from. They simply didn't care.

The day after that fateful interview with De Beers, Charmian worked for 30 hours straight. This latest information needed to be incorporated into what was already meant to be final text, which meant that Dan Brown, the designer, needed to totally rejig the report's layout and be ready for the printer who was expecting it early the next day. Charmian, Alex, Simon and I were all there, tinkering with edits, discussing what photo should go where. Occasionally we got fractious with each other as tiredness set in. I left around midnight – I had early work on the Cambodia campaign the next day – but the others saw the report through.

On the morning of 14 December 1998, Charmian and Alex arrived at our freezing offices at 6am to get the report out. Like a ship being freed of its ties to the dockside, *A Rough Trade – The Role of Companies and Governments in the Angolan Conflict* began spilling from fax machines into the newsrooms of major media outlets across the world. We had done everything we could, had put in an enormous amount of work and invested even more hope in what it could do. Just 16 pages of recycled paper. The cover photograph depicted a heavily armed Angolan soldier standing in front of a ruined, bullet-spattered building, over which Dan had superimposed a photo taken by an early enthusiast of Global Witness's work, Marc Schlossman, of a couple of hundred diamonds in the palm of someone's hand. Now all we could do was wait.

After the flurry of activity, silence descended and Charmian and Alex sat looking at the phones, which were stubbornly silent. Alex was nervous, wondering what was going on, and despite having the same feeling herself, Charmian tried to reassure him that these things always took time. And then one of the phones began to ring. And then another. By midday, it had gone ballistic.

It was on that day that diamonds lost their lustre. The sparkling gems immortalized in De Beers' hugely successful 'A Diamond is Forever' advertising campaign got a new name. Blood diamonds. The company's US$180-million-per-year advertising spend was being torpedoed by a campaign costing around US$100,000.

The office became like a newsroom as we fielded phone calls from journalists around the world, shouting across to each other, asking questions, booking in interviews for Charmian and Alex, and faxing out supplementary materials. We were unused to this. International press interest in our work on Cambodia was pretty minimal, but now we were deluged.

'I really hadn't appreciated how people are fascinated by diamonds,' Charmian said. But sadly this was only part of the explanation for the extraordinary press interest we were receiving. We had unknowingly released our report at exactly the point that the latest peace talks, the Lusaka Protocol, finally broke down and Angola re-exploded into full-scale war. On the day the report came out, UNITA launched a major assault on the key town of Cuito, raising the spectre of the 1993–94 siege there which resulted in 30,000 civilian deaths. Three days later, UNITA massacred over a hundred civilians in a disused railway station. Years of international efforts to bring peace to this tragically war-torn country looked like they had been in vain.

But the accidental timing of our report served to wake up the international community to the role that diamonds played in funding UNITA's war effort, and the industry came under the spotlight like never before. *A Rough Trade* didn't contain all the answers, although it did suggest some, but it had raised questions that in the blaze of international attention the diamond industry would have to answer.

'That was the Belgian ambassador,' Charmian said as she put down the phone. 'He was shouting at me!' Some people felt we were a small organization and that they could push us around, but he had picked the wrong person in Charmian. Reacting against the pressures of authority that had motivated her all those years ago, she calmly pointed out to the ambassador the role of De Beers and Antwerp in funding the conflict. It was not long afterwards that the diamond trade would brand Charmian Attila the Nun.

But we still faced an uphill struggle. We were beginning to learn the lesson that all entrepreneurs have to learn. No matter how good or convincing the idea, it is really hard to get people to buy in until you have absolutely proved the concept. In our case, our reputation and efficacy depended on two things. The veracity of our information and evidence was the essential glue that held the concept together, but it was the concept itself that was the most difficult thing to get across. We were breaking new ground. We were neither an environmental group nor a human-rights group. By linking those two things and adding the ingredient of corruption – a word that in those days even World Bank staff weren't allowed to use – we were doing something completely new and it took people quite a long time to get it.

The election of Tony Blair's New Labour government in 1997 brought an end to 18 years of Conservative rule, and in those heady days before Blair's illegal and disastrous incursion into Iraq, Britain embarked on an ethical foreign policy led by the new Foreign Secretary, Robin Cook. Although far from perfect, it had meant that the FCO had opened up and was exploring new ways to address seemingly intractable problems. Moreover, they had another diamond-funded war to think about.

Sierra Leone, a former British colony, had been ripped apart by civil war for most of the 1990s, and in January 1999, less than a month after our report was released, the forces of the Revolutionary United Front (RUF) rampaged through Freetown. Infamous for hacking the limbs off their victims, offering them only the choice of 'long sleeve or short sleeve', the RUF had long been funded through trading diamonds with the regime of Charles Taylor in neighbouring Liberia, another country immersed in civil war. International media attention to conflict diamonds reached a peak when the RUF took nearly 500 peacekeepers hostage in May 2000 to demand the release of their leader, Foday Sankoh.

Diamonds had become big news.

The other key slice of happenstance came in the unlikely guise of 'market forces': throughout the 1990s, De Beers' share price had been sliding – under new European Commission rules, it became illegal to have a dominant market position. They began to grasp that the days of the cartel were numbered.

Charmian is a great strategist, but she was also caught on the hop because international reaction to our report far exceeded our expectations and she had to make some hard choices about how to run the campaign.

Diamonds flowed out of Angola and into countries theoretically bound by UNSC Resolution 1173, but nevertheless they continued to flow: into Israel, the US and into Europe, where Antwerp was the main hub. And most of them ended up in the vaults of the CSO in Charterhouse Street. To stop the flow of conflict diamonds, we needed to get the UN interested.

At the invitation of the Brazilian ambassador to the United Nations, Charmian and Alex flew to New York in January 1999 to address an informal meeting of members of the UN Security Council. It was one of the first times an organization like ours had been invited to do so and we were pinching ourselves that our influence was climbing so high.

'We need to concentrate on one main target,' said Charmian. Counterintuitively, we needed to get De Beers on side because they had the power to sort the rest of the industry.

In 1999, Charmian and I went to Tel Aviv, itself a major diamond-trading centre. There we met Martin Rapaport, a leading diamond trader and chair of the Rapaport Group. Sitting in his utilitarian office in front of a wall full of pigeonholes containing plastic boxes that I like to imagine were full of diamonds and probably were, we listened, fascinated, to get an inside track into how the diamond industry felt.

'Listen, people have been killing people in Africa for centuries, so why is it our issue?' he asked. 'It's because of the diamonds that they are killing them,' Charmian answered. She hit home.

Martin told us that the diamond supply chain was highly segmented, and no one wanted to be bothered by problems that were not seen to be in their sphere of influence, 'or more importantly their sphere of responsibility'. But Martin realized that what we were bringing to the table was the idea that the diamond industry, manufacturers and dealers, needed to be concerned about what was on their horizon.

Martin had checked us out and had been impressed by our work on the Khmer Rouge, and the fact we had risked our lives tackling conflict resources, and he had decided to help. He confirmed what Charmian had found out in Antwerp. 'The minute the diamonds arrive in Switzerland, which is where most of them arrive at, there's no difficulty at all,' he said, describing the importation of diamonds into Europe. 'Does the industry want to know? That's the question for Global Witness. Why is it in their interest to know? Did the German people know the Nazis were killing Jews? I guess they could smell the smoke from the camps...'

Martin's energy and enthusiasm for diamonds, and for the issue of conflict diamonds, was infectious, and his role as an influential figure in the industry was to prove a vital ingredient to the campaign. Especially given that we usually met blank and certainly unapologetic faces when we talked to the dealers.

We also had a meeting with the boss of the Tel Aviv Diamond Exchange, the world's largest diamond-trading centre. Having negotiated the strict security protocols, we were guided by the bourse's president past rafts of tables where dealers hunched over trays of hundreds of diamonds, appraising them and haggling over prices. Our host was helpful and welcoming; and as we left we held out a copy of *A Rough Trade* with the stock cover photo of the cupped hands cradling a few score of yellowish stones. He took one look and asked, 'If your report is about Angola, why does the cover photograph show diamonds from the DRC?'

We were flabbergasted. Despite De Beers' denials that you could identify the source of diamonds, and all the work we'd done to counter them, this guy could tell the origin of rough diamonds just by glancing at a single photograph.

*

Passionate about tackling poverty and conflict as policy director at Oxfam, Dianna Melrose answered Foreign Secretary Robin Cook's call for policy advisers, a key part of his recently announced ethical foreign policy, and joined the FCO. It was February 1999, just a few months after *A Rough Trade* had been launched, and our investigations, analysis and debut report on conflict diamonds had catalysed an international process that took on a momentum all of its own. Charmian and Dianna got on.

Over the next year, they were chasing each other around the world. In July, Dianna flew to Washington and met with Canadian ambassador Robert Fowler together with officials at the State Department to talk about conflict diamonds. A key outcome of this meeting was that these governments felt it would be 'a fatal error for the UK and US to front these efforts – it should be led by southern African countries, because for them it was a key industry that needed to be protected'.

In January 2000, the Canadian NGO Partnership Africa Canada (PAC) released a report about the role of conflict diamonds in the brutal war in Sierra Leone. *The Heart of the Matter* was hugely influential and Global Witness gained a powerful ally in PAC and the report's lead author, Ian Smillie. We were no longer going it alone.

In March 2000, Dianna went to South Africa with two of her US counterparts, Howard Jeter, US Deputy Assistant Secretary of State for African Affairs, and his colleague Steve Morrison. They met with Botswana's President Festus Mogai, an old friend of Jeter's, and asked how they could bring serious political pressure to the issue of conflict diamonds; what steps could be taken to be rid of the illicit trade. Mogai said, 'South Africa needs to lead this.'

On that visit, Dianna and her colleagues also met with Nicky Oppenheimer, the powerful chair of De Beers. They had previously met with De Beers in early 1999 but the looming end of the company's cartel model had changed things massively. 'This danger came with good timing,' Dianna said. Nicky Oppenheimer was welcoming and subsequently De Beers began to provide the FCO with useful information on the diamond trade in Sierra Leone, DRC and Angola – something they had never offered us. It was great that De Beers came on side, but it's hard to escape the irony surrounding their offer to provide expertise on something they had said was impossible just a few months before.

In May 2000, Charmian and Alex flew to South Africa to attend what would prove to be a turning point for the issue of conflict diamonds. Chaired by the South African minister of minerals and energy, Phumzile Mlambo-Ngcuka, the meeting took place in the diamond-mining town of Kimberley, the birthplace of De Beers. It had the potential to close down the trade in blood diamonds once and for all.

It brought together key diamond-producing countries, the diamond industry in the form of De Beers and Martin Rapaport and a few NGOs. Charmian told us when she got back that the meeting finished with 'an agreement to work together, civil society and governments and trade industry, to tackle the problem and do something about it'. This was real progress. Having been forced into a corner, the industry had begun to put its collective heads together to come up with solutions.

One dealer, Willie Nagel, whose own family narrowly escaped the holocaust, said the industry should have a chain of warranties, according to De Beers' Andrew Coxon. His colleague Tim Capon suggested a simple solution: if they stopped outside buying, they could truly say their diamonds were conflict-free. 'I realized the issue was too big for any one sector to solve...and everyone went down to Kimberley,' Coxon told me.

Charmian, tenacious, sharp and convincing, demonstrated the essential role of civil society in multi-stakeholder processes like this. Something that was uncommon then, and often remains an unwelcome addition resisted by many governments and industry alike, regardless of the issues being discussed. Most of the wrangling so far had been over the role of producer countries, but Charmian took a different stance. 'The majority of the responsibility should lie with consumption and demand, not production. It's my view you should know what you're buying. You should know, whether you are a company or a consumer, where something you are buying has come from and what went into making it,' she told the meeting.

'There was pushback from almost everyone, even producers, but South Africa, Botswana and Namibia were convinced that inaction was not an option,' Dianna Melrose said. She was challenged by a Belgian colleague at the Kimberley meeting, who asked, 'Would this damage the interests of the Antwerp market?' This highlighted the industry's money-over-lives mindset that had inspired Charmian to take on this campaign in the first place.

'Belgium was very nervous about sanctions being put on Belgian diamonds,' said Charmian. 'And they were angry with Global Witness, because I had pointed out they had open buying with no controls. They talked about how they had great controls.' But Charmian had seen these controls in action in Antwerp when she was researching *A Rough Trade*.

'They proudly showed me that everyone who declares diamond imports has to sit down with an official and show them the diamonds and say where they've come from. And I noticed that there was no sound recording, so anything could have been said, so it was a completely unreliable control system. They changed that when *A Rough Trade* went public. We showed that they claimed to be doing something they weren't. The system was ripe for laundering and corruption.'

After around six weeks of behind-the-scenes negotiations, the parties decided to create an international agreement, named after the town in which the idea had been born. The first meeting of the Kimberley Process took place in Luanda in June 2000. Our first battle was to resist a move by some people there to exclude civil society altogether. The charge was led by the man that the diamond industry had chosen to represent them, Ted Sorensen.

A former speechwriter for John F Kennedy, known for coining the president's famous line, 'Ask not what your country can do for you – ask what you can do for your country,' Sorensen was openly hostile to NGOs. 'I was really shocked and disappointed,' Charmian said. 'The diamond industry was asking, "What right do you, civil society, have to be here?" and Ted Sorensen was saying, "It's completely undemocratic, having civil society in the room."'

Charmian gave as good as she got. 'I am so deeply disappointed to hear you, of all people, say this; I can't really comprehend it,' she retorted in open session. 'On what basis are you here? If the industry hadn't been lying to everybody and trading in conflict diamonds all this time and funding war, then we wouldn't all be in this room right now. At the point that the industry sorts itself out, then that is the point perhaps when civil society doesn't need to be involved.'

'I think it is better to have the NGOs inside the tent pissing out rather than outside the tent pissing in,' Dianna Melrose added. 'The FCO pushed back very hard and made sure NGOs and civil society stayed a part of the process [otherwise], they argued, there would be no credibility.'

But Russia was proving to be the real problem. 'The real push-back was coming from Moscow,' Dianna said. 'We hadn't factored in what Russian interests were. They were profoundly suspicious of what the UK was up to and that we were acting for De Beers, but we stressed our concerns were around suffering, illegality and corruption.'

At a critical conference in October 2000 at Lancaster House in London, the possibility of an international control regime for conflict diamonds still seemed pretty remote. Dianna Melrose's ambition was to get the UN General Assembly to pass a resolution submitted by the UK government on conflict diamonds when they met in December. She had just two months in which to achieve this and only a handful of countries were supportive. Then the Russians threatened to boycott it altogether for reasons that are somewhat unclear, rather cryptically saying that they were resisting what they called 'any attempt at supranational enforcement'.

Dianna spoke to Peter Hain, the UK's Africa minister, who in turn spoke to Foreign Secretary Robin Cook. 'Do not let the Russians do this; we must go ahead,' Hain implored Cook. The FCO learned that the Russians were pressuring many African countries to stay away from the London conference, but one of Dianna's colleagues at the British Embassy in Moscow was bullish. 'Don't worry. If you go ahead, the Russians will come,' he told her.

'Then as soon as we said, "It's definitely going ahead," the Russians were onto the UK Embassy sorting their visas,' Dianna smiled. And at the conference as a Russian official went around the table, lobbying all the African governments in turn, Dianna followed and re-lobbied everybody he had spoken to.

On 29 January 2001, the United Nations General Assembly passed Resolution A/RES/55/56 – The role of diamonds in fuelling conflict: breaking the link between the illicit transaction of rough diamonds and armed conflict as a contribution to prevention and settlement of conflicts.

ANGOLA – BLOOD ON THE ROCKS

It had been four years of incredibly hard work and just two years since we had published *A Rough Trade*. Global Witness's two-person campaign had started a process that had brought in many allies, like Partnership Africa Canada, Dianna Melrose and others. The UN resolution represented international recognition of the severity and importance of the issue, and of the responsibility of the diamond industry.

Despite initial opposition from his administration, President George W Bush signed the Clean Diamond Trade Act into law on 25 April 2003, pressured by intense advocacy from us, Partnership Africa Canada, Amnesty International and Oxfam. The act bound the US, the world's largest consumer of diamonds, to implement the Kimberley Process Certification Scheme and UN Resolution 55/66 aimed at breaking the link between the transaction of illicit diamonds and armed conflict.

On 18 March 2002, three American politicians, Congressmen Tony Hall and Frank Wolf and Senator Patrick Leahy, nominated Global Witness and Partnership Africa Canada for the 2003 Nobel Peace Prize 'for their work to sever the funding link between diamonds and war'. We didn't win, but we had an exciting few months of anticipation.

Charmian, who had worked herself into a state of total exhaustion, was diagnosed with chronic fatigue syndrome and was off work for six months.

Has De Beers really changed? In 2006, in the lead-up to the release of the blockbuster movie *Blood Diamond*, the company was running scared. 'De Beers' response,' Ed Zwick, the film's director, told me, 'was to mount a kind of very glossy ad campaign, with full-page ads all over the place, including the major papers and magazines and such, about all of De Beers' good works. These actually had become a part of their programme. However, at the time of the story we're telling, they were *not* part of their programme, very conspicuously not part of their programme.'

3

WARLORD

The men waiting at the quay raised their heads almost as one as the relative silence of Liberia's easternmost port, 12 miles from the border with neighbouring Côte d'Ivoire, was broken by the distant throbbing of a powerful motor. The shadows cast by their soft, olive-green bush hats and the ubiquitous sunglasses they all wore obscured any emotion they might be feeling.

Growing louder, the rhythmic thud-thud-thud of rotor blades reverberated through the heavy tropical air, whipping up a whirlwind of red dust that forced the men to bow their heads and cover their noses and mouths with their scarves. The Russian-built Mi-8 military transport helicopter touched down next to a cluster of port buildings, in one of the few spaces not filled with the trunks of thousands of tropical trees stacked in piles across the hardstanding.

These heavily armed troops from President Charles Taylor's feared Anti-Terrorist Unit – the ATU – fanned out around the machine as its blades slowed and the dust settled, coating everything with a fine powder, like red icing sugar.

Shortly afterwards a small cargo ship out of Dakar, Senegal, slowly took form as it emerged from the shimmering heat haze over the ocean. Some 45 minutes later it moored alongside the quay. A Lebanese man, the representative of the logging company that controlled the port, walked from his office to the ship, mounted the companionway that had been lowered to the dockside and went on board. He shook hands with the captain of the Belize-registered vessel, then the two men entered the captain's cabin and closed the door.

Soon, their conversation over, the representative disembarked and the ship's crane, mounted just forward of the bridge, began unloading a number of wooden crates onto the quay.

At a barked order, the dock workers began loading the crates into the helicopter. Then, to the horror of the onlookers, a cable holding a number of the crates snapped, whiplashing across the deck and slicing into a member of the crew, killing him instantly. The crates crashed down onto the dockside and one of them splintered open, disgorging 20 B40 rocket-propelled grenades onto the concrete. After a few moments of stunned silence, some of the soldiers rushed forward to gather up the deadly cargo.

Despite the best efforts of the ATU, news of this horrific incident quickly spread across the town. In Liberia, news spreads fast.

Loading completed, the Mi-8's engine fired up. With rotors straining to lift the load, the helicopter rose sluggishly from the ground and soon disappeared over the surrounding jungle into the hazy tropical air. Then a series of trucks started delivering the massive rainforest logs to the quayside and the crane began to hoist them into the ship's hold.

COITUS INTERRUPTUS, MILAN, 4 AUGUST 2000

On a hot August night in a hotel room in Cinisello Balsamo, just north of Milan, a pallid, naked, corpulent Ukrainian, the hotel's owner, was freebasing cocaine with four prostitutes and was becoming increasingly violent. Scared, one of the prostitutes phoned her friend who was working a nearby street. She in turn called the police.

Shortly afterwards, a squad of officers passed through the grandiose arched entrance of the otherwise nondescript hotel, made their way up to the third floor and burst into room 341. So began a chain of events that would help end one of Africa's most brutal wars.

Leonid Efimovich Minin was a senior figure in the Ukrainian Mafia. His police mugshot shows a man who had lived the hedonistic life for far too long and looked like he had topped it off by losing a bout with Muhammad Ali. The photo also depicted a man evidently unhappy at being caught with his trousers down. Off, in fact. The angry and bewildered stare captured by the lens was probably trying to mask Leonid's emotions about his immediate future, given what else he had stashed away in that hotel suite. His blue eyes were devoid of emotion. Cold.

In addition to the cocaine, the police found US$150,000 in cash, Russian diamonds worth US$500,000 and around 1,500 documents detailing Minin's businesses trading oil, diamonds, tropical timber and arms. Brochures extolling the virtues of various deadly weapons jostled with emails between Minin and some of his customers. One of these was one Charles 'Chucky' Taylor, namesake son of the warlord president of Liberia, and commander of his father's feared Praetorian Guard, the Anti-Terrorism Unit, better called the 'Terrorizing Unit'.

This routine police raid had opened a rare window into an organized crime and arms-trafficking network intimately involved in the resource wars that were then ripping numerous West African countries apart.

The eyes of the preliminary judge assigned to the case widened as she realized the significance of the contents of room 341. She picked up the phone and dialled a colleague of hers. 'Walter, you'd better get over here.'

Dottore Walter Mapelli, a young prosecutor whose usual beat was investigating financial crime, had much the same reaction as the judge. 'It was an accident,' he told me. 'We knew nothing about the man until the police took the call from the prostitute who was worried about an increasingly violent client, and suddenly I was pushed into a world I had no idea about. I had people from the American Embassy turning up at my office. There was the "retired" Mossad agent – she was a colonel based in Paris – who told me how useful Minin was to their intelligence services.'

The transcripts of Mapelli's interrogation of Minin began with the Ukrainian's almost comic denials, explaining away the incriminating documents by saying they belonged to the occupant of the neighbouring room who really was an arms trafficker, and that they had somehow got mixed up in his own briefcase. But Mapelli's incisive questions soon cornered Minin and by the end he'd given a rare insight into the workings of the Mafia's operations in Odessa, the turf war that tore them apart and that had led to a contract being taken out on him. Already rich, he fled to Spain, where he bought the usual trappings of a retired gangster – the villa, jet and yacht, plus a house in Switzerland for good measure.

Mapelli again: 'And then a Spanish guy approached Minin and said, "You'll get bored doing nothing," and suggested he start a timber company in Liberia. Of all things, a timber company in Liberia? So he did, with his Spanish friend as a major shareholder.' So Minin went to Liberia and met President Charles Taylor.

'Minin was a grand corruptor,' Mapelli said. 'He visited Liberia many times, always accompanied by the same beautiful Ukrainian woman. Her job was to seduce senior Liberian leaders.'

It worked. Taylor told Minin that he could help with the timber licences he needed, but in return he wanted weapons. He had found the right man.

The events that brought Minin and Taylor together began on the night of 15 September 1985. A former government official, awaiting extradition to Liberia on charges of embezzling a million dollars, tied some bed sheets together and lowered himself down from the window of a non-secure part of the Plymouth County Correctional Facility in Massachusetts. And vanished. He next surfaced in Colonel Gaddafi's Libya, where he was trained in guerrilla warfare and began to form a small army, the National Patriotic Front of Liberia. Charles Taylor's career as West Africa's most notorious warlord had begun.

In 1989, Taylor's army, now based in Liberia's neighbour, Côte d'Ivoire, launched an invasion of his homeland. The objective: to overthrow the dictatorial regime of Samuel Doe, who had taken power in a coup nine years previously.

Taylor's incursion into Liberia unleashed a civil war of almost unrivalled brutality. The population divided along ethnic lines and thousands flocked to Taylor's cause. Child soldiers, high on narcotics and blood, were led by men with cartoonish names like Captain Marvel, Jack the Rebel and General Butt Naked – names all the more chilling because of their comic-sounding innocence. These leaders encouraged the children to break almost every societal taboo, including raping and killing their parents. They created unquestioning, mindless, killing machines.

In 1991, Taylor took the war into Sierra Leone in a bid to take control of the country and its resources. His brainchild was the

Revolutionary United Front – the RUF – led by a fellow alumnus of Gaddafi's training camps, Foday Sankoh. Although ostensibly a Sierra Leonean rebel group, the RUF was dubbed 'Taylor's Foreign Legion' by the International Crisis Group. They marched under the banner 'No More Slaves, No More Masters, Power and Wealth to the People', and took control of the alluvial diamond fields in the south and east of the country. Soon the major diamond-buying centres of Europe, Israel and elsewhere were flush with Sierra Leonean and Liberian stones and money flowed into Taylor's coffers.

Whether or not the RUF ever believed their pro-democracy rhetoric, the reality was a reign of terror that possibly exceeded that of Taylor's forces next door. The barbaric conflict that ravaged Sierra Leone horrified the world. A West African peacekeeping force comprising mainly Nigerian troops intervened to help the Sierra Leonean Army against the rebels. The battle lines moved back and forth, but by 1999 most of the country was approaching some kind of stability. The United Nations Security Council authorized the intervention of the largest UN peacekeeping mission of that time, the UN Mission in Sierra Leone (UNAMSIL).

UNAMSIL began to help the Sierra Leonean government restore peace. Combatants, including child soldiers, began to hand in their weapons to UN disarmament programmes in return for some cash and food. It was critical to find employment for them, but work was hard to come by and the only living they had known was making war. Unemployed, they were a time bomb.

In Liberia meanwhile, Taylor had achieved his military aims by 1995 but the cost had been high. Doe had been tortured and executed and the three countries of the Mano River region – Liberia, Sierra Leone and Guinea – had been sucked into Taylor's war. A quarter of a million Liberians had lost their lives and the country's infrastructure had been almost totally destroyed. There was no running water or mains power even in the capital, Monrovia.

Elections were held and Taylor won the presidency in 1997 with 75 per cent of the vote. Many people evidently figured that only a victorious warlord could bring peace and people sang 'You killed my ma, you killed my pa, I'll vote for you'. But the peace was not to last for long.

Various dissident groups comprising fighters who had fled Taylor's forces into Guinea, Sierra Leone and Côte d'Ivoire coalesced in Guinea, to the north, under the banner of Liberians United for Reconciliation and Democracy (LURD). In 1999, they launched attacks into Liberia and began gaining ground. Within two years of taking power, Taylor's regime was under threat.

Taylor ordered the RUF to recruit more fighters. Unemployed men, refugees and disarmed ex-combatants were offered cash to fight for Taylor and more children were abducted to make up numbers. Just as the nine-year-old civil war in Sierra Leone was coming to an end, a resurgent RUF struck south and were advancing on the capital, Freetown. In force. Fears were high that the bloodshed they had wreaked before would be repeated.

Britain's prime minister, Tony Blair, ordered a widely welcomed military intervention into the former Crown colony. A Royal Navy taskforce, including an aircraft carrier, were deployed to the region, and British Army regular and Special Forces units landed in the country. Lungi Airport was secured and, following the successful evacuation of non-combatants, the British forces remained and fought alongside United Nations troops and the Sierra Leonean Army.

But the key to destroying Taylor's forces was to destroy his war chest. Until that happened, the future of the region was always going to hang in the balance.

The international community's first attempt to stem the flow of cash to Taylor came on 7 March 2001, when the 15 members of the United Nations Security Council entered their ornate chamber at UN headquarters in New York and took their seats around the circular wooden conference table. By the time their meeting was over, in a rare display of consensus, they had unanimously voted to adopt the Resolution 1343 (2001).

This resolution placed Liberia under a swingeing sanctions regime. The Security Council had imposed an arms embargo, the grounding of all Liberian registered planes and a ban on diamond exports into or out of Liberia. The council's intention was to block the supply of military hardware to the regime of Liberia's president, Charles Taylor, and cut off the diamond revenues that were paying for it. The objective was to bring an end to one of the most brutal wars ever known.

But diamonds were not Taylor's only source of funds.

*

A few months before Leonid Minin's sex party was brought to an abrupt end, I had been invited by Yale University's School of Forestry to give a talk about how the timber trade can be used to fund conflict, based on our experiences in Cambodia.

'Can you come to Liberia and do what you did in Cambodia?' The question came from a former World Bank staffer who knew West Africa well. It was flattering, and although it appeared there were many parallels with our Cambodia work, we were still a tiny organization with few staff and less money, and we knew nothing about Liberia. It was a non-starter. But I wasn't going to get away with it that easily. The man approached me after the meeting and laid out the bones of an intriguing story.

While the international community were focusing their attention on his diamond revenues, Taylor had been diversifying. During his time as a rebel warlord, he was often seen with foreign and local businessmen in his remote jungle camps in Liberia. These men were among scores of carpetbaggers trying to get rich on the back of conflict. The most easily marketable resources under Taylor's control were the rich tropical forests his army lived in and struck from.

Tropical timber is a luxury product in high demand, and the tropical-timber industry is renowned for its criminal behaviour and its amoral stance, much like the oil and mining industries. Liberia was ripe for the picking. These businessmen were contracted by Taylor to log the forests and export the timber. Despite the high risks of doing business in a war zone, there was money enough for both Taylor and these parasitic businessmen to make it an attractive prospect. Like maggots they began feeding off the carcass of war, and they were banking on Taylor's victory.

They knew that Taylor's accession to the presidency wouldn't end his need for money – quite the opposite. When he took power, he awarded vast areas of forest to those key businessmen whose logging companies had helped fund his war. Now they were able to operate openly under the façade of legitimacy conferred by a warlord turned head of state.

Chief among these was Guus Kouwenhoven, a Dutch businessman with a shady past, including links to a stolen Rembrandt, before he wound up in Africa. During the war he set up the Royal Timber Company; now, with Indonesian backing, he established the

Oriental Timber Company (OTC), known locally as Only Taylor Chops, or Old Taylor's Children. One of the few images available of Kouwenhoven at that time was captured from a promotional video shot in the Port of Buchanan, where he extolled the benefits that the timber industry would bring to Liberia. Kouwenhoven, a fattish man approaching 60, with wavy grey hair and wire-rimmed spectacles, spoke to the camera against a backdrop of heavy logging machinery being unloaded from the moored ships.

OTC was the biggest logging company in Liberia by far, and their huge yellow logging trucks were hauling thousands upon thousands of logs to Buchanan for export. But Kouwenhoven had a lucrative sideline. Rumour had it that before their holds were filled with logs, many of the ships first unloaded a more deadly cargo: arms.

GLOBAL WITNESS OFFICE, LONDON, 2001

Two weeks after returning from Yale, I received an email out of the blue from Liberia. Silas Siakor ran a small environmental organization called Save My Future (SAMFU) and, like the guy at Yale, he too asked if we would take on the Liberian logging industry. It seemed fate was taking a hand in what Global Witness should do next.

Many of the rambling discussions that had led to the creation of Global Witness had taken place in pubs, and it was over lunch at the St John's Tavern that Simon, Charmian and I debated Liberia. Our relationship was born of a strange alchemy whereby gut instinct trumped logic, we erred towards doing what seemed right rather than what seemed sensible, and the more insurmountable a problem seemed, the more likely we would be to embark upon it. This approach had served us well so far.

Within the space of two weeks, two people had asked us to take on Liberia's logging industry, and by default Charles Taylor's war machine. With our work on the Khmer Rouge timber trade and exposing the issue of diamonds funding war, we had identified resource-funded wars as one of the critical issues of our time. We also knew that the UN Security Council would be meeting soon to consider sanctions on Sierra Leonean diamonds due to their role in funding Taylor and the RUF. We thought: if they can sanction diamonds, why not timber as well?

We were fortunate enough to attract a stream of volunteers who, whenever possible, we would absorb into our slowly growing organization as full-time members of staff. One of these was Alice Blondel. Twenty-seven, tall, blonde and multi-lingual, she possessed a quirky sense of humour and a steely resolve. She was our fund-raiser, but campaigning was where her ambitions lay.

'Who wants to write a briefing on timber for the UN Security Council on Liberia?' I asked when we got back from the pub. 'I do,' she answered immediately in her soft Canadian accent. I had guessed she would. It was a Thursday afternoon and she grimaced when I told her we would need it by Monday. I had ruined her weekend, but she gratefully pushed away the business plan she'd been working on.

Among the best sources of information at that time were the reports from the rather Orwellian-sounding Panel of Experts, a body appointed by the UN Security Council, whose task was to report on the security situation and monitor the implementation of sanctions. These panels had proved their worth in Angola when Robert Fowler, the Canadian ambassador to the UN, ensured that the report of the Angola panel was incredibly hard-hitting, naming names that included those of various heads of state connected to the illicit trade in diamonds and therefore to breaking the sanctions against UNITA.

The panel on Liberia consisted of five people with expertise in arms trafficking, diamonds, air transportation and law enforcement. Further information had been furnished by Silas and others, while activists from Greenpeace and French environmental group Robin des Bois had been poking around various European ports and had reported a dramatic escalation of timber imports from Liberia.

Hunched over her computer, dressed in a thick jumper, with a scarf wrapped around her neck and her head immersed in a woollen hat, Alice braved the chill of the office as she laboriously translated a report from Greenpeace Spain. She cross-referenced this with the UN Panel of Experts reports and added in fresher details that we had been able to obtain.

On Monday morning, she presented me with a nine-page briefing and our Liberia campaign was born. Its primary recommendation was that the UN Security Council should impose sanctions on Liberian timber exports. At this stage our information was not revelatory – frankly, it was scant – but it was important to make our mark. It is easy for faceless policymakers to make momentous decisions behind the scenes, but if they know journalists and NGOs are taking an interest and will probably hold them to account, then they need to be able to justify their decisions.

Although we were a tiny organization and known only in the narrow circles of Cambodia and blood diamonds, our work had earned us respect in some important corridors of power. We sent the briefing to influential media outlets and mailed it to the 15 members of the Security Council in New York. Then we began to arrange meetings with key government officials, starting with our own.

Given the UK's military intervention in Sierra Leone and the close links between the RUF and Charles Taylor, we figured that the Ministry of Defence might be interested in our plans for Liberia and could prove helpful.

Alice and I were ushered into a large, grey, light-filled office over-looking the Thames and offered seats at a desk, on the other side of which sat an army colonel. The only other person present, a man in a smart blue pinstripe suit standing on the far side of the room, was introduced to us as a member of the Defence Intelligence Service, the MOD's own spy agency. We were never given his name.

We did most of the talking and outlined the little we knew about the importance of the revenue Charles Taylor was receiving from log exports, which had been omitted from the UNSC sanctions, and the links between the timber business and arms trafficking. The relevance of the RUF's godfather acquiring more weaponry was not lost on the colonel; he asked various questions but didn't give much away. The other man, haunting the fringes of the room, didn't speak until the end.

'If you ever happen to be in the vicinity of Freetown, I'd recommend you drop in at the High Commission and have a chat with the military attaché there, just if you happen to be in that neck of the woods.' He smiled enigmatically as he shook our hands.

Back on the street, we realized we had been doing all the talking and been given little in return. However, the meeting proved to have been more important than we knew.

We were in email contact with Silas and had begun to understand the almost impossible circumstances he was operating under, and to appreciate how incredibly courageous and resourceful he was. Ever grateful to the Catholic Church for his education, he had fled the worst of Liberia's civil war for a refugee camp in Ghana, returning as soon as it was safe to, determined to help rebuild his country.

The rural population depended on the forests for much of their culture, traditions and livelihoods, and Silas could see that Taylor's assault on these forests was one of the greatest long-term threats facing the country, especially because the logging operations directly contributed to the conflict. But to be an activist intent on targeting one of a warlord's main income streams was literally a matter of life and death.

Silas was an arch strategist. He knew what had to be done, and he knew the limits of what he could do. Under his leadership, SAMFU could highlight issues relating to the environment, but Silas could not even mention the individuals with close connections to Taylor, the companies they owned or the corruption at the centre of this business. He could not be seen to be in communication with a foreign organization like ours. Like all dictators, Taylor was paranoid about foreign intervention. Also, Taylor had one powerful factor on his side: back then, communicating with Liberia was virtually impossible. There was no mains power, landlines were non-existent and there was no internet. The average Liberian had no access to the outside world.

But Silas was not the average Liberian. He had access to the UN offices in Monrovia, and they had satellite internet. We established a secure email protocol using state-of-the-art encryption software to ensure Silas's security, and from that time onwards we were receiving regular intelligence about the timber industry. We learned the names and areas of operation of the logging companies, the ports they exported logs from, and which companies were linked to arms trafficking.

Johan Peleman, a slim, tallish man in his thirties with thinning dark hair and the pale skin of someone who spends too much time poring over his research, worked for the International Peace Information Service. Educated as an expert in medieval literature, he made his reputation in a most unexpected field. During his research he noticed that various airlines belonging to a Russian man called Victor Bout always seemed to operate in or near war zones. Bout provided services to all sides in a conflict. He chartered planes to transport UN relief supplies and would use the same plane to flout a UN arms embargo. After all, his main business was as an arms trafficker. It was Johan's work that exposed Bout's networks and as a result, his expertise was in high demand. He was soon snapped up to join the UN Security Council's Panel of Experts as their guru on the arms trade.

Johan had a reputation for being a walking encyclopaedia and we wanted to pick his brain, and so it was that Alice and I found ourselves climbing the narrow staircase to his small cluttered offices, which were based in a Franciscan monastery in Antwerp. Shelves stacked with bursting box files lined the walls and papers were strewn over the desks. Johan was affable and helpful, and he had been one of the first people to knock on Walter Mapelli's door after Minin's arrest.

He took down one of the overstuffed box files full of documents that had been seized from Minin's room in that August police raid. I leafed through advertising brochures extolling the virtues of various missile systems, deals between Minin and a Chinese state-owned aerospace company, and another document that went to the heart of the matter. This was a *certificat d'achat* – an 'end-user certificate' – signed by Robert Gueï, the president of Côte d'Ivoire, Liberia's next-door neighbour. My eyes widened as I read through a list of enough weaponry to fight a war. Which was exactly what it was.

Itemized here were 10,500 AK47 assault rifles, 5 million rounds of ammunition, 200 RPG7 rocket launchers, 50 sniper rifles, night-vision telescopic sights, thermal-image binoculars and 2,000 .45-calibre semi-automatic pistols.

There were also documents related to Exotic Tropical Timber Enterprise (ETTE), the logging company Minin had set up in Liberia. Presumably, like Minin himself, now defunct.

Other documents laid out the ownership structure of OTC, or detailed bank transfers made by their Indonesian mother company, Djanjanti. One of these was a payment of US$500,000 to San Air, a company linked to Victor Bout via another arms dealer, Sanjivan Ruprah, whose actions had been described by British Foreign Office Minister Peter Hain as 'equally odious as those of Victor Bout'. Proof that OTC was funding Taylor's arms imports.

The only times I had seen material like this was in the pages of fiction, but this was very real and I tried not to think too hard about the kind of adversaries we'd taken on. These kingpins of the arms-trafficking world were up to their necks in the carrion of West Africa's wars and they became famous by proxy, as the inspiration for the 2005 Hollywood movie *Lord of War*.

We left Johan's office, my briefcase bulging with this trove of documents, and headed out to Antwerp's tiny airport for the one-hour flight to London City. We sat at the bar for a few minutes sipping cool Belgian beers, and I eyed my fellow travellers. I wondered what they all did. Some were doubtless diamond dealers, given that Antwerp is a diamond town. Some were probably sales-people, or bankers, or tourists…but my eyes had been opened to a shadow world. There were undoubtedly some very bad characters out there and, other than the extraordinarily ugly Minin, they must all look just the same as anyone else.

A strategy was forming in my mind. The problem was simple enough to identify: a pariah state led by a power-crazed but intelligent and charismatic warlord was funding two civil wars with money ob-tained from selling natural resources. The solution was trickier: how do you stop him? How do you bring down a dictator? Well, we had delivered a mortal blow to the Khmer Rouge, so bringing down a dictator couldn't be that hard. Could it?

Virtually every form of international pressure had already been applied to Liberia or was irrelevant in the circumstances. Using leverage on international aid wouldn't work because Liberia wasn't getting any. No legitimate business was investing in the country, so no dice there. The same for international trade – Liberia was broke, and there were virtually no legal imports or exports. Except timber.

As far as I could see, there were only two possible courses of action: a military intervention – but no one was going to rush into the conflagration that that would be – or further sanctions, as we had recommended in that first briefing Alice had put together. And the only entity that could impose sanctions that could have any chance of biting was the United Nations Security Council.

It was while we were in France that we heard that the Security Council had placed sanctions on Liberia's diamond imports. While this was good news, they had ignored the two other businesses that Liberia was still engaged in: the timber industry and the important but less significant shipping registry. Counterintuitively, this was run by a company based in the US, whose job it was to register merchant ships as Liberian. This controversial practice of selling 'flags of convenience', often the domain of poorer countries like Liberia and Panama, earns a respectable sum, imposes far fewer rules on the ship owners and is far cheaper than registering vessels in their home ports in Europe or the US, for example. These omissions seemed inexplicable from our perspective, given the Security Council had had an inkling earlier than we did about the links between timber and arms trafficking.

If we could stop the timber exports, we would cut Taylor's main economic lifeline and his seaborne arms imports in one fell swoop. So that was the challenge. A two-person Global Witness campaign team together with Silas's networks in Liberia were going to have to come up with information good enough to convince the UN Security Council.

BORDEAUX, FRANCE, MARCH 2001

Alice and I touched down at Bordeaux Airport, packed our luggage and secret-camera gear into the small red Citroën we'd hired, and embarked on our first field investigation into Liberia's timber trade. We knew from Customs statistics that, after China, France was the world's second-largest buyer of Liberian timber, so we planned to tour some of its major ports to see if we could find evidence of the trade. It was a job of basic detective work.

We fixed on La Pallice, the commercial port of La Rochelle, as our first stop. We were nervous as we entered the outskirts of the port because security in these areas differed. Some ports could be totally open, others totally closed, while some were open if you had legitimate business there – and the secret of those was behaving as though you did. Alice and I put on our confident faces and promptly got lost in a maze of roads, wharves, warehouses, dockside cranes, shipping containers, the massive Second World War German U-boat pens that formed the real-life set used in the film *Das Boot*, and the dead-ends of the quaysides themselves.

But eventually, in an open area of the port, we found stacks of logs piled up under the French sky, forlorn casualties of Charles Taylor's war on his own country. The ends of the logs were marked with the letters 'RTC' and an identification number in black paint on the red wood. The Royal Timber Company was run by Guus Kouwenhoven and was the sister company of OTC, and we knew from the UN reports that they were linked to arms trafficking. We counted the logs, photographed them and noted the identification numbers: proof of France's complicity in financing Taylor's war.

Further north on this Atlantic coast, we found more RTC logs at Nantes. We stopped the car a short way from a large, white-painted, iron-clad warehouse with the word 'PINAULT' emblazoned across the front in 2m-tall letters. Founded by François Pinault in 1963, this timber company was the stepping stone that led to him becoming one of France's richest men – owner of luxury brands such as Gucci as well as Christie's auction house. Whether he retained any interest in the company when we visited it, we didn't know.

Alice had arranged a meeting in advance. I checked that the secret camera was powered up and working, snapped the recorder lid closed and zipped up the bag; then we walked past two rows of logs that lay in front of the building and knocked on the office door.

'This is really funny,' Alice said. 'When I spoke on the phone to the guy we're meeting, he said he'd never heard of RTC. Why doesn't he look out of the window?'

We were ushered into a small office and seated ourselves in front of a desk behind which sat a Monsieur Pierrick. I placed the camera bag on a small cupboard next to me, the lens facing his desk. Alice did the talking. She told him how we were interested in buying timber and enquired what species and quantity they had available. I resisted a smile as Alice knew nothing about timber species, and had said they were like Latin to her. Which wasn't far off the mark, really. 'I memorized species' names before travelling over and was always worried that I would mix up *seppuku*, the Japanese word for suicide by disembowelment, and *sapele*, the African wood species,' she said with an alarming smile.

Pierrick detailed the species they could obtain and said that quantity was no problem – they had ready sources of supply. He had little choice but to admit that they sourced some of their timber from Liberia.

As we left, we walked along the rows of logs, and most were marked 'ILC'. The Inland Logging Company was owned by two brothers who were close confidantes of Taylor, Maurice and Oscar Cooper, and maintained its own armed militia.

Our final stop was Bassens, the port of Bordeaux itself. As we arrived at the docks, we saw logs being hoisted from the hold of a bulk freighter moored alongside the quay by the huge white dockside cranes. We asked a stevedore who the buyer was, and he gestured across the hardstanding towards an office marked 'F Jammes' – and as luck would have it, Monsieur Jammes was in.

Jammes evidently didn't think there was anything odd about importing logs from a war zone. Perhaps he didn't even know Liberia *was* a war zone. It was with an air of pride that he invited us onto the ship where we could photograph the vast hold, which was the size of an Olympic swimming pool but one that was 12m deep. It was still half-filled with logs, each with a diameter of 2–3m, dwarfing the members of the crew who were attaching heavy lifting cables to them.

Perhaps hoping for a sale, Monsieur Jammes rather foolishly showed us the ship's manifest, which accounted for just 20 logs, several hundred less than were actually in the ship.

A look at the company's website today tells you that it is one of the oldest timber importers in France, and that they are concerned about the sustainability of supply and have been actively pursuing this policy since the 1990s. They weren't pursuing it in 2001.

By this time, we were actively collaborating with Greenpeace International, the French environmental group Robin des Bois and a Danish organization called Nepenthes. Together we were documenting logs entering France, Greece, Germany, Britain and Denmark. These groups were opposing the tropical-timber trade for environmental reasons; our speciality was corruption and the links with conflict in Africa, and for us that was the next stop.

FREETOWN, SIERRA LEONE, JULY 2001

In one of my father's photo albums from the Second World War, there is a black-and-white photograph from September 1940 of a street in Freetown. Two-storey block-built houses with corrugated-iron roofs line a road steeply descending towards the sea. Apart from the odd motor vehicle, the road contains only foot traffic – locals carrying merchandise in sacks on their shoulders and heads. In the distance, my father's ship, the battleship *Royal Sovereign*, lay at anchor in Freetown's port.

Almost exactly 60 years later, I could still recognize the city depicted in that photo, but it bore the deep scars of war. The two-storey houses were still there, but now there were also a few modest high-rises and apartment blocks, some burned out and most in poor repair. Virtually the only vehicles on the road were the white Toyota Land Cruisers of the UN Mission in Sierra Leone, UNAMSIL.

Our host was Tommy Garnett, a handsome, tall, fit Sierra Leonean with an infectious laugh who had spent much of his youth as a civil servant in London before marrying a woman from Ireland and raising a brood of children there. Towards the end of the civil war (which still had a year left to run at this time), Tommy, like Silas, had returned to the country of his birth. Also like Silas, he was a passionate environmentalist; and so Tommy had set up the Environmental Foundation for Africa.

Alice and I had added another Global Witness staffer to our team for this investigation. Valerie Vauthier, daughter of a French schoolteacher, was born and brought up in Côte d'Ivoire. Her local knowledge would prove invaluable. With typical generosity, Tommy put all his resources at our disposal. We stayed with his new family and later at the bunkhouse of his office, set just back from the glorious Lakka Beach, an almost endless strip of palm-fringed sand along the Atlantic shore. We also had the use of his vehicle, another white Land Cruiser, which, given the number of UN vehicles on the road, was effectively invisible.

Making good on the recommendation of the Defence Intelligence Service agent we'd met in London, we soon found ourselves sitting across from the defence attaché at the British High Commission. A colonel in immaculate tropical uniform, dark-haired and complete with a neatly trimmed military moustache, briefed us on the military situation. UN peacekeepers were stationed across the country and Freetown was secure; but overall the situation was far from stable, especially the closer you got to the Liberian border.

In Liberia itself the situation was looking far from rosy for Charles Taylor's regime, which was facing attacks from various newly created rebel groups operating out of Guinea and Côte d'Ivoire. Moreover, the UN-imposed sanctions on diamonds were beginning to bite. Alice asked why the UN didn't consider sanctions on Liberia's timber exports. 'I can't answer you that,' he said. 'Timber doesn't seem to be their priority.'

As our meeting ended, he rose and said that he'd like to introduce us to a colleague. He led us down a brightly lit corridor and knocked on the wooden door of a political officer in the Chancery Section.

'Hi, you have some visitors.' With that the colonel shook our hands and walked briskly back to his office. The political officer rose from his desk and greeted us. He could have been aged anything from mid-twenties to mid-thirties and wore an open-necked white shirt with the sleeves rolled up to his elbows. He was welcoming and listened attentively as we explained what we were doing and that we wanted to pick his brain about the situation in Liberia and Sierra Leone. Especially the movement of fighters and weapons. When we had finished, he pulled out a large paper chart from his drawer.

'Let's have a look at my mind map.' He cleared some items from his desk and unrolled the chart. It was filled with simple icons depicting men, women, governments, companies and military units with a myriad of lines connecting them. This was my introduction to a sophisticated software called i2 that visually mapped intelligence.

'What do you want to know?'

'How about where Sam Bockarie is now?' Bockarie, *nom de guerre* Mosquito, was an RUF leader with a particularly gruesome reputation and who played a major role in smuggling RUF diamonds to Taylor in Liberia.

The political officer's finger traced one of the lines ending in a simple representation of a male head.

'Here you go. Our best bet is that he's at Gbandilo, Kailahun District, right here in SL. That said, he moves around a lot. He divides his time between here and Liberia.'

The following hour passed quickly as the political officer guided us through what he knew. His finger moved back and forth across the chart, highlighting links between various people, the strengths and objectives of various armed groups, and hotspots of activity. A picture formed that brought these incredibly complicated regional dynamics together into a vaguely understandable whole. More than anything, it reinforced the strategy that we had embarked upon. Until Taylor was denied access to arms and money, the war would carry on.

Under the diplomat's tutelage, we began to get an insight into the dynamics of Taylor's rule. It was clear that his regime was facing fundamental threats as the strength of dissident rebel groups grew, just as his own allies like the RUF were getting weaker. Although the UN Security Council's sanctions on Liberian diamonds were routinely broken, they had ceased to be his most significant funding source. Taylor was now dependent on timber revenues to maintain power. And we knew that he had some parasitic allies who had thrown him a lifeline: the timber importers of Europe and China.

Just as we had left that meeting at London's Ministry of Defence sucked clean of information, we left this one gorged on it. I have met many diplomats in my time, but neither before nor since this meeting in Freetown has any of them divulged this kind of information so freely. I couldn't help thinking back to the Defence Intelligence Service agent who had recommended we visit the High Commission in Freetown, and whether he had lent a helping hand. I subsequently learned that i2's customers included the secret intelligence services of numerous countries, including the UK and US, as well as numerous police forces. I had little doubt that the political officer was MI6's man on the ground in Sierra Leone. And like him, another contact we met in Freetown would have been worth the trip to Africa on its own.

We were ushered into the office of a senior Sierra Leonean government official, Alex Palmer. Alex was a heavyset man with close-cut grey hair and a moustache, dressed in a rumpled grey suit. A small clear patch at the front of his desk was under siege from the piles of papers that occasionally made bids for freedom in small and unpredictable avalanches. Miraculously, he seemed to know where everything was.

Palmer had been to Liberia many times and had specialized in developing his own extracurricular line of intelligence gathering. He knew more than anyone else I met about the regional dynamics, the players involved and the goings-on deep behind the scenes. After we'd outlined what we were doing and what we knew, he said in a deep sonorous voice: 'Hmmmm, you're on the right track, but it's a lot more complicated, and goes much deeper than you'd believe.' With that he started delving into his filing system, unleashing more avalanches as his fingers probed the stacks of paper on his desk. 'It's my security system,' he smiled. 'No one except me can find anything in this lot.'

He continued, 'Things are getting better here in Sierra Leone. I think the enemy is on the run, but they're not beaten yet. The links between Liberia and the RUF have not been severed. What's more, the border between us and Liberia is fading. Liberia has begun logging operations in our country in cooperation with the RUF, and they are fighting alongside Liberian forces in Liberia's Lofa County.'

'Samuel Bockarie is now a senior member of the ATU and has a fake Sierra Leonean passport to help him avoid sanctions.' Alex went on to name several other people on the sanctions list who had acquired more convenient passports.

'I think the biggest worry is that the RUF is on a recruitment drive.' He thrust a bundle of papers towards us.

The first document listed 20 members of the 'RUF Vanguard' – the original members of the organization, he explained, who were now based in Liberia. Another list comprised the names of 22 members of the RUF who had gone to fight with its founder, Foday Sankoh, near the Liberian border in Kailahun District. The political officer at the High Commission had just told us that Sam Bockarie operated from here too, so this checked out.

A further list of 85 names told the story of ex-combatants who had been re-recruited and were now serving with the ATU under Charles Taylor's son. Separately, a short and poignant handwritten note documented 8 women kidnapped from their homes in Sierra Leone and gave their last-known locations in Liberia.

Palmer's final list, comprising 6 neatly typed columns, named 36 Sierra Leonean refugees who, in 2000, had been recruited in the various countries they had fled to – Nigeria, Côte d'Ivoire and Guinea – for military training in Libya. They had returned to Liberia armed with emergency travel permits issued by the Liberian Embassy in Tripoli. The last column listed their occupations: car washer, painter, student, tiler, mechanic – jobs that had no future in a war zone. Taylor conferred them with Liberian citizenship, and then they too were drafted into the RUF.

This trip to Sierra Leone had furnished us with amazing information and given us an insight into how fragile the peace process was there. We were in little doubt that Charles Taylor, like Hitler in his bunker in Berlin, intended to fight until he no longer could, regardless of the cost to his own people, his country or its neighbours.

Only when he had nothing left to fight with would the fighting stop, and it was our task to see that he did indeed have nothing left to fight with.

The UN Panel of Experts remained focused on diamonds and the logistics of arms trafficking, but for us this was becoming old news. Unless they widened their horizons to include timber, the war would carry on. We had begun to piece together various aspects of the timber trade, but we needed to convince the Security Council that this was now *the* pivotal issue, and to do that we needed to convince the Panel of Experts, and to do that we needed to have better sources of information than they did, and we needed to get them to realize that they didn't know what they didn't know.

And they didn't know the timber business.

The next day we were heading to Côte d'Ivoire, which seemed like a good place to start, and there we would have our first meeting with the enigmatic Silas. From there, together, we would head towards the country's border with Liberia. Bandit country.

ABIDJAN, CÔTE D'IVOIRE, MARCH 2001

Weasua Air Transport went out of business in 2006, an event that has probably saved numerous lives. Unfortunately, the airline was still in business in 2001 when we booked seats for the short flight to Abidjan. Daylight was clearly visible around the main cabin door of the ageing propeller-driven plane and the warm air coming in condensed in the slightly cooler air inside, producing clouds reminiscent of dry ice at a Black Sabbath concert. The lack of cabin pressurization was mitigated by the fact that the plane couldn't climb to any great altitude because the starboard engine failed just after take-off. The only thing we could do was laugh. Nervously.

Somewhat surprised to be alive, we arrived in Abidjan and checked into an anonymous business-type hotel. After freshening up, we took seats at a table in the garden and waited for Silas. Until now, disembodied encrypted email exchanges had been our only form of contact with this faceless person who had been navigating perilous waters to gather intelligence on his president's sources of money. We didn't know how he hid himself or how he got around. He was an enigma.

We had chosen a table as far from the others as possible; we didn't want any eavesdroppers and we wanted to have clear sightlines of the immediate area. After a short while, a man in his early thirties appeared from the building. He paused, scanned the garden and then walked towards us. Around five-foot-eight, wiry and with close-cropped hair, he came to the table.

'Patrick, Alice...?' Although he was from one of Liberia's ethnic groups rather than a descendent of the freed slaves that gave the country its name, Silas's accent was a rich drawl that owed much to the southern states of the US – the accent that the former slaves brought with them when they colonized the country in the 19th century.

'Silas!' We stood and shook his hand warmly. The first thing was to get the handshake right, the West African way, he taught us. A complicated mixture of two different handshakes rounded off by snapping your fingers around the other's index finger. The click at the end is the critical bit, and hard for beginners. We ordered coffee and began to get to know each other.

Silas's journey to this rendezvous had been far more hazardous than ours, despite Weasua's best efforts. He had entered Côte d'Ivoire via the unpoliced and porous land border near the western port of San-Pédro. 'No one travels those roads except the logging companies,' he told us. 'There were just the trucks loaded with logs headed for [the port of] Greenville.'

As he headed east towards Côte d'Ivoire, he got closer to Liberia's Harper Port, just a few miles from the border, and was very alone indeed. 'The roads there are dangerous, and there's virtually no traffic on them. If you get stuck, you could be stuck for days.'

These hazards increased in Harper itself. The port was controlled by Maryland Wood Processing Industries, and it was one of the major entry points for illegal arms shipments. The town was in the grip of various armed militias who had looted all the available transport, which in turn they used to loot from the town and its surrounds, and to sell what they'd looted.

'The only other activity at Harper was the ships coming and going, exporting logs and bringing stuff in for Taylor,' Silas said. 'People won't flinch to do you harm. Ignorance and innocence are our best cover.' But I don't think he realized just how dangerous it was. It reminded me of the time Simon and I had taken a boat trip behind Khmer Rouge lines in Cambodia. If we'd known what we were doing, we would have been terrified, and Global Witness could well have ended there. Luckily, we had been in blissful ignorance.

As we were talking, a bunch of noisy and cheerful young guys, maybe ten of them, arrived in the garden and sat a few tables away. Silas froze. 'Those guys are speaking Creole, which means they're from Sierra Leone.' Young, fit-looking Sierra Leoneans could well be RUF, who we knew roamed freely around the whole region. I rushed up to our room and set up our secret-camera gear. Back downstairs, we concentrated on this exciting but potentially dangerous situation until, suddenly, Silas laughed. 'Ha! It's a football team – they're here for a match.'

Two plus two had made five, but it illustrated the nerves and paranoia of investigations like this.

We had come to Côte d'Ivoire with a roughly worked-out strategy. We needed to gather evidence around the relationships between Liberia's timber barons and Charles Taylor's elite, the dynamics of the logging industry and, most difficult of all, arms trafficking.

The major spanner in the works was that we couldn't go to Liberia ourselves. It wouldn't pay to stick out like a sore thumb in a failed state just entering another civil war. Very recently four journalists from Channel 4 in the UK had been arrested in Liberia. In an interview with CNN, Taylor said that the TV journalists had accused Liberia of arms trafficking and diamond smuggling. 'That's grounds for the United States and Britain to start military action against Liberia. That's grounds for sanctions,' he said, and the journalists were charged with espionage, a capital offence. Fortunately they were released, but if we got into bother we would have a harder job convincing Liberia's government of our bona fides, given we were absolutely guilty of what the journalists had been accused of.

The heart of our strategy depended on Silas. We could do many things that he couldn't because he was far more vulnerable than we were. From outside Liberia, we could take a hard-nosed approach and accuse Taylor and his acolytes of anything we could find out. We could take information to Western governments and to the UN, while Silas was pretty much confined to Liberia with virtually no communication with the outside world. If Charles Taylor's regime knew what he was up to, he would be a dead man.

But we could only do what we needed to do if we had information, and Silas could get information that we never could. This meeting was the one chance to have a real conversation with him, so around that table in Abidjan we thrashed out a long-term plan. At Silas's request, we agreed to provide funds for him to place a colleague in each of Liberia's sea ports for a period of several months, to monitor what ships came in and out and what they were carrying. Because there was no internet and phones were insecure, communications were difficult. So every month, these four guys would travel to Monrovia, a journey that could take days from the more distant ports, to meet with Silas, and he would then communicate the information to us through secure means.

The *pièce de résistance* was also Silas's idea. He would infiltrate Guus Kouwenhoven's logging company, OTC, by getting another one of his team to apply for an office job at their Buchanan headquarters. There, we hoped, he would gain access to shipping manifests, bills of lading, invoices and other export paperwork. If Silas could pull this one off, it would be a real coup.

Our planning done, Silas needed to return to Liberia the same way he came, so we thrashed out the next steps. We would drive the 300km to the Ivorian port of San-Pédro, a known import point for Liberian timber. From there we would head northwest as far as the town of Danané, which we'd heard was a major hub for timber smuggling. There we would try to document any timber trading and keep an ear open for movements of rebel soldiers who apparently crossed the border pretty freely.

The next day, Silas, Alice, Valerie and I climbed into the battered, non-descript yellow saloon car we'd hired along with its owner, a sometimes loquacious, sometimes morose man called Youssef. Usually wearing the long Muslim robe and finely worked cap, the taqiyah, Youssef proved himself reliable; although as time went on, he made it increasingly plain that we were asking him to go well beyond the call of duty. In that, he was probably right.

Côte d'Ivoire was becoming increasingly unstable. A coup in 1999 had seen army general Robert Gueï seize power, only to be ousted himself by elections in late 2000. In January 2001, just six months before we arrived, a failed coup attempt was blamed on Gueï and the situation was tense, with escalating political, religious and ethnic violence. We needed to watch our step.

We headed west out of Abidjan on the road to San-Pédro. We broke the journey to spend the night at a forlorn and deserted tourist resort on the coast run by a grumpy, heavily built Frenchman in a pale-blue patterned tropical shirt who looked too much like Gérard Depardieu for his own good. We enjoyed a beer sitting under the palm trees along the beach, gazing at the Atlantic waves breaking over the sand, and went to sleep in insect-infested palm-thatched bungalows around an empty swimming pool. By eight in the morning, we were on the road and arrived at San-Pédro in the early afternoon.

San-Pédro lies just about 100km east of the Liberian border and is Côte d'Ivoire's second-largest port, occupying the western side of a mile-long inlet. An anarchic profusion of low, brightly painted fishing boats resembling kayaks occupied the northernmost recesses of the inlet. The southern end, with its cluster of quays and ware-houses, lay in the embrace of two concrete moles that protected the port from the sea, and we could hear the Atlantic breakers crashing into their walls.

The port didn't seem to be doing too much business. There were a few piles of logs stacked on the concrete, but the place was virtually deserted. The rusted rumps of old winches, cables and other port machinery gave the place an air of neglect. No ships were moored there, and swirls of dust were propelled along the wharves by the Atlantic breeze.

We located an official in the dilapidated port office and told him we were timber importers. We presented our business cards, which identified us as representatives of Universal Export. Old habits die hard. We walked across the quays together, probing the official for information. Dressed in sagging, once-smart dark slacks, grubby, sweat-stained shirt and flip-flops, with the metal bracelet of his cheap gold-coloured watch hanging loosely from his wrist, a slightly hangdog expression on his face, he mirrored the sense of decay that pervaded the port. He pointed to the pile of logs we'd already seen and confirmed they were from Liberia but said that not much timber was coming into San-Pédro. We believed him.

We felt we were unlikely to discover much more there and decided to drive north, parallel to the border, towards Toulépleu, a small town about 300km away. According to Silas, there was a big sawmill there processing Liberian logs. Just on the other side of the border was the territory of Bureaux Ivorian Ngorian (BIN), a logging company run by one of the kingpins of Liberia's arms supply chain, the Liberian ambassador-at-large, Mohamed Salamé.

We had good reason to approach the area with some trepidation. After seizing power in the 1999 coup, General Gueï needed weapons to shore up his powerbase. Like anyone in need, he first asked his neighbours, and Charles Taylor was happy to oblige. But with his eye on the long game, Taylor sent Ambassador Salamé, who was based in Abidjan, to see what else they could do to help. General Gueï was about to find out that there's no such thing as a free lunch.

According to the UN Panel of Experts' report, Salamé produced an end-user certificate and asked Gueï to sign it. This was for the shopping list of weapons we had seen in Johan Peleman's office in Antwerp. An end-user certificate is an essential element of a legal arms deal, an assurance that the weapons in question were solely destined for use by the state in question. To effect an illegal arms deal you also need an end-user certificate – a forged one. Leonid Minin had several in his possession when he was arrested.

Taylor's gambit was simple. Salamé and Gueï agreed to split the arms between them.

On 2 June 2000, Côte d'Ivoire's ambassador in Moscow authenticated the end-user certificate and in turn the government of Ukraine authorized the export. On 14 July, an Antonov An-124 plane took off from Ukraine's Gostomel Airport loaded with part of the deal: 113 tons of 7.62mm ammunition. After a quick refuelling stop in Libya, it landed at Abidjan the next day and was unloaded by the Ivorian military. Five million rounds of ammunition for over 10,000 assault rifles would likely have been trucked into Liberia along the same road we would be travelling.

It was too risky to explore the road that ran southwest from Toulépleu towards Liberia, so we decided to see what we could find along the border-hugging road that ran north of the town. The wide dirt road was flanked by low forest and cultivated fields and felt very remote. Then ahead of us we saw a military checkpoint. A thick pole was suspended across the road from a wooden guardhouse, and soldiers in bush hats and camouflage uniforms walked into the centre of the road and flagged us down, each cradling an AK47.

I have hated checkpoints ever since I met my first ones in Cambodia. You never know whether you're in for a shakedown, worse, or a legitimate military purpose. Beads of sweat had broken out on Youssef's brow and Silas was tense. The soldiers' eyes widened as three white Westerners, two of them attractive women, climbed out of the car. We were all nervous.

We had strayed into a military area and our explanation that we were tourists didn't cut any ice. The guards motioned us to stay where we were while one of them walked over to the guard house and radioed for instructions. To be detained so close to the border was a real problem for us. If they rumbled our secret-camera gear, they could probably arrest us for espionage.

Our best weapon was our skin colour, as the troops were prepared for almost anything except an unknown quantity like us, and after 40 minutes or so they reluctantly let us go on our way. We all breathed a sigh of relief, especially Silas, who said that on this border a Liberian sticks out like a sore thumb, and that if it hadn't been for us he would likely have been taken for interrogation. After a couple of kilometres, Youssef stopped the car, switched off the engine, laid his prayer mat down by the side of the road and gave thanks to his God. And then he complained about our foolhardiness. He was right.

As we drove further, the checkpoints became more frequent. Having got through the first one eased the others, but progress was slow as Youssef prayed after each one.

Finally we arrived at Danané and found a semi-abandoned hotel that still possessed the architectural flourishes that had arrived with the oil boom of the 1960s. The pale-blue two-storey structure was built around a pool. My room was a retro-lover's dream: the bed head was a richly veneered console with built-in bedside tables and fitted with constellations of spherical lights, half of which were broken and hanging from alarmingly naked wires. Sean Connery's James Bond would have stayed in a hotel like this. The place had now fallen on hard times, and only half its rooms were habitable, but Silas and I took a swim in the pool and we all had a beer in the bar. It was a welcome break in an area of ferment.

In addition to the sense of impending trouble that pervaded the whole country, Danané was close to both the Liberian and Guinean borders; and, like every border town in times of war, it attracted the perpetrators of violence, the victims of it and the service industries of conflict. Sam Bockarie and his RUF cadres frequented the town and mercenaries from Liberia, Sierra Leone and Guinea passed through. Armaments were trucked west into Liberia and timber was trucked the other way. Refugees, not for the first time, trudged down that same dirt road fleeing the escalating violence, and Danané expanded to accommodate them.

At Danané we said goodbye to Silas. As we parted, we gave him a secret-camera kit that we had brought over specially. We said farewell and meant it, our fingers clicking as we shook hands, and then he started on his hazardous trip back home. Our hearts were in our mouths as we watched his slim form melding into the crowds along the border road. Still affected by some superstition from my childhood, I turned my head away before he disappeared from view.

LONDON, SUMMER 2001

Back in London, we opened the large padded envelope that Silas had given us when we met in Abidjan; not wanting to get caught with it in Africa, we had couriered it straight to the UK. It felt like Christmas had come early as we found ourselves in possession of a month's worth of OTC's timber-export paperwork. There were bills of lading, ships' manifests listing the ship's name, destination and the identity of the buyers of the logs, together with invoices detailing log volumes, value and species.

We also pulled out packs of colour photographs that showed OTC's massive yellow trucks stacked high with logs, and others depicting the wide dirt roads snaking into Liberia's imperilled forests.

Perhaps most evocative of all were images of the ghost town that Buchanan, Liberia's main port city, had become. Wide, unsurfaced roads vainly resisting the advance of the scrubby grasses that were engulfing them, lined by once-white houses that were now window-less and streaked black, sometimes with mould and sometimes by fire, topped with peeling and rusting iron roofs. Forlorn telegraph poles leaned at crazy angles, long stripped of the valuable copper wire that was their *raison d'être*. These photographs told a story that couldn't really be told any other way to outsiders who couldn't enter the country.

Out of one of the photographs loomed the image of a huge, black-hulled bulk freighter towering over the quayside next to stacks of OTC logs awaiting export. The *Antarctic Mariner* had arrived in early July from China via Singapore and, according to one of Silas's lookouts, was not being treated like an ordinary ship. It was unloaded at night amid heightened security, with the work being carried out not by stevedores as usual, but by armed troops and OTC personnel. Our eyes on the ground didn't know what exactly had been unloaded, but the cargo included numerous wooden crates that were stored in one of Buchanan's warehouses under guard, awaiting onward transport. Word spread fast and the rumour mill in Buchanan was that this was a shipment of arms. It wasn't the first one they had seen.

Alice, Valerie and I cloistered ourselves away in the office, working late into the warm summer night checking and rechecking the information that we and Silas's team had gathered. We thought we had enough to enter into the next phase of our strategy.

Our second report on Liberia, *Taylor Made*, was published in September 2001. Unlike our first hurried effort 9 months before, the report's 41 pages were crammed with evidence documenting Taylor's dependence on the timber industry for the funds he needed to prop up his regime and to import the arms essential to the multi-fronted war he was now fighting. We highlighted that in 2000, around US$100 million of the country's timber revenue was unaccounted for. One hundred million dollars buys a lot of guns.

The report went on to accuse 7 out of Liberia's 25 timber companies of trafficking arms in contravention of UNSC Resolution 1343 (2001). These companies also maintained their own private militias, private armies available to Taylor's war machine. OTC was even reputed to operate its own prison.

And it exposed their customers. Prominent among these were China-based Global Star Asia and two major European companies: one of the world's largest timber dealers, Denmark's DLH Nordisk, and various subsidiaries of the Swiss-German Danzer Group. Any buyer of Liberian timber at this time had a lot of questions to answer.

Our message was simple: Charles Taylor was playing with the international community. Behind a façade of compliance with UN Security Council Resolution 1343, he was breaching virtually every requirement of it. Arms were continuing to flow into Liberia and Taylor continued to pump money into the war machine. He continued to support the RUF and was actively recruiting new fighters for it.

Our job was to get the UN Security Council to cop on; but unknown to us the timber industry was mounting a behind the scenes PR campaign – a campaign that would likely cost thousands more lives and prolong the war.

On 16 July 2001, a couple of months before *Taylor Made* was published, a letter addressed to Jørgen Møller-Rasmussen slid out of the fax machine at his office in Taastrup, a suburb of Copenhagen. Signed by me and colleagues at Greenpeace and the Danish NGO Nepenthes, it informed Møller-Rasmussen, the chief executive officer of DLH Nordisk, that his company was helping fund the wars in Liberia and Sierra Leone. It was unequivocal:

A report by the UN Expert Panel on Sierra Leone cites OTC as being implicated in arms trafficking to the Revolutionary United Front (RUF) rebels in Sierra Leone. The RUF is responsible for the murders of hundreds of civilians and the mass amputations of limbs from thousands more. The UN Expert Panel states that the chairman of OTC, Guus Kouwenhoven, has been 'responsible for the logistical aspects of many of the arms deals involved in arms trafficking between Liberia and Sierra Leone'. [...] Buying from these companies is clearly incompatible with your public environmental and timber purchasing policies. It also flies in the face of your status as a company member of Amnesty International Denmark.

DLH had a headache. Initially they responded positively, saying that they would cease to place new orders from companies named in the UN reports, and would reassess their position later, but they said that they 'do not want to purchase wood from companies which violate human rights or have destructive logging practices as this would not be compatible with DLH's basic values'.

We thought this was too good to be true. It was. But it is always a good tactic to get a company to spell out its own standards. From there it is easier to expose both their failings and their hypocrisy with key decision makers and in the court of public opinion.

UNITED NATIONS SECURITY COUNCIL, NEW YORK, OCTOBER 2001

The United Nations Security Council is tasked with maintaining international peace and security and it possesses awesome power. A Security Council decision can authorize member states to go to war, or require them to police the peace through missions like UNAMSIL in Sierra Leone. Barring the authorization of war, one of its most powerful weapons is the crippling sanctions it can impose on a member state, which could bring it to its knees.

In practice, the Security Council is notorious for failing to agree on almost anything. Old loyalties, the legacy of Cold War politics, internecine rivalries and member states' vested interests usually thwart assertive action. The question for us was: how did we get the most powerful body in the United Nations to do what we wanted it to do?

The Security Council comprises 15 UN member states, represented in New York by their country's mission – their embassy to the UN. Five of these are permanent members – the P5 – comprising the great powers that emerged from the Second World War: China, France, Great Britain, Russia and the United States. The other ten 'non-permanent' members serve on a rotational basis, with five being replaced each year by new members.

Our task was to get the majority of members on our side at the same time, and to avoid any of the P5 using their power of veto. Two of the P5, China and France, were the world's biggest buyers of Liberian timber. Added to these hurdles was that it was incredibly hard for civil society to get direct access to the Security Council at all. But on 17 October 2001, armed with the evidence compiled in *Taylor Made*, Alice and I joined three colleagues from Amnesty International, Médecins Sans Frontières and Oxfam in a dimly lit, windowless conference room in the bowels of UN headquarters. This was an Arria-formula meeting. Named after a former Venezuelan ambassador to the UN, these are informal and confidential meetings that enable the Security Council members, as individuals rather than as representatives of their countries, to hear and engage with experts on issues of interest to the Security Council. Less than one NGO per year had been invited to present to an Arria-formula meeting since they were instituted in 1992.

We waited nervously as the various members filed in. The Russian representative, dressed in a dark suit, sat down and looked about him. His eyes rested on the Toblerone-shaped block on his desk that bore the name RUSSIA. He suddenly leaned forward and flipped it over, obscuring the name.

'I am not here as a Russian,' he snapped. 'I am here in my personal capacity. It's outrageous.' Everyone, including the other members, looked at him bemusedly, and at least one person rolled their eyes. The meeting's chair, Jamaica, calmed the situation and remarked that it was noted that the Russian wasn't representing Russia.

Somewhat unsettled by such arcane protocols, we each presented our concerns about the situation in Liberia. I pressed the message that the timber industry was enabling Taylor to survive the Security Council's sanctions on diamonds and arms imports. The Chinese representative launched into an interminable speech as we listened in vain through our headphones for the simultaneous translation to enlighten us. When he finally finished, the translator summed it up in just three words. 'He doesn't agree.' I glanced sideways at my colleagues and thought to myself that this looked like it might be an uphill struggle.

The first big reversal was quick in coming. The UN Office for the Coordination of Humanitarian Affairs (OCHA) had been asked to assess the potential humanitarian impacts of timber sanctions and the key findings of their eight-page report were stark. And wildly misinformed. Ten thousand jobs would be at risk, with severe implications for the estimated 90,000 dependents of these employees. Sanctions would deprive Liberia of the US$50 million that it earned from the timber industry the previous year.

That most of OCHA's intelligence had come directly from Guus Kouwenhoven's OTC was evident to us from the paean of praise the company received in the report. This was confirmed to us shortly afterwards by one of Alice's sources. Alice met him at Balthazar, an upmarket restaurant in New York's SoHo district, where Woody Allen and his wife Soon-Yi Previn were sitting at the next table.

In the comfort of the wood-panelled dining room, with its over-sized wall mirrors and ornate ceiling, the source confirmed that the report's figures were highly inaccurate. The employment figures were overstated by at least 100 per cent, and the revenues by eight times the true figure of US$6.6 million. If OCHA had bothered to look at the Liberian government's official statistics, they could have seen this for themselves. He also confirmed that the authors' main information source had indeed been OTC.

I have no idea why OCHA produced such a dangerous report, but Alice had a theory. 'I think this was an overhang of the sanctions on Iraq and the humanitarian consequences there…OCHA were shit-scared to be seen by the public to be providing data that would lead to humanitarian disaster. France and China used the stupid thing for ages…as their alibi – to cover up that they were in fact putting business interests in their own countries first. And it was infuriating. All the bureaucrats using a cover-up of "We want to avoid suffering", while the humanitarian catastrophe was worsening because of their sloth-like speed on sanctions…their fear to be perceived as "the bad guy".'

It was a stitch-up with real life-and-death consequences, but the damage had now been done. When the Security Council reviewed the sanctions regime later that same month, timber was left alone.

Round one to Taylor and his timber barons.

THE MEDITERRANEAN, 26 FEBRUARY 2002

With his quiet demeanour and round wire-rimmed spectacles, Filip Verbelen had the air of an academic, and it was true that he published in learned journals and disappeared for weeks at a time pursuing his passion for ornithology. But in February 2002, Filip was doing his day job. As a leading campaigner at Greenpeace International, he was taking part in a long-planned action to high-light the importation of illegally logged tropical timber into Europe just ahead of the annual meeting of the G8 countries. Following Filip's investigations into illegal logging in Cameroon, Greenpeace's flagship, the *Rainbow Warrior II*, had just intercepted two illegal timber shipments into Portugal and was ready to head for Spain to take part in more actions.

Simultaneously we and Silas had been feeding Filip specific information about imminent shipments of Liberian timber. Because this trade was funding a killing war, we felt that stopping imports of this 'conflict timber' was more of a priority than the Cameroonian trade, especially because France was both a major importer of Liberian timber and a permanent member of the UN Security Council. But diverting the *Rainbow Warrior II* and the whole Greenpeace campaign at short notice was not a small ask.

Filip called Yannick Jadot, now a Green MEP but then the man who coordinated Greenpeace's actions in France. He also contacted his counterpart on the *Rainbow Warrior II*, lead campaigner Tim Birch, and made the case that the Liberian shipments were 'timber funding a war machine'. Filip emphasized to Tim that it was rare for them to have a ship in a position to be able to be diverted at the same time as possessing the intercept information they needed. Filip asked whether the *Warrior* could divert to France. Immediately.

Tim consulted the *Warrior*'s captain to see if this tough call could be made. The decision came back unusually quickly. 'Yes, that's the big story – let's go after that one,' the captain told Filip, and the iconic state-of-the-art three-masted schooner changed course.

The bulk freighter *Agia Irene* had no sooner moored at the French Mediterranean port of Sète when four Greenpeace Zodiacs swiftly drew alongside. As Greenpeace activist Ludovic Frère told the press: 'We had been following him for a long time, we waited until he arrived in French territorial waters. When he wanted to anchor, we blocked the anchorage.' Ten Greenpeace crew members in orange wet-weather gear slung ladders along the ship's sides and stormed her with the precision of a commando raid; two skilled climbers hoisted themselves up the two tall gantries fore and aft of the hold and slung an enormous banner between them: 'Stop Rainforest Destruction', and stayed there, paralysing the cranes. Then the *Rainbow Warrior II* blockaded the ship.

The Greenpeace activists began documenting the identification letters and numbers of the logs on board the *Agia Irene* and relayed them to Filip in his office in Brussels. In turn Filip called me and I cross-checked the information with the paperwork provided by

Silas. We needed to confirm both the logging companies and the buyers. Events were moving fast.

A Gendarmerie Maritime launch belatedly followed the Greenpeace inflatables but the officers on board were helpless. Without the climbing skills or equipment of the Greenpeace activists, they couldn't even reach them – that was a job for Special Forces – so there was nothing they could do to stop the action. Greenpeace rejected a judge's order for them to withdraw and the standoff lasted for three days. Three days that the *Agia Irene* couldn't unload its cargo. Three days for the global media to film and photograph the action. Finally, the activists were arrested but they had done their job. The role of Liberian timber funding a war was becoming global news, and the French mission to the UN had a major headache.

This interception was one of many that took place across Europe and the resulting publicity from these and from Global Witness's investigations was raising public awareness of 'conflict timber' – and that awareness increased the pressure on politicians to act.

The logging companies and their customers were on the defensive, and they were also becoming more evasive. We knew from Silas's source in the offices of OTC that the company simply didn't know how we and Greenpeace were tracking their shipping movements and they began to disguise the origin of the logs.

OTC notified its customers that neither the logs nor the associated paperwork would bear the name 'OTC' any longer. Instead they would bear the (rather ironic) name of 'Evergreen'. In addition, the buyer and seller identification marks on the logs were changed to a series of colour-coded dots. But as soon as OTC and its customers settled on this subterfuge, we were tipped off. The risks for Silas's source were mounting: how long would it be before someone realized there was a mole and come looking for him? But still the information flowed. We were winning the game of cat and mouse, and the interceptions continued. OTC's attempt at deception was a victory in itself – a tacit admission that Liberian timber was toxic.

Pretty soon our strategy – and our footprint – expanded across the Mano River Union and beyond as we charted what was happening in terms of the trafficking of arms, of people, of resources. Our team was on the road to West Africa, New York and Asia for about four months every year. 'There are so many people who're risking their lives to help and support our investigations,' Alice told me as she described meetings in back alleys, being handed documents, photos, CDs burned with downloaded data charting corporate structures in Hong Kong and tracking ships with the help of the International Transport Workers' Federation. And of course, our mole in OTC was risking his life every day, and his own success increased his risk.

KAILAHUN, SIERRA LEONE, 2002

Alice had been joined by a new teammate. Mike Lundberg was a fresh-faced, clean-cut young American lawyer and together they were researching what would be the most incisive Global Witness report documenting the continuing arms shipments into Liberia, and Taylor's increasing dependence on timber revenues.

Piggybacking on UN-operated helicopter flights over Sierra Leone, Alice was accessing the still unstable territory close to the Liberian border. She was investigating arms movements in the Kailahun District when the Sierra Leonean police picked up two child soldiers who had slipped across the border and were caught in the act of hiding a cache of arms for future use. They were hauled into the local police headquarters for questioning and the police chief invited Alice to witness the interrogation.

One of the children was 13, the other a year older, and they went by the names Snake That Bite and Mission. Both had been kidnapped and press-ganged. Snake That Bite had risen through the ranks and was now a 'captain'.

'Do you have a religion?' the police chief asked. Snake That Bite nodded.

'What religion?' Snake That Bite said he was a Christian.

'How can you kill people and be a Christian?' the chief asked.

'I pray for their souls,' he answered in a flat voice, devoid of emotion. 'And then I kill their bodies.'

For Alice it was a deeply emotional experience. 'What a horrible face of war,' she said. 'These two children had absolutely no life left in their eyes.'

'Do you know what we do with snakes that bite?' the chief continued. 'We crush them and kill them.' The child's face broke into a wide-toothed smile, the same reaction a normal child might have when talking about a computer game. Violence was the only thing he could relate to.

The police chief permitted Alice to ask some questions. 'I asked about what they'd seen, about arms and weapons, and it was Snake That Bite who told me that the boxes of ammo had the words "Libya a Parti", or some such [on them]. This meant that the ammunition was sent from Libya...and ended up in Lofa County. Also, "aid" was being shipped to Liberia by ship. Aid being rice on top, arms at bottom. So many people have gotten away with murder in this saga,' she told me. 'Some other kids I met had been kidnapped from their farms outside Monrovia and helicoptered, probably on OTC choppers, to Lofa and told to kill or be killed. There was a girl that was given a broken, rusty AK that she used to cook bushmeat over an open fire. She was alone.'

THE ENDGAME

Information was arriving at Global Witness daily: from our own investigations, from Silas's team in Liberia, from the UN Panel of Experts and our NGO colleagues. Even the UN missions were forwarding us confidential information they were receiving. Once you stoke a hornets' nest, lots of stuff comes out.

'Time and relationship building,' Alice said, 'are the keys to getting the Security Council on side.' Alice and Mike continued to probe deeper into Sierra Leone, interviewing combatants, UN personnel, government officials and diplomats. Meanwhile, Silas's reports continued to flow in.

Alice had built a network of her own as her investigations took her to Hong Kong, China, Ghana and Singapore. 'Our sources are risking their livelihood at best, and their lives at worst,' she told me in one of our regular briefings. 'There are people I meet every time I go over, who provide me with lists, dates of transactions, names, photos and data that they had taken out of Liberia to give me. Then they go back and collect more. They have become friends – strange friends – friends in hushed tones, but I know and they know that if they're found out we won't meet again.'

I listened in awe as Alice regaled me with her stories of long, convoluted trips to cloak-and-dagger meetings. 'These [people] are the unsung heroes, the ones the world will never know about,' she continued. They included a cab driver and a source close to Taylor, who had been left high and dry by the international community. They were the people who gave information from refugee and internment camps; they were members of the Sierra Leone police, members of the military, a border guard, the brother of a friend who saw his family killed by the ATU and wanted only to tell us everything he knew. And there was the standard pompous diamond dealer sipping rum and Coke at the bar while bragging about his latest deal. 'It's gone far, far beyond anything we could have imagined at the start,' Alice said.

Alice and Mike's investigations had enabled us to chart a network across the Mano River Union of rebel movements, child trafficking, arms trafficking, diamond-sanctions violations and bank transfers.

We had to be extra vigilant with those who were providing us with information – not least Silas, who we had to get out of the country on at least one occasion. 'The underbelly of the dragon is the timber industry,' Alice smiled. 'The more we tickle it, the more it awakens, the more I know we are on the right track. Then we tickle it some more. We're outwitting the dragon.'

Very quickly we became known for the quality of our reporting and sources. The international community began to approach us for accurate information on Taylor's breaches of UN sanctions, the links between the various business and military groups and the role of the timber industry. This became key currency when we engaged with UNSC members.

We made visit after visit to the members of the Security Council, making sure they had absolutely no excuse not to be aware of what was going on, on the ground and on the oceans. Some members truly wanted to know; others actively didn't, but we told them anyway. Similarly, we and our NGO partners at Greenpeace, Robin des Bois, which was targeting the French buyers, and Nepenthes in Denmark force-fed information to the timber companies who were living in self-imposed denial. They knew that their money was supporting Taylor's war. They knew, but they didn't act. Rather than make a decision based on the facts, or, God forbid, actually make a moral judgement, they professed helplessness – 'The UN needs to tell us what to do,' was their empty refrain. 'Until then, we trade.'

Alice struck up a great rapport with many members of the Security Council, but none more so than the Russian ambassador to the UN, Sergei Lavrov, who went on to become foreign minister under Putin. An extrovert and combative debater, he had read our reports and those of the Panel of Experts. He was one of the few people at that level who knew his stuff.

Alice and he had fun. 'We would fight, interrupt each other and interrupt the interruptions.' They would raise their voices and then suddenly Lavrov would stand up and say, 'It's good that we have these fights,' and later give Alice a bear hug as they said goodbye. Alice described being ushered down the corridor: 'I would look at the posters lining the walls – Russian soldiers dressed in camouflage uniforms lifting smiling children into trucks. They were captioned "Children in Chechnya being sent to a health resort." It was so weird.'

Lavrov eventually confided to Alice that Russia was generally anti-sanctions, but in this case they would not oppose them. Alice had charmed the Russian bear.

But France was a constant thorn in our side and definitely needed force-feeding, just like a goose being raised for foie gras. Our contact at the mission, a pompous First Secretary, was 17 minutes late for our first meeting and was subsequently exactly 17 minutes late for every meeting going forward. Alice and Mike would sit in the waiting area laying bets as to whether it would be 17 minutes this time. It always was.

The Frenchman evidently didn't care about the subject, instead patronizing Alice by saying, 'It's good for you tree huggers to have a cause.'

'Arse,' Alice said to herself.

The non-permanent members were a tricky proposition. Colombia and Spain were on side, others less so. Over time, various members became supportive but did not want to put their heads above the parapet. Sanctions are an unpopular tool and no nation wanted to take a publicly supportive position alone. Ironically, they were handicapped in their decision-making because they didn't know what their fellow members were thinking, because they too were unwilling to air their views.

So Alice became a self-appointed go-between and began to create an informal coalition that was so secret that its members didn't actually know they were part of it. By mid-2002, Alice knew the mood of most of them.

Her final coup was China. Alice had sat through many meetings at their mission, sitting on the opulent red velvet and silk armchairs that were set so far apart from their interlocutors that the only way to communicate was in a borderline shout, making meetings difficult and formal. She was always met by the same two representatives, who were polite but non-committal and who listened more than they spoke as they sat rigidly on their distant chairs.

But at one meeting there, on the same chairs, a new diplomat took her seat. She was younger and more junior, which Alice initially thought was not a good sign. This diplomat said China was not convinced by the desirability of sanctions, citing the humanitarian consequences. Alice felt that the real reason was the fact that China was the biggest importer of Liberian logs, so she took the young diplomat through her country's own timber-import statistics. Although it was true that China was the world's greatest importer of Liberian logs, these made up less than half a per cent of China's total log imports. Liberia was an insignificant speck on the big picture.

The young diplomat's eyes widened with understanding – this was something she could use to consult with Beijing. Alice's stratagem worked and the Chinese came on side. They later emailed Alice to say that it was her work that swung their decision. It's hard to emphasize Alice's achievement enough: Russia and China are almost impossible nuts to crack.

Another critical development was the Panel of Experts' belated acknowledgement that they did not understand, and had never understood, the timber industry. This changed when they appointed to the panel a young Canadian forester who had been working at the US Forest Service. We heard that Art Blundell almost didn't get the UN job because his surname was so close to that of our very own Alice Blondel, a fellow Canadian. The Security Council evidently feared a plot. Art needed little convincing that Liberia's timber exports should be sanctioned, and his expertise brought critical arguments into the panel's thinking.

As 2002 drew on, many of the UN missions continued to feed us intelligence from their various embassies and sources on the ground in Africa. Others were still not convinced about the need for sanctions or, like France, were implacably opposed: both because they were Europe's biggest importer of Liberian timber, and because politically and economically France was so invested in Central and West Africa.

Our reports *Logging Off* and *The Usual Suspects*, published in late 2002 and early 2003 respectively, contained bang-up-to-date hard evidence and the insights gained over three years of investigations and campaigning. The weight of evidence was becoming difficult to ignore. Perhaps the best compliment our work received was when one UN mission cabled their counterpart in Sierra Leone: 'Alice from Global Witness was here again. We need to get our stuff in order, we don't know what to say anymore.'

UNITED NATIONS, NEW YORK, 6 MAY 2003

On a fine spring day, the 15 members of the UN Security Council took their seats around the circular table that had seen so many momentous decisions over the past half-century, and voted to adopt Resolution 1478 (2003). This resolution extended the existing sanctions regime on Liberia, with one addition. Article 17 announced that the Security Council had decided that 'all States shall take the necessary measures to prevent, for a period of 10 months, the import into their territories of all round logs and timber products originating in Liberia'. The sanctions would come into effect on 7 July 2003. We had done it.

But the show isn't over until the fat lady sings. The sanctions wouldn't take effect for two months and the timber industry didn't waste any time. DLH Nordisk embarked on a flurry of activity. The rebels were advancing on Monrovia and with sanctions on the horizon they were determined to get as much timber out as possible. Despite the fact they had now received the clear guidance they had asked for, senior managers focused their efforts on channelling ships into Liberian ports and loading up the orders they had still been taking. They would obey the letter of the law, but not until they absolutely had to. Confidential sources told us that frantic conversations were taking place as DLH managers in Denmark communicated with their people on the ground in Liberia to load every last log they could onto the waiting ships in order to beat the sanctions deadline.

My disgust at these men still brings up bile when I think about them.

MONROVIA, 11 AUGUST 2003

A month after the sanctions bit, Charles Taylor had run out of money and friends. As rebel forces laid siege to Monrovia, Taylor resigned the presidency and fled into exile in Nigeria.

Silas, Alice, Mike, Greenpeace, Nepenthes, Robin des Bois, our sources and all of our colleagues in our loose coalition of organizations, and the allies we'd made in various diplomatic missions across the world, had played a critical role in cutting Taylor's money supply and his ability to fight. On one level, we were elated. We had come a long way from those initial contacts from the World Bank staffer and Silas. I was proud of that. And surprised.

But we had also learned how the wheels of change at an international level move painfully slowly, even when lives are at stake. The tragedy for the people of the Mano River region, who had so long yearned for peace, was that the timber sanctions hadn't been imposed two years beforehand. How many lives that would have saved we can never know.

We had gleaned a painful insight into this shadow network – how the vested interests of countries and companies conspire to thwart the right outcome in the interests of their own power and profit. This is the way the world turns, but we had also learned that a small group of people can stick very large spokes into the wheels.

GBARTALA, BONG COUNTY, LIBERIA, 2006

The war had been over for three years and with two Global Witness campaigners, Natalie Ashworth and Sofia Goinhas, I was heading from Monrovia to the town of Yekepa on the Liberian border with Guinea. Accompanied by Silas in his organization's dark-blue Mitsubishi Pajero, we had covered around two-thirds of the distance and were nearing the town of Gbartala.

'Do you want to take a detour?' Silas asked. 'There's something interesting to see here.'

The truck took a right turn down a short track that opened up into a large area of cleared land, fringed by trees. At its southern boundary stood a long roofless two-storey building, surrounded by scrubby plants and tufted grass. Its windows had long lost their glass and frames and the blank holes stared out at us from walls that were painted in fading camouflage colours.

A massive slogan, in green letters a metre tall, was emblazoned along the whole frontage at first-floor level: 'College of Knowledge'.

'The headquarters of the ATU,' Silas said simply.

This was where Charles Taylor's son, Chucky, had presided over a reign of terror. Silas pointed out pits in the ground where people detained by the ATU had been tortured and left to die. The atmosphere of the place was chilling. I don't think I believe in ghosts, but like other scenes of torture and massacre that I've visited – often remote and derelict – the atmosphere was heavy with menace and pain, and as we drove out onto the main road, it felt as if a smotheringly heavy weight was being lifted from us.

Charles 'Chucky' Taylor, Jr, former head of the Anti-Terrorist Unit, was arrested for passport fraud while entering the US at Miami from Trinidad in 2006. He was sentenced by a Miami court to 97 years in prison for torture. In 2014 he apologized for his crimes, saying, 'I am sorry if I had done anything to offend anyone.'

On 26 April 2012, his father, former president Charles Taylor, wearing oval wire-rimmed spectacles and smartly dressed in a neat blue double-breasted suit, a yellow silk tie and matching pocket handkerchief, was asked to stand by Judge Richard Lussick of the Special Court for Sierra Leone. Taylor's face was impassive as he was handed a 50-year sentence for war crimes and crimes against humanity. He is serving his sentence at HMP Frankland, a high-security prison near Durham, in the north of England.

In contravention of the Security Council travel ban, Guus Kouwenhoven fled to Côte d'Ivoire, where he took up the logging business and also benefitted from World Bank-funded road-building contracts. He continued to do business with Danzer.

The Dutch police cited UN Security Council and Global Witness reports when they brought about his prosecution in 2005. After conviction, acquittal, appeal and counter-appeal, on 26 April 2017 he was finally convicted of aiding and abetting war crimes and illegally trading arms and sentenced to 19 years in jail. He continues to live in his mansion in Cape Town, South Africa, while he fights his extradition to the Netherlands.

'Minin was a man at the end of his trajectory,' Chief Prosecutor Walter Mapelli said. 'Totally cocaine-addicted. Women-addicted, too. The funny thing is, he was a man who was always able to pay everyone to fix things, so he was genuinely unable to understand why he had been arrested.'

Leonid Minin served two years for possession of cocaine. When he was arrested in August 2000, Italy and Ireland were the only two countries in Europe where brokering an arms deal was not illegal, as long as the arms themselves didn't transit their territory. Italian law changed as a result of the Minin case.

Minin's current whereabouts are unknown.

4

KLEPTOCRATS AND SHOPAHOLICS

Every time I visit Washington, DC, I walk past the old Riggs Bank building on Dupont Circle. Now the PNC Bank, the only clues to its once prestigious past and ignominious collapse are a few small stubs of brass set into the walls, the remains of the metal fixings that once held its name to the grand stone portico.

When I was 16, I was captivated by Frederick Forsyth's 1974 novel, *The Dogs of War*: a story of adventure, war, money, lost love, crooks and rough justice, it sits on the shelf next to me as I write. A prospector for a British mining company discovers a mountain of platinum in a tiny poverty-stricken West African nation, Zangaro. Rather than pay a fair price for this vast mineral wealth, the company's ruthless boss hires a bunch of mercenaries to overthrow the country's brutal dictator. Thinking back, maybe that book sowed one of the seeds that led me to co-found Global Witness. In any event, art meets life.

Forsyth's Zangaro was based on the former Spanish colony of Equatorial Guinea, on the west coast of Africa. Its brutal post-colonial president, Francisco Macías Nguema, presided over a country of just half a million people, around 80,000 of whom he slaughtered. The rest lived in abject poverty and fear. But Macías came to a sticky end when he was executed by his nephew, who took the top job in a 1979 *coup d'état*. The new president, Teodoro Obiang Nguema Mbasogo, who became Africa's longest-serving dictator, inherited a cripplingly poor country that resembled its fictional counterpart in almost every respect. Except for one: its wealth lay under the sea.

Equatorial Guinea's oil boom came in the 1990s with the arrival of 'Big Oil' – companies like Exxon, Marathon Oil and Amerada Hess. According to the IMF, the country saw the fastest GDP growth in the world. Oil revenues increased from around US$3 million a year in 1993 to over US$210 million in 2000, according to the World Bank, which predicted that this figure would reach US$700 million by 2003. Equatorial Guinea became Africa's third-largest oil exporter, with an economy growing at around 37 per cent per year.

With this level of growth in national wealth managed by a responsible government, the population should be able to look forward to massive investments in schools, hospitals, housing and roads, as has happened in Saudi Arabia and the Emirates. But, as the World Bank stated: 'there has been no impact on the country's dismal social indicators'. In fact, the IMF noted these were actually going backwards, leaving the bulk of the population scraping by on less than a dollar a day.

So where was all this oil money and what was it being spent on?

John Bennett, former US ambassador to Equatorial Guinea, had a theory about this: he told Televisió de Catalunya in a 2003 interview that the US$1.5–2 billion the country had earned over the preceding decade was being put offshore by the ruling elite. True or not, the answer evidently wasn't going to come from President Obiang, as he stated that the country's oil revenues were a 'state secret'.

It seemed the proof may have to come from the outside.

Why was Equatorial Guinea important to us? Well, for some of the same reasons as Zangaro was to Frederick Forsyth. Hugely powerful Western conglomerates and the countries that spawned them wanted a pliant head of state who would keep the oil taps turned on. For a price. We and our NGO allies wanted countries' natural resource wealth to benefit their citizens. What was happening in Equatorial Guinea was a grotesque story that told in the right way could benefit the citizens of resource-rich states all over the world. It was a story about the power of oil. And for us, that story had begun 1,500km to the south.

Shortly after Charmian began working on diamonds, Simon began working on oil.

The oil and gas industry is the most powerful industrial sector on the planet and, according to the Organisation for Economic Co-operation and Development (OECD), one of the most corrupt. In its short history, it has become an unofficial arm of many governments and been the cause of numerous wars and untold suffering. The CIA and MI6 coup that in 1953 toppled Iran's secular prime minister Mohammad Mosaddegh, replacing him with the brutal Shah Reza Pahlavi, primarily benefitted British Petroleum, an injustice that ultimately led to the Iranian Revolution. The French oil company Elf Aquitaine had been dubbed a 'secret branch of French foreign policy in Africa' before being engulfed in a huge corruption scandal. The 2003 allied invasion of Iraq and the ousting of a head of state, albeit an egregious one, was a war about oil. The oil industry wrecks just about every country it sets foot in.

Simon's task in Angola, Africa's second-largest oil producer after Nigeria, was to find out where the country's huge revenues from oil actually went. There were no publicly available figures, despite Angolan law stating that the country's oil and gas 'belongs to the Angolan People'. But the Angolan people didn't know where the money went. The IMF didn't know. In fact, the only people who did know were a corrupt clique surrounding President Dos Santos and the senior figures who ran the state oil company, Sonangol. And they weren't telling.

What was obvious to anyone in Angola during the 1990s was that the money was not being spent on hospitals, schools, roads and other infrastructure. And it certainly wasn't being spent on the people, who were living in conditions of unimaginable squalor. It was also obvious that the government was funding its war with UNITA from its oil revenues. It's a sovereign right of a government to fund its defence from the national coffers, but just how much were they spending? Again, no one knew. Simon's best guess, having talked to the IMF and others, was that around a quarter of Angola's oil revenues – around US$1.4 billion per year at the time – was unaccounted for.

What was also startlingly clear was that the ruling elite and the entire apparatus of the state were utterly corrupt. And wherever the international oil majors drilled in the Global South, the story was almost always the same. While the companies were pumping billions of dollars of oil and making their shareholders rich, the populations that as the ultimate owners of the oil should have been the first to benefit didn't see any of this wealth. Instead, they continued to live in grinding poverty, suffering the rule of oppressive regimes only interested in stealing as much cash as they could while the oil flowed.

As Simon was exploring the dark side of oil, many people told him, 'Forget it. You will never change the oil industry.' Simon just hated being told what to do.

And he was a fast learner. We released our first report on oil, *A Crude Awakening*, in December 1999, almost exactly a year after *A Rough Trade* marked our debut in Angola. It shone a spotlight on the corruption of the country's oil sector. The government was taken by surprise but its censors moved quickly, suppressing all mention of the report by the local media. Angola's *Folha 8* newspaper went ahead with its print run, with each one of the five pages previously devoted to the story left completely blank except for the photographs that would have accompanied the exposé. The censorship sparked street protests that highlighted the venality of the government and the anger of the people more poignantly than the report itself could have done. In any event, we were one step ahead.

When the daily delivery of one of Portugal's major newspapers, *Público*, hit the streets of Luanda, it carried the story. We had been working on it with Pedro Rosa Mendes, the intrepid Portuguese reporter who had joined Charmian for the diamond investigation in Zambia. It's always good to have a back-up!

Having regarded us as an ally because our diamond campaign had targeted their political opposition and battlefield enemy, the MPLA government now accused us of being part of 'a global Machiavellian plot' as well as being funded by the French secret service. But that wasn't all.

The day after we published, a meeting was held in Angola's London embassy, at which the decision was made to put up Antonio 'Mosquito' Mbkassi to sue us. He was one of the cabal we had labelled 'the untouchable oily-garchy'. 'For some reason he doesn't like it,' Simon laughed. But receiving our first libel threat as an organization became a very scary time for us all and caused Simon many sleepless nights, thinking he had brought down Global Witness. But our fear was replaced by anger. If they wanted a fight, they could have one.

Our next oil-focused report, *All the Presidents' Men*, appeared in 2002 and dissected the corruption and vested interests of Angola's ruling elite, exposing its innards to the light. Its cover was in the style of the poster for the Hollywood film of the same name. Under the list of directors and cast, it said, 'and introducing the notion of Publish What You Pay' – a slogan that was to become a movement.

As the MPLA government didn't respond to our calls to publish what they earned from oil, we knew that there was another group of people who did have the answers. The oil companies themselves. After all, they were writing the cheques. The report called on them to publish what they paid to the Angolan government. It was not an unreasonable request – it's something they routinely do when operating in the US or Europe. But oil being a notoriously corrupt industry, the opacity afforded to these companies in Angola and other corrupt mineral-rich states suited them well and they wanted it to stay that way.

In 2000, Simon, Charmian and I met George Soros for the second time, at his home in London. The first meeting had been brokered by Aryeh Neier, the president of Soros's Open Society Institute (as it was then called), just a few months before. They had provided a small amount of funding to cover some of the costs of our Angola work but as one of the world's richest foundations, we knew they could be a key partner for us.

On a trip to New York, I'd asked Aryeh if he would like an update on our work. As I was ushered into his large office, I can truly say that Aryeh was one of the few people in the world I was scared of, because of both his air of authority and the sheer scale of his achievements. After fleeing Nazi Germany as a young boy, Aryeh finally reached the US via England and became a titan of human rights.

'Have you thought about growing Global Witness?' he had asked me. As an organization then consisting of perhaps ten people scarcely able to cope with what we were doing, I had said no, we didn't really want to be big.

'That's what I thought when I founded Human Rights Watch,' he replied. Blimey, I thought to myself, he founded Human Rights Watch?

'I'd like you to meet George,' he said. 'I think we could be giving you a lot more support than we are.'

In preparation for this meeting, George had asked us to put together a business plan and come back to him when we had done it. We had never written a business plan. We didn't even know what a business plan was. Moreover, we had never thought, 'What next?' Up to now, our campaigns just seemed to come along and suggest themselves, and we rather liked that. But we went away and dutifully spent the next month agonizing over the plan; all the things we could do and how much it would cost. It ran to 80 pages. We sent it to George, and he invited us back to discuss it.

On a warm spring day, we rang the bell of his stucco-fronted townhouse on an exclusive garden square in London. The three of us were led upstairs to the large and airy living room, its huge French windows looking out over the square, where we sat on a sofa, nervous as hell.

George Soros and his family had survived the Nazi persecution of Jews in their native Hungary. In 1947, George escaped the new Soviet-backed government by fleeing across the country's snow-covered borders to the West. He was 17, broke and had had his fill of dictatorships. He made his way to London, where he took menial jobs, including as a railway porter and a lifeguard at the Caledonian Road swimming pool, to fund his studies at the London School of Economics. Here, George not only picked up the economic skills that would make him one of the world's richest men but also received the inspiration that would shape his life's work. Professor Karl Popper was one of the most eminent philosophers of science of the 20th century, a champion of open societies and a passionate supporter of liberal democracy. Popper's teachings fell on fertile ground with his new student, a survivor of two totalitarian regimes. George became not only one of the most generous philanthropists in the world, giving away an astonishing US$32 billion or so, but one of its most well-resourced anti-corruption campaigners.

George walked in with our business plan in his hand. He greeted us warmly, sat down opposite us and paused reflectively for a moment. Then with a mischievous smile he said, 'Like all business plans this one is very long and doesn't really say anything,' and tossed it to one side. There was a pause – we weren't sure whether he was joking or not. We knew that this could be a seminal moment for Global Witness. If George decided to support us it would mean we could take the step from being an extraordinarily poorly resourced organization to the next stage. To build some kind of financial security instead of the near hand-to-mouth existence we had experienced so far. Horrified, we leaped in to explain the nuances of this section or that idea, but he cut us short. He was already a vocal opponent of the corruption that was beginning to erode the hopes of the post-Cold War former Soviet states, and he had been enthused by one of the issues we had raised in our plan: the need to tackle corruption in the oil and mining industries.

He sat forward on the sofa and quizzed us about our work. Simon did most of the talking on this subject; it was his baby. He pointed out the levels of corruption in the industry, which was something new to George and he listened intently, interjecting with the odd question. Occasionally he came up with an idea, some of which were very bad indeed. How do you respond to a billionaire who could make such a difference for Global Witness when he comes up with a dud? 'That wouldn't work,' Simon said, and explained why. George nodded and continued listening.

We hadn't known what to expect, but George was curious and wanted to learn. It turned out that he liked a challenge, an argument and information he could work with. And he didn't tolerate 'yes men'. Maybe that is what clicked – we got on really well.

As we got close to time, he said, 'Look, I will fund you. I will give you 35 per cent of your annual budget, regardless of what your budget is. I won't give you more than that – I don't want to create dependency.'

As Simon, Charmian and I piled out of his front door and walked to the Tube, we were ecstatic. Global Witness's future had been changed so much in that 90-minute meeting. As we sat having a coffee in Carluccio's opposite South Kensington station, I said, 'Do you think the idea of asking us to put together a business plan was his idea of a practical joke?' On balance, we thought it was. Although his funding never actually exceeded 25 per cent of our budget, it was transformational; more importantly, he became a fellow campaigner.

Simon had been banging his head against a brick wall to get oil companies to even meet with him, but at his behest George wrote to Prime Minister Tony Blair and to US president George Bush, suggesting they convene to discuss corruption in the oil industry. Global Witness was a tiny, virtually unknown NGO but George was an international financial titan. He had already proved this in

1992 when he made a £1 billion profit shorting the pound on what became known as Black Wednesday. Politicians listened to George.

Simon's conception of Publish What You Pay (PWYP) in *All the Presidents' Men* was a simple idea. If oil and mining companies were forced to publish what they pay to governments then at least this income stream would be open to public scrutiny; then the country's citizens had the ammunition to hold their leaders to account. The concept of PWYP was launched in London in 2002 by us, George, the Catholic Agency for Overseas Development (CAFOD), Transparency International UK, Oxfam and Save the Children UK. It now numbers over 1,000 civil-society organizations across the world.

The tenacious advocacy by the members of PWYP paid off when Tony Blair launched the Extractive Industries Transparency Initiative (EITI) in 2002 in Johannesburg – the first international good-governance and anti-corruption mechanism to tackle corruption in the oil and mining sector. The theory was simple: countries publish what they earn from oil and mining; the oil and mining companies publish what they pay to the governments. These figures should match. If they didn't, something was wrong. The third and most innovative element of EITI was that civil-society organizations had an equal place at the table, so they could hold both their government and the companies to account.

But the EITI has a couple of flaws. Firstly, it is a voluntary mechanism. If a country chooses to join, then the companies operating there are obliged to play by the rules, but the more corrupt the country, the less the incentive to join. Secondly, in non-democratic countries, 'civil society' does not have the ability to change the status quo. So our ultimate aim was for legislation: laws that would have the teeth to prevent corruption, to prosecute the corrupt and, failing that, at least to seize the money they had stolen. This is why we were interested in Equatorial Guinea.

Among the volunteers I depended on when I was organizing street collections as a fundraiser for EIA was an eccentric, fast-talking, hyperactive, gawky schoolboy called Gavin Hayman. He was invariably dressed in black, and his pale face shone brightly between his polo neck and his mop of dark hair. His intelligence, weirdness and crazy theories about almost everything endeared him to us. We lost contact for almost a decade but in 2001 he eventually came to work for us, with a Ph.D in International Environmental Crime under his belt.

Working together, Simon – still fresh from his exposés of the massive oil-fuelled corruption in Angola – and Gavin began to realize that what was happening there was perhaps not a one-off but was likely being replicated across Africa's new oil boom. The seas off the West African coast were attracting the survey vessels of the world's biggest oil companies on the hunt for more reserves.

And most of the world's biggest oil companies were in the United States.

On a visit to Washington, where we had established an office catalysed by the need to pursue our oil-related advocacy in the US, Gavin told us he'd been talking about this phenomenon to a contact of his, Ian Gary of Catholic Relief Services (CRS). 'We were talking about how American companies were doing deals with African countries with brutal human-rights records, the usual abusing dictators and kleptocrats.' One of those countries was Equatorial Guinea, and it was Ian who introduced Gavin to someone with an interesting story to tell.

Gavin met up with this new and anonymous source in central Washington. 'I stumbled on what was evidently an open secret among the international financial institutions like the IMF and the World Bank,' Gavin told me.

'You know where all Equatorial Guinea's oil money is, don't you?' the source asked Gavin, who shook his head. 'It's just up the road, maybe between US\$300 and US\$500 million of it, in the Dupont Circle branch of Riggs Bank. Under the president's sole name.' Gavin was wide-eyed.

If it was true that the president of one of the poorest countries in the world could syphon off all of his nation's wealth into a personal bank account in the richest country in the world, then it would not just be a momentous injustice but a fantastic scandal. And great scandals make great stories.

Known as the 'Bank of Presidents', Riggs Bank was one of America's most prestigious. Abraham Lincoln himself had banked there. Riggs was also the bank of choice for many of the foreign embassies based in DC.

Many investigations begin like this: a source providing information they don't know what to do with or that their jobs prevent them from acting on. We believed the information was credible, but we had no proof. Gavin started digging, together with a new volunteer, Sarah Wykes, who joined us in 2002 from Amnesty International. A fluent French and Spanish speaker, she soon became an invaluable part of our oil-corruption work, focusing on the oil-rich Francophone countries of West Africa. They started trawling LexisNexis, an online source of legal documents. They began searching with the only two key words they had: Obiang and Riggs. But where to start? After going down a few dead ends, Gavin thought to himself, 'What would you do with a lot of money in the US?' Well one of the obvious things you would do is buy a house. So they started searching the database for property records. It turned out to have been a good route to follow.

In late 1999, President Obiang spent US$2.6 million on a luxurious house in Potomac, Maryland, an exclusive suburb of Washington. It was our introduction to conspicuous consumption. 'It's got ten bathrooms!' Gavin exclaimed. 'And seven fireplaces. My God, this is amazing.'

Apart from anything else, this was in stark contrast to the lot of Equatoguinean citizens, the majority of whom lacked clean drinking water. Of course, the house also came with an indoor pool. A year later, Obiang's wife forked out a more modest US$1.15 million for another Maryland house, using a US$747,500 mortgage from Riggs Bank, which she paid off nine months later.

Gavin was excited. A president's salary doesn't run to this kind of high-end property, so where did this money come from? A larger organization might have hired an investigator to ground-truth a few of the facts, but instead one of the staff members in our Washington office asked her mother, who lived in Maryland, to go take a look. The photographs she took on that cold clear winter's day in late 2002 depicted two large mansions, their extensive grounds framed by the high iron railings that kept outsiders off their snow-covered lawns.

Tax filings and contact details for both purchases were given as Simon P. Kareri, c/o Riggs Bank NA, 1913 Massachusetts Avenue NW, Washington, DC, 20036. With Simon Kareri, we had a name and we could carry on our sleuthing. Meanwhile Gavin heard that a leading US investigative reporter, Ken Silverstein, working for the *LA Times*, had also come across the Riggs Bank story, and we decided to see if we could link up with him.

Working well with journalists is a brilliant way to get a story told, but it can be a tricky path. Journalists are understandably protective of their stories – they always want the scoop – so they play their cards close to their chest. Gavin remembers the to and fro of one of our first conversations with Ken: '[He said], "Well, do you know where the money is?" And we're like, "Yes, we know where the money is." And he's like, "Well, you tell me and I'll tell you."'

Through our joint sources, we were able to start painting the picture of how the Obiang family were looting their country. As a significant oil producer, Equatorial Guinea was just the kind of example we needed to demonstrate the need for the nascent EITI, and to expose just the kind of criminality it seemed the country was involved in. Gavin and Ken agreed that we would break our stories on the same day: 20 January 2002.

In his *LA Times* article, 'Oil Boom Enriches African Ruler', Ken told the story of how upwards of US$300 million of Equatorial Guinea's oil wealth was stashed in Riggs Bank's Dupont Circle branch under the personal signature of President Obiang. Riggs also held an account for Obiang's younger brother, Armengol Ondo Nguema, one of the most feared members of the ruling elite. As the head of national security, he had a reputation as a murderer and torturer. In 1999, the US State Department reported that he had ordered five prisoners to be beaten to death in the notorious Black Beach Prison. 'Police reportedly urinated on prisoners,' the report stated, 'kicked them in the ribs, sliced their ears with knives, and smeared oil over their naked bodies in order to attract stinging ants.' The president and senior officials blamed rogue elements in the security forces. 'However, according to credible reports, this torture was approved at the highest levels of the Government and was directed personally by the chief of presidential security, Armengol Ondo Nguema...[who] allegedly taunted prisoners by describing the suffering that they were about to endure.'

Riggs Bank's account manager, Simon Kareri, the man who had helped Obiang and his wife buy the Maryland houses, had also assisted the charming Armengol to buy a house in Virginia, describing him in his reference to the real-estate agent as 'a valued customer of Riggs Bank'.

We placed heavy reference on Ken's article in our press release, while Ken quoted Gavin, enabling us to get our broader point across that what was happening in Equatorial Guinea was happening in every oil-rich African state. But the elephant in the room wasn't an African one, it was American. Much of the hundreds of millions of dollars in the account at Riggs had been put there by US oil companies, including Exxon, Marathon Oil and Amerada Hess.

Our exposé had received wide coverage – it was a salacious scandal, after all. But Gavin knew this wasn't enough. That one of the United States' supposedly most respectable banks was helping corrupt dictators loot their countries and spend the money in Washington was surely something law enforcement should be interested in.

Gavin wrote to Carl Levin, the chairman of the US Senate's Permanent Subcommittee on Investigations (PSI). Sometimes described as the most feared committee in Washington, its mandate included keeping foreign corruption out of the US. It was a long shot, but Gavin asked them to investigate the role of Riggs Bank in the Obiang family's property deals in the US.

The PSI had been investigating various banking scandals since 1999 that had led to the enactment of Title III of the Patriot Act of 2001, which, among other things, required US financial institutions to conduct enhanced due diligence when opening private banking accounts for foreign political figures, and to refuse to deposit funds suspected of a connection with foreign corruption.

Meanwhile Elise Bean, deputy staff director and chief counsel for Senator Levin on the PSI, had seen Ken's article and its mention of Simon Kareri, a man who had already crossed the PSI's radar during previous investigations. She and the PSI's chief investigator, Bob Roach, began working closely with their Republican colleagues on the staff of then PSI chair Senator Norm Coleman, probing into the Riggs Bank case.

Just over a month after the news about Riggs Bank had broken, Gavin and Katherine Astill, a colleague from CAFOD, had the chance to meet just the people who could answer some of our questions relating to the money in Riggs Bank. The Equatoguinean ministers of the Treasury and of the departments of Justice and Energy had been invited to a meeting at the prestigious London think tank Chatham House.

The meeting started off cordially enough, with the ministers seemingly keen to help. They invited Gavin to visit Equatorial Guinea – because although information about the oil revenues was freely available, they said, it was only available in-country. They confirmed the existence of the account at Riggs but wouldn't confirm that Obiang had sole control of it. They showed them an oil-production contract and Gavin pointed out that Article 10 stated that all oil receipts are to be deposited directly in the country's Treasury, and queried why the money was all in Riggs Bank in Washington.

'The ministers told us the Treasury building was insecure and it didn't have a safe,' Gavin said. 'They also told us that as the payments were in US dollars it was best to park the money offshore to avoid commission charges.'

Gavin and Katherine pressed home question after awkward question, and then the meeting started to go downhill.

'One of the ministers leaned forward,' Gavin told us, 'and he said, "Mr Gavin. You have to remember that these things are complicated and dangerous and people can get hurt." And it was weird, because he then talked about how aeroplanes can fall out of the sky.'

Gavin continued, 'Then they got up and stormed out.' But not before they had accused Global Witness of being terrorists and racists.

In 2004, we released a report called *Time for Transparency*. Our research and field investigations into five countries in regions ranging from the Caucasus to Africa and the Pacific highlighted the common denominators of corruption in natural-resource-rich countries. With poverty came a criminal lack of investment in health, education and infrastructure at the same time as billions of dollars of state revenues were channelled offshore into the bank accounts of the elite. In these nations, which statistically should be among the world's richest, ordinary citizens were condemned to a life of squalor and fear. At the same time as they trampled all over their populations' human rights, the ruling elites lived lives of extraordinary extravagance, mainly spent in the world's pleasure spots. After all, cities like Equatorial Guinea's run-down capital Malabo don't have too much to offer the international jet-setter.

But their criminality was only half the story. It was the banks and real-estate agents and lawyers that helped our mammoth corporations, in league with corrupt leaders, to loot entire states. *Time for Transparency* focused on what should and could be done to address these problems. It rammed home our message that governments should publish what they earn from their natural resources while companies should publish what they pay. Only when that information is available can citizens hold their governments to account.

Meanwhile it seemed that Gavin's letter to Senator Carl Levin, the then chair of the US Senate's PSI, may have helped. Under the leadership of Elise Bean and using their subpoena powers, the PSI were trawling through Riggs Bank's records. I imagine even they were shocked at what they found.

Their report, released in July 2004, was utterly damning. What the bank was doing for the Obiangs it was also doing for another murderous dictator. Chile's notorious General Augusto Pinochet's only declared income was his US$90,000-a-year pension as a senator for life, but his family held numerous accounts at Riggs' Dupont Circle branch containing between US$4 million and US$8 million at any one time. Riggs' meagre defence was that this money came from 'private investments'.

When Pinochet was arrested in the UK in 1999 at the request of a Spanish judge to face charges of torture and murder during his rule, the UK courts froze his assets. But this didn't stop Riggs Bank from moving US$1.6 million of his money from the UK to the US. The subcommittee found that Riggs had 'deliberately assisted him in the concealment and movement of his funds while he was under investigation and the subject of a world-wide court order freezing his assets'. The report further stated that 'Riggs Bank concealed the existence of the Pinochet accounts from the federal bank examiners for two years' and reminded the reader that Pinochet was 'accused of involvement with human-rights abuses, torture, assassinations, death squads, drug trafficking, arms sales, and corruption'.

And on Equatorial Guinea the report was equally damning. It confirmed that the bank held anything between US$400 million and US$700 million at any one time, in over 60 accounts held by leading members of the Equatoguinean government. Not once did the bank ask any questions about where the money came from. The bank had also opened an account that oil companies were able to pay directly into and that required only two signatures to withdraw the money: those of Obiang and his son or nephew. On this basis the bankers sat back and relaxed as US$35 million was wired from the account into those of two unknown companies based in secrecy jurisdictions – countries who guaranteed that the real owners of companies would be protected by anonymity.

The subcommittee's report was not without drama as it detailed Equatorial Guinea's faithful account manager Simon Kareri carrying suitcases of cash into the bank for deposit. One bank employee told the investigators that

> most of the cash was in unopened, plastic-wrapped bundles which did not have to be counted, while the remaining bills were counted using high-speed machines. Since US$1 million in hundred-dollar bills weighs nearly 20lbs, the currency brought into the bank would likely have weighed at least that much on each occasion. On the last two occasions involving [deposits of] US$3 million, the bank would've had to accept nearly 60lbs in currency. The bank employee indicated that the large cash deposits he witnessed were not treated as unusual or requiring additional scrutiny.

Riggs' more regular customers probably felt a quiet pride as they passed through the grand Palladian entrance of honey-coloured stone into the hushed banking hall of Riggs' Dupont Circle branch, unaware that the bank's top executives would probably be more suited to banking in Palermo. The report noted that the bank's chairman had written a brown-nosing letter to Obiang in May 2001, saying:

> We would like to thank you for the opportunity you granted to us in hosting a luncheon in your honor here at Riggs Bank. We sincerely enjoyed the discussions and especially learning about the developments taking place in Equatorial Guinea...we have formed a committee of the most senior officers of Riggs Bank that will meet regularly to discuss

our relationship with Equatorial Guinea and how best we can serve you.

Meanwhile an email exchange between bank staff asked: 'Where is this money coming from? Oil – black gold – Texas tea!'

Another memo from Simon Kareri to his boss Larry Hebert read: 'Regarding the issue of the president of Equatorial Guinea being corrupt, I take exception to that because I know this person quite well. We have reviewed...the transactions of Equatorial Guinea with Riggs since inception and not once did Riggs send any money to any "shady" entity or destination.'

I wonder whether he carted around suitcases of cash for his other clients and considered it to be a normal way of doing business. Maybe the bank's slogan suggested that he did: 'For over 165 years we've been developing innovative, custom-tailored solutions to improve the lives of our customers.'

Sarah Wykes told the international press, 'Although Equatorial Guinea has the world's fastest-growing economy on paper, its human development is actually going backwards. Now we know why: the money is offshore, out of sight and out of control. Allegations in the Senate report imply that, far from being a force for development, some oil companies are making this problem worse.'

Riggs's senior leadership, together with representatives from ExxonMobil, Amerada Hess and Marathon Oil, were hauled up before a hearing of the PSI. It can't have made comfortable listening for Riggs's chairman, Lawrence I Hebert, to hear that Riggs Bank had been fined US$25 million for money laundering. This fine was the largest ever under the Bank Secrecy Act, but $25 million is loose change for a bank. What Riggs Bank couldn't survive was disgrace; and it was sold shortly afterwards to PNC Bank, its name disappearing for ever.

'The 2004 Riggs Bank investigation led by Senator Levin was the first to test how US banks and federal bank regulators were implementing the new anti-corruption provisions enacted in 2001,' Elise Bean told me. 'As a result of the inquiry US bank regulators finally got serious about implementing the new anti-corruption safeguards and forcing US banks to strengthen their anti-money-laundering controls and review and close some suspicious accounts.' Elise is evidently not someone to mess with. For his part, Simon Kareri was sentenced to 18 months in jail and, along with his wife, who was also found guilty, paid US$631,000 restitution.

The terrible publicity the Obiangs received was undoubtedly a set-back, but their attempts at defending their reputation ultimately backfired, perhaps because their long years in power coupled with their fantasy lifestyle had left them completely out of touch with reality. It's hard to think of any other way to explain why President Obiang told an interviewer from the UK's Channel 4 that the country's oil money was under his personal control because it was the only way he could be certain it was safe.

In a move to placate their critics, the Equatoguinean government said that they would become more transparent in the management of public funds and pledged to join the EITI. But despite this and the furore surrounding their corruption, the Obiangs somehow got their money out – or US$700 million dollars of it – though where it went remains a mystery.

Regardless of the huge publicity surrounding the collapse of Riggs Bank, there were other banks still prepared to work with the Obiangs. What, for example, was account number 30588 61204 61483680101 at a branch of Barclays in Paris being used for? An account belonging to President Obiang's eldest son, Teodoro Nguema Obiang Mangue, TNO for short.

It soon became clear that Equatorial Guinea's ruling family had no intentions of curbing their lavish lifestyle at all. And this was a lightbulb moment for us. Although it had been patently obvious, it hadn't occurred to us or to any other organization that *every* corrupt deal needs a bank.

Anthea Lawson is very tall, with long dark hair and tons of charisma; the kind of person who commands a room. A former journalist with *The Times*, she joined Global Witness following her work with child soldiers in Sierra Leone, where she remembered a film producer patting her on the head, telling her, 'It is so great that you work for an NGO.' Of all the people you don't want to patronize, Anthea comes close to the top of the list, and patting her on the head is likely to unleash a scything torrent of foul language.

Anthea was the ideal choice to develop this new campaign. Her boss was Alex Yearsley and working with him was 'like dancing in a whirlwind'. Within a month of joining, she was with him in New York and Washington, being introduced to all of his contacts. 'People who investigate offshore companies, people who would end up being amazing sources of information and great teachers to me,' Anthea enthused.

She met with Jack Blum, a US attorney and leading authority on corruption; she met John Christensen and Richard Murphy of the Tax Justice Network; and she met Elise Bean. She learned everything she could from all of them.

Anthea was trying to get her head around the role of banks in corruption. She knew there was something really, really wrong, but actually proving it, linking what these people were saying to the small pieces of evidence that she had so far, was another matter. 'I've got half-arsed things, like a bank-account number for Deutsche Bank,' she told us. 'It's like, Jesus, how do I even conceptualize what's wrong here?' However, unknown to Anthea, some stars were beginning to align.

In 2007 three French organizations embarked on an unprecedented legal case against the heads of state of Angola, Burkina Faso, the Republic of Congo, Gabon and Equatorial Guinea. Association Sherpa, founded by a crusading lawyer named William Bourdon; Survie, an NGO tackling hunger and corruption; and the Fédération des Congolais de la Diaspora alleged that the Paris mansions and country chateaux belonging to these men and their families could not possibly have been bought with their government salaries.

In response, the French police began an investigation that became known as the *Biens mal acquis* case; literally 'ill-gotten gains'. The objective was to get the assets seized and the looted money returned to the populations of the countries it was stolen from. But the case was dropped by the public prosecutor on the grounds that there was insufficient proof. Then Transparency International France, also working with Sherpa, stepped in with a complaint of its own.

Sarah Wykes seemed to have a special knack for obtaining leaked evidence from court cases and police investigations. In late 2007 she went to Paris and was shooting the breeze with her friends at

Sherpa when one of them gave her a sheaf of documents. Back in London she made a couple of copies and handed one to Anthea, who needed some live examples of bank shenanigans to use as case studies for the new campaign. An emblematic case study would be invaluable in helping her lobby for far more stringent laws to prevent banks laundering the proceeds of corruption and other crimes.

'I read the file over the Christmas holidays. Oh, my goodness... my French isn't fluent, but I can read it and it's like, holy shit, I can see what we've got here. This is unbelievable. This is killer.' Anthea was looking at the 200-page French police dossier detailing their investigation into President Obiang's eldest son, TNO. And it came with a bonus prize, because on 4 September 2007, Stewart C Robinson, deputy director of the Criminal Division at the US Department of Justice's Office of International Affairs, wrote to the French police with a formal 'Request for Assistance'.

Written on behalf of the Fraud Section and the Money Laundering and Asset Recovery Section of the US Department of Justice, together with the US Immigration and Customs Enforcement (ICE), this request stated that 'the [US] prosecutors suspect that most, if not all, of Teodoro Nguema Obiang's assets are derived from extortion, bribery or the misappropriation of public funds'.

The US investigation had 'identified numerous suspicious transactions originating from or transiting the French financial system' with the money ending up in US banks. It was a fascinating glimpse into very high-end shopping.

And then came one of those delightful incidences of happenstance. While Gavin was sitting in our latest office in Holborn one afternoon, his phone rang and he picked it up to hear an American voice at the other end. Calling from California, the man told Gavin that he had until recently worked as one of TNO's domestic staff. He had been employed at a vast mansion in Malibu where his boss lived a life of extreme profligacy and decadence. He had a private jet, owned a fleet of luxury cars and divided his time between Europe and the US, where he spent his life partying and in amorous pursuit of rap stars. He treated his staff like dirt and they, like the caller himself, were disposed of at a whim. Treatment like this didn't engender loyalty.

Gavin and his team immediately got back onto LexisNexis and

this time there was no need for a wide search. We went straight to property records.

In 2005, a company called Sweetwater Malibu LLC paid US$35 million for a vast horseshoe-shaped mansion set in a 16-acre estate with its own golf course in Malibu, California. And who owned Sweetwater Malibu? Teodoro Nguema Obiang Mangue. Even for the Obiangs this level of extravagance seemed excessive, but we hadn't seen anything yet.

Anthea must have been drooling as she read through the US documents. They detailed that the US investigators suspected that the Malibu mansion had been purchased with money sent by Obiang into the US in April 2005 via five wire transfers of US$5.9 million each 'from Société Générale de Banques en Guinée Équatoriale to Banque de France, account # 2000193528235, to a correspondent account at Wachovia Corporation Atlantic to account # 2000055333 at First American Trust FSB in the name of First American Title'.

A year later, TNO moved another US$10.3 million into the US via the same route into a correspondent account at Wachovia Atlantic and then to a Bank of America account in the name of a law firm called McAfee & Taft*.

Between May and June 2006, another US$33.8 million was transferred into an account at UBS under the name of Insured Aircraft Title Service Correspondent. The investigators believed this was the money used by a BVI company owned by TNO, Ebony Shine International Ltd, to purchase a luxury Gulfstream jet.

Between November 2006 and June 2007, the 'suspected money laundering continued…through the use of an intermediary'. TNO's attorney, Michael Jay Berger, received at least four wire transfers totalling about US$800,000.

The US request included a PowerPoint presentation prepared by the special agent in charge of ICE's Miami bureau. In addition to the intelligence that TNO's Malibu mansion was 'undergoing a multimillion-dollar renovation', it also catalogued yet another stable of cars belonging to TNO, stored at the Peterson Automotive

---

* When we called them, McAfee & Taft denied that TNO was a customer of the firm and said the firm did not have direct knowledge of the transactions, which must have been on behalf of another client.

Museum in Los Angeles. All in all, between Europe and the US, TNO owned three Bugatti Veyron sports cars worth US$1.3 million each, a Rolls-Royce Phantom for US$350,000, a Maybach with a minibar for another US$350,000, four Ferraris at US$250,000 each, a Bentley Arnage for a cheaper US$240,000 and a Rolls-Royce Park Ward.

'Good shit like this doesn't emerge unless you've got a whistle-blower or it's emerged from legal proceedings, or both,' Anthea said, telling us about this goldmine. This time we had both.

Our aim was to make life as difficult as we could for the klep-tocrats who committed these crimes. We wanted to make it harder to perpetrate the crimes and even harder to get away with. These documents and the Riggs Bank case demonstrated that tackling grand corruption was impossible as long as the banking sector was a willing partner in crime. And these were crimes. There were laws in place to prevent all the things the Obiangs and the banks were doing, but they were not being enforced. This evidence would be powerful ammunition for our campaign. Anthea wrote to Sherpa. They had obtained this information for their court case against the African heads of state. Anthea wanted it for a different purpose and started working out a formula for communicating with the banks: 'To say, "We have evidence that this account was used for this purpose"...and we ask them what due diligence they did. And then they tell us to fuck off.' Which is effectively the banks' usual response, but at least we would give them a chance to defend themselves, an important point if a case ever came before the libel courts.

One of our chief allies in this campaign was an unlikely one: Teodoro Nguema Obiang himself. The French police investigation had shone a light on his outrageously profligate lifestyle. It made for fantastic copy – a journalist's dream – and most revelations about TNO resulted in reams of news coverage. But could what worked for journalists also work for a more powerful constituency?

Anthea was joined by a new team member. Fresh out of university, Rob Palmer joined us as an intern in 2008 aged just 22 and started putting together our first report on the banking sector with Anthea. Intelligent, fresh-faced and clean cut, Rob had begun bucking the system at Cambridge, where he edited one of the student newspapers.

'I started in August and Lehman Brothers collapsed in September,' Rob said. As the financial world collapsed around us, it was clear that what they were working on was at the heart of the problem. 'It just felt so incredibly relevant and was a story that hadn't been told before,' he said.

Anthea was trying to work out how to get to the Financial Action Task Force (FATF), an intergovernmental body that was a crucial target for our advocacy, because it was the FATF that set the internationally endorsed global standards against money laundering and terrorist financing. She knew that we needed to be on the inside of global standard setting, but there was no precedent for this because civil society hadn't spoken out on this issue before. These issues were regarded as technical and bureaucratic and not a matter of public interest until we started working on them. We needed to woo this bureaucratic body.

Our flirtation with FATF was very Global Witness, although it started conventionally enough. We began to get to know enough of the delegates and FATF's president, and we knew a couple of the people who were running FATF's small secretariat, which was based at the OECD in Paris. 'But we still weren't in the room,' Anthea said. So we got some advice that maybe we could organize something *outside* the room and settled on one of their gatherings in Paris, where together with Transparency International we set up a side meeting. The big challenge was how to tempt delegates, weary after a long day's negotiation, to come to our event at all.

This is one of the secrets of successful advocacy: just like we had to know as much as possible about the subjects of our investigations, we also needed to learn as much as we could about our friends. Anthea, who was in Paris with Rob, had done her homework. 'We knew that the American delegate, a guy from the US Treasury who was running the main meeting, was really into karaoke,' she said. 'So we were like, fine, we'll do an evening thing. We organized karaoke, we laid on a load of wine. It was in a very small room, smaller than we'd anticipated. And it was a basement and it got quite hot.'

Anthea and Rob prepared the room for the meeting, but the arranged time came and went. They waited anxiously and still no one had showed up. Then they texted the American to learn that his meeting was overrunning. 'And we were thinking, Oh, this isn't gonna happen, you know; maybe we'll just get five of them, we would do a presentation, give them some wine, talk about the problem as we saw it,' Anthea said. If they were the right five people, a close meeting like this could really make a difference.

'Damn it, about 50 of them turned up and the room was rammed, it was suddenly like a sauna in there. They were all swilling our wine,' Anthea went on. 'And then I stood up at the front and gave them a PowerPoint presentation.'

Anthea's presentation was satire and comedy, suspense and shock – delivering a story that, unless you're in our world, seems too fantastic to be true. Anthea's audience, more used to slides of dry narrative, bar charts and columns of figures delivered in a monotone, settled back to watch.

The first slide was a photograph of a sports car.

'This is a Bugatti Veyron,' Anthea said. 'It costs US$1.3 million dollars.'

'This is another Bugatti Veyron,' she said as the second slide – exactly the same photograph – flashed onto the screen, piercing the darkness of the increasingly hot room.

'At its top speed of 407km/h, the tyres burn out in 15 minutes, but this doesn't matter as you empty the fuel tank in 12 minutes.'

For this factoid she had Rob to thank, who'd been watching *Top Gear*. The delegates had never seen a presentation like this.

'This is another Bugatti Veyron,' Anthea continued. 'Only 30 of these cars have been made, and Teodoro Obiang, the son of the president of Equatorial Guinea, owns 3 of them.'

And then slides of his other cars, the US$35 million mansion in Malibu and the private jet slid across the screen. Then came the logos of the banks against the transfers they had made as they laundered TNO's stolen cash around the world. This was the sensational stuff, and then came the horror.

Slides depicting the squalor endured by the ordinary people of Equatorial Guinea: a narrow refuse-filled muddy alleyway between ramshackle wooden huts; a child peering shyly from the doorway of a darkened hovel. 'One in five children in Equatorial Guinea won't live to see their fifth birthday,' Anthea relentlessly continued her presentation.

She told us, 'You could see their faces. Something got them, something was working. Showing them the material snapped them out of their world of smooth technocratic law: they were seeing the real implication of what they were dealing with. And the FATF people, they got it. After that we were invited into the room to make a nuisance of ourselves when they were actually having their discussions.'

Anthea's first major report remains one of Global Witness's fattest. The cover of *Undue Diligence – How banks do business with corrupt regimes* depicted three pink piggy banks captioned 'See No Evil', 'Hear No Evil' and 'Speak No Evil'. The report's 134 pages outlined case after case of banks laundering money for the corrupt heads of state in six countries, ranging from Congo-Brazzaville to Turkmenistan.

Launched in March 2009, *Undue Diligence* sent shock waves through the banking sector and the reverberations reached the highest levels of decision-making in the world's leading financial centres. Within two months of its release, Anthea was asked to provide written testimony for a hearing by the US House of Representatives Committee on Financial Services, on 'Capital Loss, Corruption, and the Role of Western Financial Institutions'.

Our follow-up advocacy work with FATF and others resulted in strengthened international anti-money-laundering mechanisms and contributed to the historic UK Bribery Act that passed in 2010. And perhaps the greatest compliment to the work of Anthea and her team came from an unexpected quarter. As we said in our 2009 Annual Report: 'We are not sure whether to be flattered or dismayed to hear that some financial institutions are using *Undue Diligence* to train their compliance officers.'

Before long, Anthea herself was asked to speak to bank staff. As she showed the same presentation that she'd given that evening to the delegates of the FATF in Paris, she saw the same look on people's faces. 'People at these sessions would sometimes cry; somebody would get emotional about realizing what they were doing.'

Anthea had set her team to producing a follow-up report to *Undue Diligence*. 'We knew that US law enforcement knew about TNO's corruption,' she said, 'so how come he could still come and go to the US at will? How come he could enjoy all those assets he'd purchased with money stolen from his own people?' Anthea knew we needed to shame them into action.

Simon and our team in DC had been engaged with a lot of behind-the-scenes lobbying that had resulted in the dryly named Presidential Proclamation 7750, which empowered a tiny office in the State Department 'To Suspend Entry as Immigrants or Nonimmigrants of Persons Engaged In or Benefiting From Corruption'.

Corruption is a notoriously difficult crime to prosecute due to the complexity and opacity of the cases, but PP 7750 set a lower standard – essentially that if there were grounds to suspect someone was corrupt then they would be denied entry into the US. We and other organizations submitted a series of names of people on our books, but the list of people suspended under PP 7750 was confidential. We had no way of knowing whether TNO's name was on the list – the Equatoguinean Embassy in Washington said it wasn't. What we did know was that he was still entering the US.

The US could also prosecute under other anti-corruption and money-laundering legislation, but nothing seemed to be happening. We thought it was time to give the authorities a little nudge.

We commissioned Ken Silverstein to help us put together our next report, which was one we hoped would tip the balance against TNO. Simultaneously we began working with *New York Times* journalist Ian Urbina, who specialized in corruption stories. On 16 November 2009, the day we published *The Secret Life of a Shopaholic*, Ian's article was splashed across the front page of the *New York Times*: 'Taint of Corruption Is No Barrier to U.S. Visa'. This level of prominence was a major coup for us.

Together we documented, theft by theft, car by car and house by house, the gargantuan scale of TNO's corruption, and Anthea called on the US to act. US law requires the State Department to deny visas to foreign officials when there is credible evidence they are involved in corruption; yet the authorities continued to allow Teodoro to come and go as he pleased.

Despite everything, it seemed there was absolutely no way of finding out whether the US would follow up on our demands. We would just have to wait and see.

The details of the earlier US investigation into TNO had been a goldmine of hard facts, yet there had also been a tantalizing loose end. Stewart C Robinson's request for assistance from the French police had mentioned that, based on reports from two separate sources, the US authorities suspected that TNO had also ordered a

200-foot superyacht complete with a shark tank. Now, to an investigative organization like ours, this was like a red rag to a bull.

GERMANY, 2010

It was freezing on that December morning as Karl climbed into a borrowed car and took the A23 north out of Hamburg. Twenty-five centimetres of snow had fallen overnight so he drove carefully; he wasn't in a hurry. After an hour, he turned off the autobahn and headed west. After another half hour, he pulled up at the bridge that crosses the River Stör and got out of the car. About half a kilometre to his left, the Stör joined the mighty Elbe on its journey to the North Sea. Virtually straight ahead, Karl could see the river's final meander and there, on the opposite bank, were the cluster of buildings and the quay that he was looking for. The home of Kusch Yachts.

Karl had done very little preparation for the meeting he was about to have. When this opportunity came up, he'd actually taken a day out of his holiday visiting friends in Germany; but he thought he could wing it. Having collected his thoughts, he got back into the car, crossed the bridge, pulled up at Kusch's gates and pressed the entrance buzzer. Having ascertained that Karl didn't have an appointment, the security guard said he couldn't let him in. Karl, who is nothing if not charming, asked whether he could call the manager or CEO to explain the reason for his visit.

When he was put through to a staff member, Karl apologized profusely for turning up out of the blue. He said he'd originally planned to make an appointment for the following week, but the overnight snowfall had resulted in today's meetings being cancelled and he thought he would use his unexpected free time on the off-chance that he could get a meeting at Kusch. The man was very obliging and buzzed the gate open. First hurdle jumped. He was in.

Karl was directed up a narrow staircase lined with photographs of the superyachts that Kusch built, and entered a large office on the first floor, with big windows looking down onto the jetties below. There were three or four desks and a drawing table where the blueprints of the yachts were put together. Karl was introduced to the three engineers working there.

'I'm a London-based businessman and I was in Hamburg for various meetings,' Karl told them. 'One of my friends in London recently met with the yacht designer Tim Heywood, who told him about a yacht he had built that had been bought by Roman Abramovich, and my friend said, "I need a yacht like that."'

There were some elements of truth in Karl's story, but not many. Not even his name. Karl is a Global Witness investigator with a knack for undercover work. His is a job that requires charm, quick thinking and a lot of balls.

We had already exposed TNO's extraordinary profligacy, but a superyacht with a price tag in the hundreds of millions of dollars was in a different league. If we could prove this commission existed, it would be another big nail in TNO's coffin. It was Gavin who asked another disenchanted member of TNO's domestic staff who had contacted him whether they had heard about this rumoured yacht. She gave him the name Kusch, the company she'd heard would be building the yacht.

But how to get Kusch to confirm it? The companies that provide services to the ultra-rich are bound by a vow of silence akin to the Mafia's *omertà*. The ultra-rich like their privacy. In essence, the approach we took was not unlike those first basic investigations we did in Cambodia: we figured that if Kusch thought we were a potential customer, then the lure of money might loosen their lips. We realized that the chances of us pulling this off were pretty slim, but it was worth a shot. So when Karl pressed the buzzer on the gates of Kusch's yard in Wewelsfleth, he had two pieces of information that would have to serve as the foundations for his story. The first was that we knew Kusch was building a yacht for Obiang, but we couldn't admit that we knew that – Karl had to get them to tell us. The second was dropping the name of Tim Heywood, who had designed Abramovich's yacht, the *Pelorus*.

Karl, in real life as in his undercover guise, talks a lot, immersing the listener in a torrent of words. Charming and uninterruptable, this flow erodes the barriers that people might usually erect. He was in luck: the engineers told him that by coincidence they were indeed building a yacht like the *Pelorus*.

'That is amazing luck,' Karl said. 'Is there any chance I can see the plans?' Like all artists, these engineers were keen to show off their work. They brought out two big folders that contained the interior and exterior plans for the yacht and placed them on one of the desks. For the next two hours, Karl and the engineers pored over the plans as, full of curiosity, Karl asked question after question.

They wouldn't tell Karl the name of their client, but Karl had anticipated that. 'I told them that I knew somebody who is a very wealthy person in a West African state, and I know he wants to have a yacht and I might even be able to name this name. And they looked at me, and I said, "Does it begin with O?" And then they just nodded.' Karl had got Kusch to confirm what we had suspected.

Karl raised the issue that as he was a very wealthy man and the son of a president, security for 'O' had to be a major concern. The engineers proudly explained the various security measures being built in, right down to the thumb sensors that controlled entry to the yacht's corridors and suites.

Karl and the engineers were getting along well. They brought out coffee and Christmas cakes, which they munched as they hunched over the plans.

'And I know that Mr Obiang likes parties?' Karl said. Half statement, half question. And the engineers told him about the luxury bar and the cinema that could seat 30 people, and the precious woods that would be part of the boat's fittings. Kusch's main work was the building of the hull, they said, and coordinating all the specialist work and the craftsmen who together would create this monumental testament to greed.

'It must be very expensive,' Karl mused. Another closely guarded secret, but as he had done with the client's name, Karl ran off some numbers until he got a confirmatory nod. Obiang's bill for the boat would be US$380 million, give or take.

That's a lot of money anywhere, but in Equatorial Guinea it was three times the combined health and education budget. Instead, as Human Rights Watch reported, TNO alone 'spent more on houses and cars in the United States and South Africa between 2004 and 2006 than the government did on the entire education sector in 2005'.

As Karl bade his farewells, he felt bad for the engineers. 'The way they welcomed me – I came unannounced and without having an appointment, and they agreed to meet me,' he said. 'They were quite open. They didn't show any suspicion or ask "What is this guy

doing?" Probably I just talked them under the table. I don't know.'
He probably did; he occasionally does the same to me. 'I felt pity
for them afterwards because they must have got a big bashing from
their boss, Mr Kusch.' Karl's concern for them was sincere. 'They
gave me Christmas cakes and biscuits.'

One thing we discovered was the press and general public's love of
salacious facts about the ultra-rich. While wars, disease and famine
often go under-reported, there was no shortage of interest in the
criminally expensive tastes of Obiang and his peers. 'Forget health
and education…son of despot splashes out £233 million on a yacht,'
was the *Daily Mail*'s headline on 1 March 2011. It was just one
of many articles in the international press. Besieged by the media
interest, the Equatoguinean government were forced to admit that
TNO had ordered the yacht, but that he had since dismissed the idea
of buying it.

At a cost of just a few hundred pounds, Karl's trip to Wewelsfleth
had caused an international storm and cost Kusch Yachts an order,
but at least it saved them from taking money stolen from the belea-
guered people of Equatorial Guinea. I hope they feel good about that.

The work of Sherpa, Transparency International France and Global
Witness had catalysed law-enforcement investigations in France,
Switzerland and the US, but one of Obiang's continuing high-end
spending sprees ratcheted up the authorities' interest in him even
more. It all began on 4 December 2010.

A collection of rock and pop memorabilia, including several
iconic costumes from Michael Jackson's tours, was going under
the hammer at Julien's Auctions in Beverly Hills. The organizers
of this eagerly awaited auction must have been well pleased with
the results. A jacket belonging to John Lennon went to some happy
and well-heeled punter for a quarter of a million dollars, but of the
US$3 million the auction raised, US$2,270,187.50 was spent by one
man. Just who was this mysterious bidder? The Hollywood gossip
mill cranked up and it wasn't long before TNO was identified as the
buyer. But these extraordinary purchases also got noticed by others.

Created to tackle high-level public corruption, the newly formed
Kleptocracy Asset Recovery Initiative (KARI) brought together
a powerful team comprising Department of Justice prosecutors

working closely with the FBI and other federal law-enforcement agencies. Its goal was to forfeit the proceeds of corruption by foreign officials and, if possible, to return the money for the benefit of the people it had been stolen from. The organization was looking for its first case. Their interest piqued by the Beverly Hills auction, its investigators dug a little and wondered how a man with an official salary of just over US$80,000 per year from his role as Equatorial Guinea's minister of forests and infrastructure could support such an expensive Michael Jackson habit.

On 11 June 2012, they filed their first complaint, *United States vs One white crystal-covered "Bad Tour" glove and other Michael Jackson memorabilia'*, to the US District Court for the Central District of California. TNO had liked the glove so much that he paid US$310,000 more than its estimated value. The judge threw out the case, citing that it didn't reach the required standard of 'probable cause'. Not to be deterred, the investigators went on to compile a damning litany of corruption and theft of state assets that allowed TNO to spend a staggering US$600–800 million on his personal lifestyle between 2006 and 2010. Their third complaint hit home.

In October 2011, five years after we had found out about TNO's mansion, the US Justice Department seized US$70 million of TNO's assets in the US. In a bid to avoid arrest in the US, TNO reached a settlement with the US Department of Justice, handing over approximately US$34 million of his assets, including the mansion. But he got to keep the Gulfstream jet and the Michael Jackson memorabilia, which also included the famous 'Thriller' jacket.

Leslie Caldwell, assistant attorney general for the DoJ Criminal Division, said of the case, 'We are touching the untouchables. We are saying that the US financial system is not a safe haven for corruption.'

The settlement required that US$20 million of the forfeited money should go to a charity that would benefit the people of Equatorial Guinea, with the process being governed by the US. It was a nice idea, but over a decade later the citizens of Equatorial Guinea still haven't seen a penny of this money. It's not clear what the sticking point is, but a source close to the case told me he thought that the Equatoguinean government genuinely didn't want the money to benefit their people. If they remained uneducated, sick and poor, they would expend all their energy on just trying to survive, with no time left to think about 'ivory tower' issues like democracy and tackling corruption. It was a deeply cynical view, but given the Obiangs' record it was also frighteningly believable.

An FBI special agent told me this was a problem in many similar cases. It could be easy enough for the perpetrators to steal the money in the first place, but if that money was seized by the authorities in another jurisdiction, how could they be sure that if it was returned it wouldn't immediately be stolen again? And so billions of dollars looted from their citizens by the ruling elites of many corruptly led nations sit uselessly in bank accounts in the US, Europe and elsewhere. Crimes like this won't stop until the criminals are jailed.

Unrepentant, TNO himself wrote on Facebook: 'I am pleased to be able to end this long and costly ordeal. I agreed to settle this case despite the fact that the US federal courts had consistently found that the Department of Justice lacked probable cause to seize my property.' But his troubles weren't over yet.

In December 2016, another superyacht belonging to TNO, the *Ebony Shine,* was seized by Dutch authorities on behalf of the Swiss government, who were also investigating his corruption. The Swiss later dropped these charges, instead settling for confiscation of certain assets, including another 25 cars worth US$18.8 million. TNO eventually got his yacht back after three years. The government of Equatorial Guinea said it was part of their navy.

In a desperate attempt to protect his son, President Obiang named him vice president, in the hope that this would give him diplomatic immunity from prosecution, but it failed. On 27 October 2017, the court case in Paris begun by Sherpa and Transparency International France a decade previously came to its conclusion. TNO was convicted of corruption and given a three-year suspended jail sentence. The court ordered the seizure of his €107 million mansion on Paris's Avenue Foch and the €40 million of furniture, works of art and fine wines the police found inside it. In what must have been a bitter blow, they also took another of his car collections.

As Rob looked at the coverage of these events, the best thing for him was the cars: 'Just to see this photo of a truck with these outrageously fast cars lined up on it, being carted away. It was incredible.'

Despite the confiscations, trials and convictions, TNO is still a free man and still in line to succeed his father. For crimes that have cost his country hundreds of millions of dollars – money that could doubtless have saved the lives of thousands of his fellow citizens who died of preventable diseases – TNO hasn't served a day of prison time. He merely gave up some of the assets he had stolen and has doubtless stolen hundreds of millions more to replace them.

Only when the perpetrators of crimes face proportionate punishment will corrupt politicians and businesspeople think twice before committing them. Right now, the fines are a drop in the ocean. Simply a cost of doing business. Although the DoJ had said that that the US financial system was not a safe haven for corruption, it is the US – not the tropical Caribbean islands – that is the biggest secrecy jurisdiction in the world. Until the ownership of companies is publicly available, we will never stamp out corruption. And until that time comes, the least we can do is to make life very hard for criminals like these.

Global Witness, our co-conspirators and the law-enforcement investigations that followed had exposed the Achilles heel of the kleptocrats, something that's true to pretty much most of them. Despite their venal criminality they crave prestige and, more than anything, they like to go shopping. It's that simple.

5

AN ODOUR OF SULPHUR

My shirt stuck to my back in the tropical heat as I stood among the dereliction of the deserted iron-ore mine in the shadow of Mount Nimba. Long denuded of tropical rainforest, which had been felled decades before, these hills were now covered in coarse grasses and provided a stark backdrop to the scars and remnants of the hope that had once existed here. The only sounds came from the insects hovering in front of my face and the breeze whistling through the old mine workings.

As I picked my way through heaps of rusting machinery, I narrowly missed falling into a massive hole where the ground fell away into subterranean darkness; the steel girders that lined the old mine shaft fading into an eerie gloom, like a motorway into a dystopian underworld. With no guard rail between me and oblivion, I felt that tingling grip of fear somewhere between my loins and my stomach and involuntarily stepped back. Behind me, the vast yellow hulks of the trucks once used to haul away the valuable minerals that were mined here were slowly disintegrating, stripped long ago of everything removable and rotted by a quarter of a century of tropical rains, sun and wind.

I was in Liberia with two Global Witness colleagues, Natalie Ashworth and Sofia Goinhas, and our old Liberian friend and campaigning partner from the civil war days, Silas Siakor. We were there to investigate a massive mining deal struck between the government of Liberia and Mittal Steel, owned by the UK's richest man. Most of our work required immersing ourselves in the labyrinthine legalese of mining contracts and tracking the movement of profits through different tax havens: structures designed to minimize taxes paid in Liberia and to maximize profits for the company. The trip to the derelict mine site helped us understand the situation on the ground. And it helped us understand something else too.

Like almost everything in Liberia, Yekepa had been shattered by 15 years of civil war that had ended just three years previously. The company that had brought wealth to the region had long gone, leaving the surviving remnants of the workforce and their families occupying the mouldering two-room bungalows built for them in the 1960s, on the fringes of what was now a ghost town. As in Buchanan, broad and once proud thoroughfares lined with telegraph poles, stripped of the copper wires that had brought power to the town, were being reclaimed by the jungle, while the overgrown tennis courts, empty, refuse-filled swimming pools and deserted company buildings, their walls encrusted with the black mould of the tropics, were a cruel reminder of better times. Before the carnage.

To our north, beyond the mine tailings, rusting machinery and the skeletal remains of the mine buildings, lay the remote forest-covered mountains of southern Guinea. As I looked across the border, I unknowingly caught a glimpse of the future, for underneath those mountains lay the same treasure that lay under my feet: the world's richest untapped deposit of high-grade iron ore. Two and a half billion tons of it. This mountain range is called Simandou, a name that would soon send shock waves through the world's mining industry and that would draw us into one of our most complex investigations; one that would pit us against one of our most aggressive foes.

But that was all ahead of us. With a last look at this lush panorama, we retraced our steps down the grassy slope to the track and climbed into the dust-covered Mitsubishi Pajero. A Pakistani Army battalion, bored, friendly and helpful, was quartered nearby, part of the United Nations force mandated by the UN Security Council to maintain the fragile peace. We had tea with them, sitting in the back of their white armoured personnel carrier with the large black 'UN' emblazoned on its sides, before embarking on the day-long spine-jarring journey over Liberia's ruined roads back to its capital, Monrovia. I was glad that they were there.

Guinea should be rich. It possesses not just gold and diamonds, but the world's largest reserves of bauxite – the raw material for aluminium – as well as the iron ore that lay under Simandou. Iron ore is the primary raw material for the steel industry and steel is the most important construction and engineering material in the world, used in virtually every aspect of our daily life, from large-scale construction, infrastructure, energy and transport systems to our individual cars and tractors, washing machines and other electrical goods.

But I had visited Guinea before, when we were investigating the timber-for-arms trade during the Liberian Civil War, and I had seen that Guinea was not rich. It was a dirt-poor pawn in the scramble to hoover up the world's natural resources and was the target of some of the most ruthless operators on the planet – be they the country's former colonial rulers, the succession of dictators that followed or the corporate leviathans who courted them. It is a textbook example of 'the resource curse': Guinea was poor precisely because it was rich. Its citizens survived on less than two dollars a day, with only half of the rural population having access to clean water and 30 per cent of kids too poor to go to primary school. On top of this, it was home to at least 300,000 refugees who had fled the conflicts in neighbouring Sierra Leone and Liberia. It was a country whose national budget was dwarfed by the personal wealth of many of the company bosses who would seek to exploit it.

The jewel in the crown of Guinea's mineral wealth is the iron ore that lies under Simandou. It has the potential to bring the belea-guered population a standard of living that they can only dream of but which the rich world takes for granted: education, healthcare and prosperity for the many, not the few. But Simandou carries a health warning of its own, as those who have attempted to mine its riches have found out.

Mineral resources are finite – what is lying under the Earth's surface is all there is or will ever be – and they're gradually running out. And as they run out, their value increases, which is precisely why, as our investigations repeatedly exposed, the mining business can be cut-throat, competitive, unscrupulous and corrupt.

We were beginning to get a handle on how the oil and mining industries worked. Giant corporations ceaselessly patrol the world in search of new reserves, just like the fleets of the colonial powers did in their hunt for treasure in the 16th and 17th centuries. Circling

AN ODOUR OF SULPHUR   165

them are the smaller fry – the pirates and privateers who set out to prepare the terrain – doing the dirty work that will allow the leviathan to 'buy' a project, without having to do the dirty work that created it in the first place.

Nothing much has changed. In the 21st century, these pirates lie in wait just a stone's throw from the same inlets and harbours of the Caribbean islands that still bear the place names given to them by their nautical predecessors in the golden age of piracy, like Smugglers Cove or Rogues Bay. Their ships have been replaced by their modern-day equivalents – shadowy companies set up by the networks of lawyers and company-registration agents that are based there. Their activities are hidden behind an almost impenetrable bastion of stringent secrecy laws and protected by an army of international lawyers. The British Virgin Islands is one of the safest havens of this modern pirate fleet and it's not hard to imagine how another part of its coastline got its name: Fat Hogs Bay.

But these contemporary pirates don't just plunder treasure fleets, they loot entire countries. To do this, they depend on stealth, dirty tricks and deals of Machiavellian complexity – the foundation stones of corruption – and into this melee brazenly sailed a man called Beny Steinmetz. It is the new colonialism. Or rather, it's virtually exactly the same colonialism, but dressed up slightly differently. The flags of the former colonial powers no longer fly over the resource-rich nations of Africa, Asia and Latin America, but the diplomatic 'soft power' wielded by these countries – plus China now – and the lobbying pressure from mammoth corporations amounts to much the same thing.

We first came across Steinmetz when we were investigating blood diamonds in Angola. After completing his stint in the Israeli Army, he followed his father into the diamond business, forming the Steinmetz Diamond Group with his brother, and in so doing became a member of the billionaire club and one of Israel's richest men. A billionaire with the usual trappings: homes in France and Switzerland and, of course, the trophy jet and superyacht. The few photographs of this intensely private person depict a fit, tanned and casually dressed man with close-cropped brown hair, looking younger than his 60-odd years. To me, he bears an uncanny resemblance to Richard Roper, the suave but ruthless arms trafficker played by Hugh Laurie in the recent dramatization of John le Carré's

The Night Manager; and like Roper, he presides over a philanthropic foundation that carries out various good works in his home country and brings good PR. His activities overseas are less charitable.

Steinmetz's operations are carried out by a web of companies that, on the face of it, have no connection to the mothership, Beny Steinmetz Group Resources (BSGR). Even if a trail led there, he maintained the fiction that he played no role in the company that bears his name. On paper, he was simply a consultant to it. But just a few months before I was standing on that bleak mountainside in Liberia in 2006, a plan had kicked into action, a plan that would seek to propel Beny Steinmetz and BSGR into the super-league of the mining industry. It had begun with the creation of a company called Pentler Holdings, registered in the British Virgin Islands on 28 October 2005. Discovering who was behind Pentler could be the key to the mystery that we were about to be immersed in.

The three biggest iron-ore mining companies in the world are Anglo-Australian BHP, the Brazilian giant Vale, and another Anglo-Australian conglomerate, Rio Tinto. They all wanted to get their hands on Simandou, but it was Rio Tinto that was awarded the rights to explore Blocks 1, 2, 3 and 4 of the deposit by Guinea's dictatorial president Lansana Conté in 1997. The importance of this acquisition could not be underestimated. Rio's chief executive, Tom Albanese, told reporters that 'Simandou is, without doubt, the top undeveloped tier-one iron-ore asset in the world.' Rio had become one of the lead actors in what was to become a curious ensemble playing out a drama of Shakespearean complexity and intrigue.

Almost a decade later, the by now ailing Conté wrote a letter to Rio Tinto questioning the validity of their rights to Simandou. This came out of nowhere. A month later, Conté's government confiscated Blocks 1 and 2 from Rio Tinto, justifying their actions by claiming that the company had been too slow in developing them. It's true that Rio Tinto hadn't yet mined any ore from Simandou, but that wasn't the real reason. That soon became evident.

In December 2008, Conté signed over these two blocks to BSGR, for free. The only stipulation was that the company was required to spend US$160 million to develop the mine. Two weeks later, President Lansana Conté was dead.

Within six hours of his death, a young ex-army officer took power and established a military junta. Dapper in his red paratrooper's beret with its swooping eagle badge, his eyes permanently masked by aviator glasses, Captain Moussa Dadis Camara was, like most dictators, completely paranoid. Justifiably, as it turned out. His regime lasted little more than a year. In an approximate re-run of countless coups before his, he promised democracy and declared war on corruption. He closed down state institutions; his troops massacred 150 opposition members in a sports stadium and gang-raped hundreds more. And then his aide-de-camp shot him in the head. Whisked out of the country for emergency medical care, he survived but had lost his appetite for rule. One of his last acts as president was to reaffirm BSGR's right to Simandou.

And then Beny Steinmetz's BSGR pulled off a coup of its own. Just two years after Lansana Conté had awarded them Blocks 1 and 2 of Simandou for nothing, they sold 51 per cent of their stake to Rio Tinto's arch rival, the Brazilian mining giant Vale, for a mouthwatering US$2.5 billion – more than twice the country's national budget – with US$500 million paid up front, creating a joint venture called VBG. Beny Steinmetz had joined the mining Premier League, yet not an ounce of iron ore had been taken out of the ground. It was a masterstroke that the *Sunday Times* hailed 'The Deal of the Century'.

Mo Ibrahim, the billionaire Sudanese telecoms tycoon and prominent anti-corruption campaigner, held a different view: 'Are the Guineans who did that deal idiots, or criminals, or both?' It was a good question.

Around about the same time, a West Africa-based investigative journalist called Daniel Balint-Kurti was swapping stories with another hack who had just returned from Guinea's capital, Conakry, where he had been doing some investigative work. He told Dan about an intriguing experience he had had a week before. He was waiting to see someone in the Ministry of Mines and Geology when a man entered the minister's office carrying a briefcase. A few minutes later, he left without it. The briefcase was rumoured to have been stuffed with cash. Was the minister, Mahmoud Thiam, on the take? Like all good news hounds, Dan has a nose for a story, and as he sniffed this one he scented prey.

Global Witness first got to know Dan in 2006. A freelance investigative journalist for the *Sunday Times* among others, Dan had spent years in West Africa delving into geopolitics and corruption, often probing into deals to secure natural resources. We first hired him as a freelancer to investigate the role of the cocoa trade in funding the bloody civil war that was ripping apart Côte d'Ivoire. His work was brilliant and featured in our influential report *Hot Chocolate*, and it wasn't long before Dan came to work for us full-time.

A slim-built, outwardly diffident man, Dan has the air of someone who spends his time in the dusty, wood-panelled rooms of some leading university, perhaps a professor in an obscure arm of linguistics or philosophy. His air of diffidence is exaggerated as he speaks, carefully weighing up every word, balancing his arguments, facts, probabilities and subterfuges as he slots pieces of wildly complex and improbable jigsaw puzzles into place. Dan relentlessly hunts for the missing pieces in conversations, leaked documents, news articles and his vast mental archive of past cases and networks of informants. And he possesses an inherent understanding of the way a criminal mind works, of where someone with something to hide would hide it and how. His adversaries usually regret confusing Dan's polite and self-questioning demeanour with that of someone who could be brushed off.

The rumoured briefcase full of cash had set him thinking. 'If a government enters into a deal that makes absolutely no economic sense, then it's odds on that the deal is corrupt,' Dan mused.

The first truly democratic presidential elections in Guinea's history took place in June 2010. Thirsty for reform, the electorate returned the leader of the opposition, the urbane French-educated Alpha Condé. A former lecturer at the Sorbonne, he won on a ticket of security-sector reform and a pledge to tackle corruption. Condé inherited one of the poorest countries in the world, and one of the most corrupt. One of his first actions was to establish the Technical Committee for the Review of Securities and Mining Agreements to review all the mining contracts signed by his predecessors. He needed to know how BSGR had acquired the rights to Simandou and how they had scooped up US$2.5 billion while the country had got nothing at all.

*

In April 2011, Jonathan Springett, a guest lecturer at a leading US university, was in full flow when his phone started ringing. Once he'd finished speaking, he left the lecture hall and returned the call. It was from George Soros. George asked him to come to New York as soon as possible; he needed his advice.

With George was a young Guinean man sent over by Alpha Condé to seek George's advice. Jonathan listened intently as this man outlined Condé's problem. Guinea was sitting on top of fantastically valuable natural resources and there was no lack of interest in exploiting them. In fact, Guinea had the opposite problem. How could Condé know which deals were above board and which were corrupt?

George's interest in natural-resource governance had evolved from his experiences in the former Soviet Union. He tried to assist these newly formed countries through his Open Society Institute because he could see that corruption was eating their future from the inside. It was one of the primary reasons he had been so supportive of our work when Simon had conceived the Publish What You Pay movement back in 2001. George had chosen wisely when he called Jonathan Springett, because this was exactly his area of expertise. It was all about following the money.

'The information you need to track bank transfers simply isn't present,' Jonathan told the man from Guinea. 'Your law-enforcement establishment doesn't have the forensic training necessary to deal with the infrastructure of large-scale corruption. Most people think corruption is something that happens in jurisdictions in the tropics but that's not true. Large-scale corruption occurs invariably in major financial centres and involves polished lawyers, bankers, accountants and PR professionals who cover their tracks,' he explained. 'So if you want to find out what went down, the steps that would document corruption, the financial transactions will be in London, Paris, Amsterdam, Zürich, Geneva, New York...'

Jonathan's advice to President Condé was clear. Guinea would need to engage a foreign law firm and private investigators. 'You can't pursue every case, so you'll need to identify a small number of significant deals where there is convincing evidence, and which would enable you to be able to collaborate with a major enforcement jurisdiction.'

Jonathan got the job and he put together a team to review significant transactions, ones that had hit the international news. There weren't that many that reached that limit of notoriety, but one stood out: 'Simandou had an odour of sulphur about it from the very beginning.'

It was a fateful morning in 2012 when Dan exited Chancery Lane Tube station for the two-minute walk to our offices at Buchanan House, an elegant 1920s office building in the heart of London's legal district. Eschewing the lift, which was usually crammed full of students too lazy to walk up the one flight to the business school that occupied the first floor, Dan climbed the stairs to the sixth floor and pushed open the glass doors of our light-filled office, which had a view onto Holborn to the front and over the roofs of Mirror Group Newspapers to the east, where the disgraced tycoon Robert Maxwell had famously crafted the theft of his employees' pensions.

The office was open plan, with each team's desks in clusters, nestling among filing cabinets weighed down with souvenirs brought back from the many countries the team members had visited in the course of their work: maps, posters, flags and ornaments vied for space with swathes of vibrant African and Asian fabrics and photos of past deeds. Dan threaded his way through the desks to where the anti-corruption team sat and asked Anthea, by now the director of corruption campaigns, for a meeting. They walked out onto the roof terrace for privacy, and he asked her for clearance and a budget to commence an investigation into Simandou.

Anthea didn't take long to decide. 'Yes, let's do it. What do you need?'

Dan constantly scanned the international media for news on Simandou, and in 2012 it began to appear. In the year since their appointment by President Condé, Jonathan Springett and the Technical Committee had been delving into the dark heart of BSGR's Simandou deal. In 2012, they wrote to BSGR alleging that the company had obtained Simandou through corrupt means, and posed numerous questions. BSGR had 60 days to respond or, together with their joint-venture partner, Vale, they would face the cancellation of their rights to Simandou. The 'Deal of the Century' was imperilled and once again it became international news.

As the review progressed, tantalizing pieces of information were being leaked by a variety of sources. We knew we could add weight to the committee's work. Unconstrained by the formalities of government, we could enhance their enquires by obtaining evidence of our own, which we could use to advocate with policymakers or work with law enforcement. We could collaborate with the media and amplify the scandal behind Simandou. So, like a flock of seagulls hovering over the by-catch slipping into the choppy waters behind a fishing boat, we joined a whole array of actors coalescing around scraps: investigative journalists like the *Financial Times*'s Tom Burgis, others from specialist mining-industry publications and people like Dan, who began to get a whiff of something fishy being uncovered.

Among the allegations levelled by the Technical Committee was that BSGR had bribed the late President Conté's fourth wife, Mamadie Touré, to get her husband's signature on the deal. If this was true, it would be dynamite, but was it? And if it was, could we prove it? And then we began to get to know the enemy.

Dan was sitting at his desk in Buchanan House when he opened his emails on the morning of Monday 15 October 2012. Among them was a letter from the chairman of BSGR, David Clark. He accused us of 'acting with Mr George Soros in conducting an investigation into [BSGR]' and said that they understood that Global Witness was considering writing a report on the subject. The letter threatened that they would 'respond with all available legal means to prevent damaging and defamatory attacks on our company'. Dan was shocked. His investigation was still in the early stages of information gathering and we'd made no public reference to it. 'Either we've been hacked or someone's talked,' he said.

We suspected one of our sources and it was an object lesson for us: we couldn't underestimate who we were dealing with. Beny Steinmetz was rich and notoriously litigious; our legal team were on high alert and all Dan's meticulous investigations were put under the magnifying glass. Simon took top management responsibility to read and sign off most of what we would publish on the Simandou case. We went into internal information lockdown.

But the letter did show that BSGR were rattled and that they didn't want anyone prying into their business. The letter was the harbinger of their unfolding strategy: attack is the best form of defence. They set out to portray the investigations into their corrupt deal as an orchestrated plot, and like many before and after them, they decided to hang it on George Soros. George is often accused of leading plots, and it wasn't the first time we had been accused of being part of one of them, something that usually demonstrated desperation on the part of those we were investigating – resorting to propaganda when facts weren't on their side. Steinmetz was clutching at straws.

Global Witness had become an old hand at legal threats. They are an occupational hazard for us but we're not complacent – one small misstep in a swamp and you're up to your neck and sinking fast. Our resources are minuscule compared to the vast wealth available to many of those we investigate, but we invest a small fortune in top legal advice, which has enabled us to turn what could be seen as a crippling hurdle to our advantage. More importantly, we don't scare easily. Like a dog yelping in frustration as it tries to attack a hedge-hog, our adversaries can be driven into a frenzy by their impotency. They have sharp teeth but sensitive noses. Ignoring the threat, we wrote back to David Clark requesting that the company provide full details of how it gained access to Blocks 1 and 2 of Simandou. We heard nothing back. But at around the same time as David Clark wrote to us, one of the sources Dan had been cultivating sent him a bundle of documents. It was the first big break.

The papers comprised a flurry of contracts and agreements, and as Dan worked his way through them a light began to shine into the mysterious shadows of Beny Steinmetz's Deal of the Century.

In the first document, signed on 20 February 2006, a company called Pentler Holdings, registered in the British Virgin Islands, trans-ferred a third of its capital to one Mamadie Touré. The document was signed for Pentler by its representative, Avraham Lev Ran. A month later another company, BSGR's local entity, BSGR Guinea, transferred 17.65 per cent of its holdings in Simandou to Pentler Holdings. Because Mamadie Touré now owned a third of Pentler's 50,000 shares, this shuffling of paperwork meant that she now owned around 6 per cent of a mining operation potentially worth billions of dollars.

This was intriguing enough, but it got better. Another contract signed two years later, on 27 February 2008, took things into the stratosphere of intrigue. BSGR Guinea, represented by its president, Asher Avidan, agreed to pay US$4 million dollars to a BVI registered company, Matinda Holdings, as a 'commission' for obtaining Blocks 1 and 2 of Simandou. Two million dollars of this 'commission' would go directly to Matinda, with US$100,000 already paid in advance. The remaining US$2 million would be distributed among 'those people of goodwill' who would play a role in facilitating the granting of these blocks. It was signed for Matinda by Mamadie Touré. She was becoming a very rich woman.

Dan had no doubt about what he was looking at. 'These documents look like the rarest of things – documentary evidence of corruption,' he said as we leafed through them. I marvelled at the efficacy of the secrecy and complexity deliberately designed to complicate things. If you don't know that the deal is being done at all, you can't investigate it. If you do get wind of such a deal but don't possess any documentation, then there's no trail to follow. These leaked documents cast at least some light on the inner workings of the Simandou deal but they also highlighted another mystery.

In unknowing parallel with Dan, the *Financial Times* had been following the same events and broke their story on 2 November 2012: 'US$2.5Bn mining tussle…Tycoon's iron ore jackpot in peril.' The article reported that the Technical Committee set up by Alpha Condé to review mining contracts had written to BSGR's and Vale's joint venture alleging numerous instances of corruption, including that BSGR had lavished gifts, among them a diamond-encrusted gold watch, on the president himself. The most serious allegation levelled by the committee was that BSGR had paid a US$2.4 million commission to the president's fourth wife, Mamadie Touré, to help secure the rights to Simandou.

An article in a prestigious paper like the *FT* can reach a whole range of influential people, from high-level politicians to captains of industry, and from stock exchanges to law-enforcement agencies, and their top investigative journalist, Tom Burgis, was tenacious in pursuing this story.* But whereas the responsibility of a journalist for a media outlet stops with the articles they publish, for

---

* See also Tom Burgis's excellent 2015 book, *The Looting Machine*.

organizations like Global Witness the exposé is just the start. Our investigations provide the evidence we need to patrol the corridors of power, to advocate for action, to pressure law enforcement to do its job, for the introduction of new laws and, ultimately, for people to be held to account for what they have done. It is a critical dimension in the game of high-stakes chess, which is the world Global Witness inhabits. And this critical difference between a media organization and an NGO was to become part of the story.

The *Financial Times* possessed roughly the same information as we did. 'The *FT* article gave me the perfect peg to publicly pose questions directly to BSGR,' Dan said, and he penned Global Witness's first press release on the Simandou deal. In it, we called on BSGR to make public the negotiations behind their acquisition of Blocks 1 and 2 of Simandou, and to detail the terms of their contracts with the government and with their joint-venture partner, Vale.

'Our questions were perfectly reasonable, but I knew that they would rattle BSGR,' Dan said. 'They prefer to operate below the radar – we needed to get them to show their face.'

Extracts from the Technical Committee's investigation continued to make headlines. 'During the period of the military regime in Guinea from 2009 to 2010, BSGR was engaged in a strategy to improve its relations with decision-makers by making regular payments to high military figures...These payments were often distributed in cash, carried into the country in BSGR's private jet,' Reuters quoted from the Technical Committee's report. 'Thiam – [Guinea's minister of mines and the man Dan's journalist friend suspected of receiving a briefcase full of cash] – repeatedly served as a BSGR conduit for the purposes of these payments, receiving the money on arrival at Conakry Airport and organizing their distribution among the people to whom they were destined.'

'If the corruption allegations were not so insulting, I would find them funny,' Thiam told Reuters. 'To pretend that I indulged in such practices is absolutely false.'

On 22 February 2013, BSGR responded to the Technical Committee. They denied that they had made any illegal payments to get hold of Simandou, and for good measure stated that Mamadie Touré was not married to President Conté. They added that questions relating to her were in any case 'not pertinent…as BSGR has never approached Mme Touré on the subject of the Simandou project'. The wording of this denial was like a ripple in a creek that alerts the crocodile to the presence of prey.

'Why would they deny that Mamadie Touré was the wife of the president if the second point was true?' Dan asked. 'If they hadn't approached her, then it wouldn't matter who she was. It reminded me of that famous quote from Freud: "I never borrowed a kettle from you, and anyway, it was already broken when I borrowed it."'

In any event, as far as we were concerned the question was moot. Dan had already got hold of a copy of Mamadie Touré's passport, which listed her as *femme de PR* – the wife of the Président de la République.

Reinforced in his suspicions, Dan worked his networks of contacts with renewed vigour. Making calls on his mobile from the roof terrace, his favourite haunt, or holding clandestine meetings in the greasy-spoon cafés that he loved, Dan greedily hoovered up any information he could find.

Many members of the shadow network are companies that are prepared to take greater risks than their more mainstream counterparts, like doing corrupt deals in unstable dictatorships or war zones. These are the apex predators. One step down the food chain lie the companies who seem happy to service them and feast on the scraps. Firms like London-based lawyers Mishcon de Reya.

One of London's top law firms, Mishcon are perhaps most famous for representing Diana, Princess of Wales, in her divorce from Prince Charles. At the time of our investigation, they were the law firm of choice for the super-rich, notable particularly for working with PEPs. A PEP is a politically exposed person, a term coined by an intergovernmental organization, the Financial Action Task Force (FATF), to encompass politicians, public officials, their family members and close contacts. There is nothing wrong with being a PEP per se – every government minister in every country in the world is one, along with their families – but given the potential opportunities for abuse of power or misuse of public funds by those in high office, banks and other institutions are required to keep an eye on PEPs and to report any suspicious behaviour. So if a PEP with a modest government salary opens a multimillion-dollar bank account – like so many of the subjects of our investigations do – the bank is legally required to check that the source of funds is legitimate.

At Global Witness we know that PEPs feature in a disproportionate number of corrupt deals. Mishcon must know this too. 'Grubby is a very complex point for a lawyer,' their managing partner Kevin Gold told London's *Evening Standard* in a 2014 interview, which noted that 'His law firm has made it its business to deal with politically-exposed persons — think oligarchs and those that harbour the private billions that swill around Chelsea, Knightsbridge and feature in spats that flare up in unstable parts of the world.'

Our first brush with Mishcon came in April 2012 and centred around the case of a banker who had been sentenced to prison *in absentia* for transferring millions of dollars from the Kyrgyz Republic ahead of a peoples' revolution (see Chapter 7). Within a couple of years, our correspondence with the firm had grown to encompass three of their clients in different parts of the world who were subjects of three completely separate Global Witness investigations, including into the billionaire chief minister of Sarawak, who made the family fortune by corruptly selling off Borneo's rainforests to the Malaysian timber Mafia. I do wonder how the partners in law firms like Mishcon can sleep easy given that their 'politically exposed' clients, certainly as far as Global Witness is concerned, seem to represent a rogues' gallery.

Mishcon's letters are infamous within media circles for their aggressive stance and given their name pops up so often, they are presumably often successful in suppressing adverse reporting about their clients. It requires guts and good lawyers for journalists and organizations like ours to take on litigious billionaires. 'Reputation management', or reputation laundering as we call it, has become the name of the game for these firms. For us it is simply a euphemistic term for keeping the lid on inconvenient facts. The lawyers also work in league with PR companies such as Powerscourt, founded by ex-*Sunday Times* journalist Rory Godson, which, in another glorious euphemism, claims to help clients to 'prepare for and manage times of reputational stress'.

Needless to say, it was Mishcon who were the lawyers for Beny Steinmetz, and Powerscourt who, in December 2012, began to mount a PR counteroffensive on his part.

*

As the momentum around the Simandou case built up, Dan needed help, and in April 2013 we hired Leigh Baldwin, a tall, fair-haired and sardonic investigative journalist in his thirties. With his large, sixties-style glasses, he looked a little like a young Michael Caine. Together, Dan and Leigh made a formidable team.

During the first few months of 2013, Dan issued numerous press releases to turn up the temperature on BSGR, adding to other widespread press coverage. Backed into a corner, on 9 May BSGR released a 'Response to Press Speculation', which stated: 'Allegations that there was anything improper about the manner in which BSGR obtained its mining rights in Guinea are entirely baseless and motivated by an ongoing campaign to seize the assets of BSGR...The granting of exploration permits to BSGR by the Government of Guinea in February 2006 was conducted in a fully transparent manner, and as part of a competitive process during which BSGR had to consistently prove that it had the technical and financial capability to carry out exploration, feasibility studies and project development.' Hmm.

Dan and Leigh spent many hours sitting on the roof terrace plotting our next moves. That corruption had taken place was demonstrated by the contracts we had seen, but Dan and Leigh didn't believe that the signatories of at least one of these contractors, Pentler Holdings, were the people actually pulling the strings. They were dancing to someone else's tune. We suspected who it was, of course, but suspicion isn't proof. Whichever way they looked at it, all the roads led back to Pentler Holdings. 'Pentler is a vehicle for bribes and rewards,' Leigh said. 'If we can find out who is behind Pentler, then we have the key to Simandou.'

Pentler Holdings was the opaque shell company formed back in 2005 in the British Virgin Islands (BVI) and it was a party to some of the key 'contracts of corruption' around Simandou, so the first step was to check the BVI company registry. Being a secrecy jurisdiction, the only information you're likely to get from the BVI is the company name and the identity of the corporate registration agent that formed the company – but at least this would tell you if the company existed or not. Dan emailed the request to the BVI's company registry and a few days later received their response.

'Pentler and Matinda are real.' Dan was briefing Simon during one of their regular updates. It was a small first step. 'We know the companies exist, but we still don't know if the contracts themselves are genuine.' Leaked documents rarely carry a stamp of authenticity. Whether we could use them or not depended on whether we could back them up, and even then it was going to be a judgement call. This was why it was vital that Simon was kept up to date with the investigation's progress.

If our theories were correct, BSGR would need to create as much distance as possible between themselves and the contracts signed by Mamadie Touré, especially the one confirming receipt of US$2.4 million from Pentler. BSGR's 9 May 2013 statement, posted on its website, said: 'Lacking a permanent presence in Guinea, BSGR sought to work with Michael Noy, Avraham Lev Ran and Frédéric Cilins, who had extensive business operations in Guinea, which they subsequently established as Pentler Holdings.'

So was that the answer? Were these three men really the owners of Pentler Holdings?

It was a hot, wet, April day and Frédéric Cilins was sweating slightly as he made his way across the concourse of Florida's Jacksonville Airport. But it wasn't the heat that was bothering Cilins, or not that kind of heat anyway. As an old Africa hand, he was used to that. It was the third meeting here and the balding 50-year-old Frenchman walked fast towards the café. He knew the airport better than he would have liked by now; and he needed to conclude this deal, and fast, and then get the hell out.

The African woman was sitting at a table waiting for him. She ordered a cranberry juice while Cilins settled for a strawberry and apple mix. Cilins wasn't happy when he heard what had happened to the woman when she had gone to the immigration department.

'You won't believe what I have to tell you. I went to get my visa. I was waiting for the agent; they made me wait in an office. They made me wait a long time. Then I saw two people come in, a woman and a man, and they told me that they're FBI, that they're doing an investigation of bribes – of bribes from mining contracts in Guinea… and asked if had the documents. I said I have no documents. They said if I refuse to talk to them, they will give me a [subpoena]. They will bring me before a judge and Grand Jury and testify and give all documents to the Court.'

Cilins didn't like that. 'The documents, did you tell them that you had no documents?' Cilins asked anxiously.

'Yes.'

'We must destroy this, urgent, urgent, urgent. What I don't understand—'

'I think, Frédéric,' she broke in. 'It looks like the same document...that the US government is looking for. I do not know what to do.'

'You have to destroy everything there is – I told you that a long time ago – don't keep anything here, don't keep anything here, not even a photocopy.'

Panicked, Cilins asked the woman question after question about what the FBI knew. How had she come to talk to them? Did they know his name?

'You know there aren't 50 solutions,' he said finally. 'You have to destroy everything and deny it all.'

He asked her to burn the contracts. 'Everything that I am telling you comes directly from Beny,' he told her. 'He told me, "I want you to tell me, Frédéric, I want you to tell me that you have destroyed those papers."'

He was prepared to pay the woman handsomely. Very handsomely. Sitting in that simple café, Cilins offered her US$1 million dollars; US$200,000 up front, and a further US$800,000 when the deal was done.

In addition to destroying the contracts she needed to sign another document, which he placed in front of her. In so many words it said that she hadn't been bribed by the company Cilins was working for. She agreed, but for this she wanted some money immediately. Cilins promised US$50,000, which he'd bring two days later, 14 April 2013. She signed the document and they walked together to the airport's business centre to make a copy. Tidy paperwork is just as important for corrupt deals as legitimate ones, it seems.

Unfortunately for Cilins, FBI Special Agent Peter Kilpatrick's colleagues were observing his every move, including this meeting with their 'cooperating witness', who was wearing a wire. She was Mamadie Touré, the fourth wife of the late President Lansana Conté, and had already been arrested. The transcripts of this high-stakes conversation not only damned Cilins, but also contained wonderful mundanities that beset the players in their criminal deals.

Cilins began reading from a report from the law firm hired by the Guinean government to investigate the Simandou deal. The tape clearly picked up Cilins's voice as he did so. 'Frédéric Cilins moved part time to the Novotel in Conakry and [in the] name of BSGR, develops and implements a plan to enable BSGR to acquire the rights to Simandou,' he read. 'In order to get closer to the president's family, Frédéric Cilins is organizing a donation of pharmaceutical products to the Henriette Conté Foundation...'

'During a meeting attended by Frédéric Cilins, Roy Oron and three or four other representatives of BSGR, Oron gives President Conté a gold watch set with diamonds valued at US$60,000. BSGR sends a check without provision in the amount of US$10 million or US$7 million, according to the sources, to Mamadie Touré. BSGR promises a commission of US$2.5 million to Mamadie Touré, which will be paid to her if she manages to allow the company to acquire rights in the exploitation of Blocks 1 and 2 of Simandou. BSGR pays Frédéric Cilins a commission for services rendered.'

'I just give you the points where we are named, you and me, eh,' Cilins said to the woman as he continued to read the report of his own crimes.

'[Steinmetz] then developed links with Mamadie Touré, the fourth and youngest wife of the president. According to the source, the women of Conté were not very well organized and had only means of payment in cash, not using accounts abroad. Frédéric Cilins is a Franco-Israeli national who acts as an intermediary for Steinmetz in Guinea. He is deemed, according to source 1, to have details of the activities of Beny Steinmetz and the payments made by...representatives of BSGR.'

At this point Cilins's flow was interrupted as the waitress arrived and asked what they wanted.

'What do you want then?' Cilins translated for Touré.

'I do not know...Do they have a sandwich?'

'Do you have chicken with...er...?' Cilins asked the waitress.

'Chicken sandwich?' she asked.

'Chicken sandwich. Yeah. Make two of them, please.'

'It comes with lettuce and tomatoes,' the waitress said.

'Yes,' Cilins responded.

'Do you want to add cheese or mushrooms?' she pressed, evidently keen to provide the best service she could.

'Tu veux du fromage avec?' he asked Touré.

'Oui,' she replied.

'Yes, with cheese please,' he told the waitress.

'Cheddar? Swiss?'

'Cheddar.'

'Cheddar.'

'*Tu veux du coleslaw avec? Tu veux des frites, tu veux quoi avec – à côté?*' he asked Touré.

'*Oui, des frites.*'

'And the French fries, please,' he ordered.

'Okay. Do you want mayonnaise, honey mustard or barbecue sauce?'

'*Euh...Tu veux de la sauce avec? Mayonnaise, moutarde...*yes, mayonnaise. One with mayonnaise. Only one with mayonnaise.'

'Barbecue?' the waitress asked.

'No. Okay? Thank you.'

And with that, Cilins tried to pick up the thread again, as he read the litany of alleged offences in the law firm's report.

Frédéric Cilins was arrested as he left the airport with US$20,000 cash on his person. He was charged with 'tampering with a witness', 'destruction, alteration, and falsification of records in a federal investigation' and 'obstruction of a criminal investigation'. He was in big trouble: the first two charges each carried a maximum penalty of 20 years in prison.

Meanwhile BSGR's fightback, looking more implausible by the day, ground inexorably on. Mishcon de Reya and Powerscourt continued with their twin strategies of intimidation and obfuscation, but we smiled because we knew their job had got harder as Cilins's arrest in Florida sparked off another wave of press reports.

The FBI's indictment of Cilins is a publicly available document and I can recommend it as a good read. I was glued to it as page after drama-packed page captured Cilins's palpably rising anxiety levels, but the indictment kept one piece of information secret. Who was the person it simply identified as 'Co-Conspirator No.1'?

Ever since Dan's first press release on Simandou in November 2012, our tactics throughout this long-running saga had been to strategically release our findings to shatter BSGR's defences as they arose.

The proud executives of BSGR launched their Guinea operation in 2008 with a party in their new Guinean HQ. The guest list included members of the ruling elite and BSGR invited the local TV station, RTG, to film it. But the film was never shown on Guinean TV; belatedly someone realized the risks it posed and warned off journalists from airing it. But Dan had heard about the existence of the footage. He knew in his gut that this film could be important in joining some of the dots of the case, and he began to work his contacts to track it down. It didn't take him long.

'You've got to see this,' Dan said to me and Simon. He virtually press-ganged us into a small meeting room in the office. Dan opened his laptop and clicked 'play'. The blurry black-and-white footage depicted a presentation by a group of men seated behind a long table in a large and crowded room. All but one of them are white. The audience is African: dignitaries dressed in suits or the flowing robes of the national dress.

The lead presenter, a middle-aged executive with a South African accent, extols the virtues of his company's plan to mine Simandou. He is Marc Struik, then CEO of Mining and Metals for BSGR. His colleagues seated at the table include Roy Oron, BSGR's CEO, and Asher Avidan, the company's president. Translations from English to French are being made on camera by a balding man wearing a grey shirt with a button-down collar and a matching tie. Frédéric Cilins. Steinmetz wasn't there, but his top brass were, in force. Their mood seemed to veer between triumphalist, smug and somehow uneasy.

The film jumped to an external shot of BSGR's new offices, located in a white two-storey villa, a large white banner emblazoned with the company's name draped crookedly from the balcony. The equatorial night had fallen as guests spilled out of the villa and congregated under a series of awnings for a reception. A party, as it turned out, to celebrate a prospective and massively lucrative mining deal and the company's first foray into this country. The shoulder-held camera walks the viewer through the crowd and among the businessmen working the room, ingratiating themselves with the Africans that outnumber them.

There is no doubt that the guest of honour cuts an entrance. The large African woman, wearing a flowing white national costume with an elaborate matching headdress and heavy gold jewellery, sweeps into the room flanked by members of the Presidential Guard in their red berets and camouflage fatigues, followed by a

retinue of advisers and hangers-on. She brings with her the unmis-
takable aura of power. She bestows her wide and humourless smile
as only the powerful can. She nods left and right and shakes hands
with those she knows, while her brother, Ibrahima Touré – identified as the vice president of BSGR Guinea – guides her stately
way through the crowd towards the group of BSGR officials. Her
brother introduces her to each one by name and title, which seem
to impress him more than his sister, and she shakes their hands too
and moves on in regal procession.

The woman is Mamadie Touré.

Our jaws dropped to the floor as we realized the critical importance of this film.

'BSGR said they had never dealt with Mamadie Touré,' Dan said.

'Are we sure it's her?' Simon asked. Dan confirmed we were, not
least because she was with her brother in the film. 'And Cilins was
there, right at the beginning,' Simon mused.

'It seems you've pulled out the rug from under them,' I smiled. It
was hard to over-emphasize how incredibly important this evidence
was. Coming just six days after Cilins and Touré's fateful meeting in
Jacksonville Airport, this video put a lie to BSGR's claims that they
had never met or dealt with Mamadie Touré, had not hired Cilins
and hadn't made any illegal payments. We thought it was unfair to
keep the footage to ourselves, so we put it on our website under the
headline, 'Damning video and contracts show BSGR was lying in
Guinea mining scandal.'

Powerscourt's Ian Middleton, who had evidently drawn the short
straw and become Beny Steinmetz's spokesman, went into action.
He rebuffed reporters' questions regarding the FBI investigation into
BSGR as 'a desperate smear campaign'. I thought that was ironic
given that this was exactly what Powerscourt ('Our clients' success
is our success') were being paid to do themselves.

Powerscourt adopted the tactic that if PR doesn't work, get heavy.
Questions from the *Guardian* about US investigations into Beny
Steinmetz drew a threat of libel action from Middleton. It's easy to
say but, if you think about it, it is a remarkable departure from the
usual role of a PR man. Within hours of his warnings, the *Guardian*
received a threatening letter from Mishcon de Reya. With a bizarre
and rather ill-judged denial, Middleton added that 'Cilins is not an
agent for Steinmetz's company.'

*

Meanwhile the *Guardian* and countless other media organizations began to find themselves at the sharp end of Mishcon's legal
threats. Mining.com, a respected online mining-industry news site
that had got the story right, nevertheless bent under the pressure
and published Mishcon's rebuttals of a June 2013 article about the
corruption surrounding Simandou.

Mining.com: '3. The FBI probe has uncovered all sorts of
shadowy dealings including a US$2 million payment to Conté's
fourth wife Mamadie Touré (her brother Ibrahima Sory Touré was
a VP for BSGR in Guinea) to help advance the Steinmetz cause.'

Mishcon de Reya: 'Wrong: The FBI has "uncovered" nothing: the
allegations made are based on forged documents. The inaccuracy of
this sentence is illustrated by the fact that you are unaware of the
identities of the individuals, for example, Mamadie Touré was not
the fourth wife of Lansana Conté.'

And...

Mining.com: '4. Earlier French citizen Frédéric Cilins and BSGR's
agent in the country was arrested in Florida for tampering with
evidence – that is, destroying documents relating to the Steinmetz-
Conté deal – and improperly influencing witnesses.'

Mishcon de Reya: 'Wrong: Mr Frédéric Cilins is not an agent of
BSGR. The FBI probe has made allegations against Mr Cilins and a
number of charges have been brought against him in the US, and at
present these allegations remain as such.'

Mining.com had been scared into censoring the truth on an issue
of key public interest – there are not many organizations that can
afford to fight a libel suit in the UK courts, especially one against
a foe as powerful as BSGR. But I took my hat off to the website's
editor. Whether intentionally or not, the decision to repeat their
allegations alongside the replacement text insisted upon by Mishcon
only served to emphasize Mishcon's and their client's desperation,
and did more to highlight BSGR's playbook than the original article
must have done. Especially given the exposé we were about to come
out with.

Dan and Leigh had been exploring avenue after avenue trying to
find out who lay behind Pentler Holdings, but were met by dead

end after dead end. Increasingly frustrated, they pressed their network of sources in their efforts to unravel the company's corporate structure. Finally, they found what they were looking for: a series of documents that laid bare many of the secrets of Pentler Holdings. Dan called Simon and me with the news. Like the film, it was a game changer because it was information no one else had.

Pentler Holdings was set up in the British Virgin Islands on 28 October 2005 and was owned by a company called Onyx Financial Advisors, which held all Pentler's 50,000 shares. And we knew that Onyx was closely linked to BSGR. Dan and Leigh examined Pentler's certificate of authorized capital, which bore the signature of one of Onyx's directors, a Belgian national called Sandra Merloni-Horemans. A quick look at the entry for Onyx Financial Advisors on the Companies House website in London showed that Merloni-Horemans was also a director of BSGR. Onyx's CEO, Dag Cramer, was also a BSGR director and headed up two other Steinmetz group companies. Companies House recorded that Onyx was originally incorporated in 2005 as BSG Management Services Ltd before changing name in 2011. Its one hundred shares were held by Onyx Financial Advisors SA in Geneva.

Despite the fact that BSGR had made more denials than St Peter about Cilins's true role in the affair, they had been right about one key fact: Frédéric Cilins was indeed a director of Pentler Holdings. Thus Onyx's ownership of Pentler, coupled with Cilins's directorial role, connected BSGR with the bribes paid by Cilins to Mamadie Touré. The net was closing in.

Adding to the implausibility of BSGR's assertion that Pentler was simply owned by three men called Michael Noy, Frédéric Cilins and Avraham Lev Ran, Lev Ran wasn't authorized to act on the company's behalf until 13 February 2006, when he received power of attorney signed by Onyx and BSGR director Merloni-Horemans. It was just a week later that he used that authority to transfer 33 per cent of Pentler to Mamadie Touré, and it was in the following month that Pentler acquired 17.65 per cent of BSGR's Simandou holding. One of the final pieces of evidence that tied Pentler to Onyx, and therefore to BSGR, was almost comically mundane. The business cards of BSGR's president Asher Avidan and Onyx's CEO Dag Cramer both bore the same address: 7 Old Park Lane, in London's Mayfair.

These details obtained by Dan and Leigh destroyed two of BSGR's key defences: that Cilins had nothing to do with them and that they had never had any dealings with Mamadie Touré. It was a turning point.

Leigh wrote to David Clark at BSGR asking various questions regarding Pentler Holdings. If the response from Mishcon's head of Private, James Libson, was anything to go by, Dan and Leigh's strategy worked. They were obviously very unpleasantly surprised that we had pierced the corporate veil. '[Your questions] relate in part to confidential information that could not have been obtained except direct from one or two Onyx employees or from its computer systems,' he wrote. 'Please explain, as a matter of urgency, how you obtained information about Onyx and any connection with Pentler Holdings Limited and Margali Management.'

The letter amused Dan – 'We didn't obtain any hacked material, but to me, Libson's questions seemed to be a tacit admission that we had got it right' – and our press release, 'New evidence ties BSGR to company behind Guinea mine bribery', went down the wires on 14 August 2014.

Dag Cramer evidently took a sanguine approach when he copied us into what I assume was meant to be a purely internal email. His advice was perhaps misplaced:

Best thing is to ignore them.

Regards

Dag

Dag Cramer
CEO Onyx Financial Advisors

Later that year Mishcon contacted various media outlets, warning them against publishing 'hacked' material. BSGR is a highly litigious company and has very deep pockets. A defamation case in the UK courts can run up millions of pounds in costs whether you win or lose. But no one expected the counterattack that followed.

The next phase in this story had begun in 2012 and had been rumbling along in the background throughout the events I just described, so please excuse this brief jump back in time. On 6 December 2012, less than a month after our first press release raising concerns about potential corruption in the Simandou deal, we received a letter from Beny Steinmetz himself – the only direct communication we have ever had from him. Just two or three lines long and signed with a scrawled 'BS', the letter requested that we provide all the information we possessed about him personally, especially that which had been used in our communications with George Soros and with a company called Veracity Worldwide. He enclosed a cheque for £10 to cover our costs, probably the smallest legal bill he incurred since he took on Simandou. Part of Mishcon's strategy became clear, and it was clever.

This letter was a subject access request (SAR) filed according to the UK Data Protection Act (DPA). The DPA governs how organizations and the government use and store an individual's personal information, for example companies using data for marketing purposes. Every UK citizen has the right to ask a company or indeed an organization like ours what information they hold on them. But Steinmetz was trying to use the act for a very different purpose: to shut down our public-interest reporting into the corruption scandal that surrounded Simandou and the numerous serious crimes associated with it, on the basis that we were infringing his right to privacy. This was the first time ever that the DPA had been used for this purpose. Mishcon's and Steinmetz's strategy was to use the Data Protection Act – which is extremely pro-privacy and therefore a useful tool for those wanting to shut down critical speech.

The disclosure of this information could expose the identity of our sources who had taken immense risks to provide it to us, and the protection of sources is one of the golden tenets of journalism, whether you write for an NGO or a media organization. And for good reason. In this case, given the amount of money at stake coupled with the history of violence and the poor rule of law in Guinea, this had the potential to be a life-threatening issue and we had to take it seriously. This is one of the reasons that I never ask our teams the identity of their sources. If I don't know who they are, then no one can force me to expose them.

Tensions were running high as Simon, Leigh, Dan and I discussed the implications of this threat with our in-house lawyer, Nicola

Namdjou. If this case went against us, we would be legally obliged to hand over the information, with serious implications if we failed to do so. Leigh was in no doubt about his views: 'If people ask you to hand over your data there's only one answer. Fuck off.'

On the plus side we felt that Steinmetz's strategy showed that he was feeling the heat from the numerous investigations that were getting ever closer to the core of his Simandou operation. It seemed to show that Steinmetz was losing appetite for the libel suit and was looking for other solutions. But on the negative, if Steinmetz won the case it could set a legal precedent that would threaten investigative journalism not just in the UK but in Europe and beyond: think investigations by human-rights groups into slavery, or into corruption in the public services, or scandals in the NHS. Losing this case would benefit only those with something to hide, and it would be a huge win for the shadow network.

So now we found ourselves fighting two battles. One to pursue our investigations into Simandou, and the other to defend our rights to talk about the case at all. We were in no doubt about our choice. Having enjoyed a good holiday break, Dan wrote to Steinmetz on 10 January 2013, stating that we didn't hold any information on him personally and had never heard of Veracity Worldwide, and therefore we were compliant with the DPA. Dan added that any investigations we were carrying out that touched on BSGR would be subject to Section 32 of the DPA.

Section 32 provides an exemption to the usual rules and applies to information held for journalistic purposes – in a nutshell, information that is intended for publication and that is in the public interest. Our work has always been journalistic and many of our key investigative staff, including Dan and Leigh, are professional journalists. But Global Witness is not a conventional media organization and Mishcon's strategy rested on this point: could a non-profit investigative NGO be considered a journalistic organization? There was everything to play for and an awful lot to lose.

By return of post, on 11 January 2013 Mishcon followed up Steinmetz's request with the first of what was to become a long chain of letters replete with legal arguments about why we were obliged under the DPA to provide the information Steinmetz wanted. One of their letters stated that 'Global Witness's work is campaigning and investigative. It is not engaged in journalism. It

seeks to influence journalism.' Under the wise guidance of our new
in-house lawyer Nicola Namdjou, we hired one of London's top
barristers, Anya Proops, and continued to refuse to comply, and
waited. Eventually Steinmetz and his cohorts did what we thought
they would do.

In February 2013, Mishcon referred the complaint to the
Information Commissioner's Office (ICO), the government entity
set up under the Data Protection Act to protect information rights.
Steinmetz had long maintained that he played no role in the running
of his eponymous company, as illustrated by one of the other retrac-
tions Mishcon had insisted upon from Mining.com: 'Mr Steinmetz...
is not a director of BSGR and acts solely as a consultant to the business.' A useful fiction enabling him to distance himself from company
affairs when it suited him. However, the current situation evidently
didn't suit him, so on his behalf Mishcon did a reverse ferret. In the
submission to the ICO, they stated that: 'Mr Steinmetz is in fact a
consultant to these businesses, however, it is broadly perceived in the
public domain that these companies are interchangeable with Mr
Steinmetz personally.' The goalposts had shifted.

More used to ruling on data breaches by UK marketing firms, the
hard-pressed ICO staff found themselves propelled into the middle
of a major international corruption scandal under the harsh glare of
international media attention. In July, Steinmetz's stooges at BSGR,
David Clark, Dag Cramer and Sandra Merloni-Horemans, also
filed subject access requests with Global Witness. Nicola, Simon,
Charmian and I met regularly with Dan and Leigh to get the latest
updates on the ICO case and the progress of the investigation. We
needed to be very well informed and rigorous in our commitment
to winning this case.

The ICO's initial ruling on the complaint came a month later and
didn't go entirely our way. It said that Global Witness may well not
have complied with the DPA, but noted that in addition to claiming
journalistic exemption, our interest was in BSGR the company, not
in Beny Steinmetz the man. The ICO told Steinmetz that they would
not be taking any regulatory action against Global Witness, but that
we should review our processes. A slap on the wrist.

But now, with the implications for free speech and investigative
reporting more widely, we were adamant that this was an issue
we must pursue. For us it wasn't just about Simandou now. The

wider press was taking an interest as the outcome of this case would affect journalism throughout the UK, and we received many messages of support. This was about free speech and our democratic system. We hadn't asked to be thrust into the ring, but now we were here we might as well slug it out. We continued to withhold the information Steinmetz wanted. Their next salvo wasn't long in coming.

In December 2013, Steinmetz and his allies turned up the dial and filed a claim against us in the High Court in London. As their faithful PR hounds at Powerscourt put it in a press release: 'Human-rights legal action filed in London against Global Witness'. I felt it was somehow ironic that a crew who had conspired to steal US$2.5 billion from one of the poorest countries in the world was now feeling precious about the abuse of their human rights. Undeterred, we decided to enjoy the Christmas break and it wasn't until January 2014 that Simon issued our response: 'The case filed by BSGR officials is a threat to freedom of speech...it risks stripping journalists and NGOs of vital safeguards aimed at protecting sources and reporting freely on matters of public interest.'

In support of the case, in his witness statement submitted to the High Court, Mishcon's James Libson stated that: 'The Claimants [Steinmetz, Cramer and Merloni-Horemans] contend that the Defendant [Global Witness] does not process data "only" for the purposes of journalism. The Defendant is a company established with the purpose of campaigning. Any activity undertaken by the Defendant that could arguably be described as journalistic is carried out with the aim of furthering its campaigning goals. The Defendant is not a newspaper, a media organisation or even an online commentator. The fact that it publishes reports and material on its website does not make it a "journalist" within the ordinary and natural meaning of that word.'

They probably thought that compelling argument put the lid on it. However, I remembered the first ever correspondence we received from Mishcon's Mr Libson threatening us on behalf of the banker from the Kyrgyz Republic, which included the following line: 'As experienced investigative journalists you will be aware...' It would seem that Libson's witness statement contained a bare-faced contradiction with his previous evaluation of the role we played.

We had become part of the story. Coverage of the Simandou deal now focused not just on BSGR but also on 'one of their loudest critics', as the *Financial Times* had described us. Our defence argued that the case amounted to an attempt to stifle reporting on a major corruption scandal and was an abuse of British law. The wheels of justice moved slowly, and we would have to wait a year to learn the outcome.

The High Court referred the case back to the ICO and their decision came in December 2014. 'Israeli billionaire fails to silence critic over mine deal,' reported the *Financial Times*. Reuters followed with 'Data office says NGO has journalist exemption, rejects Steinmetz claim.' These were just two of a swathe of reports in the mainstream media and specialist legal and mining publications and on the websites of law firms, freedom of speech advocates and human-rights groups. Leigh told the *FT* that the decision was 'a victory for press freedom because it defines journalists by what they do, not whom they work for'. We had won.

Winning the case was only a stepping stone in our campaign to expose the scandal of Simandou, but this legal battle had struck an important blow against the shadow network and exposed the behind-the-scenes activities of their advisers. They might argue that the law is impartial, but we knew that how long and at what level you can maintain a legal fight depended on your bank balance; and in this Steinmetz had a wide advantage. Their gambit to remove key protections for organizations that investigate scandals in public life had failed. For Steinmetz and the companies and individuals he was associated with, it was the first in a long line of legal setbacks that had significant implications for him and the company that bore his name. But it was those associated with him who began to pay the price first.

In March 2014, Frédéric Cilins, ignominiously arrested after his last fateful meeting with Mamadie Touré in Jacksonville Airport, was sentenced to two years in prison for bribery and obstructing a criminal investigation. In US attorney Preet Bharara's words, 'In an effort to prevent the federal authorities from learning the truth, Cilins paid a witness for her silence and to destroy key documents. Today, Cilins learned that no one can manipulate justice.'

Perhaps Steinmetz was going to have to learn the same lesson himself. Like water trickling through a crack in the dam, Cilins's arrest was the start of a deluge. Just as Rio Tinto's Tom Albanese had six years previously, Beny Steinmetz now found himself standing on shaky ground. Only a month after Cilins was led away from Jacksonville Airport by the FBI, the Guinean government cancelled BSGR's and Vale's rights to Simandou.

Vale, now owners of a US$2.5 billion 51 per cent stake in nothing at all, took BSGR to an international arbitration court to recoup its costs, including the US$500 million it had paid up front. Was the Deal of the Century really dead?

Well, the honeymoon was certainly over. Only a few years before, Beny Steinmetz was basking in glory when he got hold of Simandou. I imagine him accepting the adulation of his peers and journalists alike, like a Roman emperor receiving tribute for another successful conquest – a testament to his business acumen and his strategic nous. But now it was all turning to ashes in front of his eyes. Many lesser men may have broken under this strain, but Steinmetz pushed himself off the ropes and began to fight back with all the means at his disposal: money, influence, dirty tricks and, probably more than anything, the sheer will to win. But his allies were still paying the price.

Mahmoud Thiam, the ex-UBS banker and former minister of mines and geology in the Republic of Guinea – the man who had said, 'If the corruption allegations were not so insulting, I would find them funny' – didn't find it remotely funny when he was arrested at his home in Manhattan in December 2016 and charged with laundering US$8.5 million paid to him in a separate corruption case. Thiam had funnelled the money via Hong Kong bank accounts to the US, where he splashed out on luxury property, including a US$3.5 million estate in Dutchess County, New York, and his children's school fees. Although the arrest was not related to Simandou, his defiant rejection of the Technical Committee's allegations of corruption – 'To pretend that I indulged in such practices is absolutely false' – now rang rather hollow. He was sentenced to seven years in jail.

A week after Thiam was picked up by the police in New York, Steinmetz himself was arrested in Israel. He appeared in court on suspicion of paying bribes in relation to the Simandou deal, as well as on suspicion of money laundering. The court ordered him to be held under house arrest for two weeks and his Israeli and French passports were confiscated. In August, he was rearrested and questioned by Israel police's Lahav 433 division, along with four other businessmen, about the forging of contracts in order to launder money. One of these men was Asher Avidan, the former head of BSGR Guinea. In a statement, Steinmetz complained that he was the victim of a 'political war' that he claimed was being financed by the investor and philanthropist George Soros.

But the only criminal charges actually filed against Steinmetz came from the public prosecutor in Geneva, one of Beny's home bases. The Swiss authorities had been investigating BSGR's role in Simandou since 2013, when they raided the offices of Onyx Financial Advisors and seized a haul of documents, but it wasn't until August 2019 that they charged Steinmetz and two unnamed associates with 'bribing foreign officials and forgery' and more specifically with paying US$10 million in 'bribes to one of the wives of former president Lansana Conté with a view to ousting a competitor and granting BSGR mining rights in the area of Simandou'. If convicted, Steinmetz and his associates would face between two and ten years in prison.

Following the Guinean government's cancellation of BSGR's and Vale's rights to Simandou in April 2014, Rio Tinto filed a racketeering claim against the two companies at the US District Court for the Southern District of New York, seeking 'compensatory, consequential, exemplary and punitive damages' and alleging that they had conspired to steal Simandou from them, with Vale being 'at the heart of a conspiracy'. Steinmetz was named in the case, as was former mines minister Mahmoud Thiam, who, Rio said, had received a US$200 million bribe from Steinmetz. The case was dismissed in November 2015 on a technicality – Rio's suit had fallen outside the statute of limitations.

Also in April 2014, following Guinea's cancellation of Vale's and BSGR's mining rights, Steinmetz sought arbitration at the International Centre for Settlement of Investment Disputes in Paris to get this decision revoked. This case rolled on for almost five years and all the indications were that BSGR was heading for a major defeat, but then something extraordinary happened. In February 2019, the government of Guinea and BSGR stunned observers by suddenly agreeing to end the dispute, in a deal brokered by former French president Nicolas Sarkozy, still one of the most powerful politicians in France. BSGR crowed that it had been cleared. Beny Steinmetz told Bloomberg: 'We were enemies. Now we are friends and partners with the Guinean government. We have both put aside the past and BSGR and its employees and advisers have been vindicated.' This was a little premature.

In April 2019, the three arbitration judges in the international court case brought by Vale awarded them a whopping US$1.25 billion. BSGR had indeed bribed Mamadie Touré, by offering her shares to secure her 'assistance in influencing [former] President [Lansana] Conté', they ruled. 'BSGR made a false representation in declaring that there had not been any bribery of Mme Touré.' In unusually outspoken remarks, the judges said it would be wrong for them 'to accept bribery as a fact of life in some countries and keep eyes shut when faced with allegations of corruption'.

But by this time, perhaps having seen the writing on the wall, BSGR had taken the precaution of calling in the administrators, presumably to protect the company should the case go against them. Steinmetz, who had risen so high just a few years before, had, like Icarus, flown too close to the sun and had plummeted back to Earth. But unlike Icarus, Steinmetz survived and he still had a few tricks left up his sleeve.

Now that he had buried the hatchet with Alpha Condé's government, Beny Steinmetz entered into a new mining deal with a company called Niron PLC, registered just nine months earlier in the UK. Its director was Sir Michael Davis, nicknamed 'Mick the Miner', then treasurer of Britain's Conservative Party and the former head of mining giant Xstrata. Under this deal, Niron obtained the rights to mine Zogota, a block south of Simandou and previously withdrawn from BSGR over corruption claims. Steinmetz was a co-investor. The deal also required Guinea to withdraw from criminal proceedings targeting Steinmetz in Switzerland and to promise not to make any 'disparaging remarks' against Steinmetz or BSGR for ten years.

A quick search of the records at Companies House to find out who controlled Niron led straight to a dead end. Niron's single share belonged to a secretly owned firm in the Bahamas, Global Special Opportunities Limited (GSOL). There was no clue as to who owned this company or, therefore, as to who owned Niron. Once again, a sizeable chunk of Guinea's iron-ore reserves was under the control of an anonymously owned company.

*

The story of Simandou is not over. Twenty-three years after Rio Tinto first obtained Blocks 1 to 4, the lure of the world's richest untapped deposit of iron ore has attracted both blue-chip companies and a gang of adventurers, like sharks to the carcass of a whale. Simandou created a feeding frenzy as, crazed by greed, these 'minovores' seemed to lose their sense of reality and began an internecine struggle, taking chunks out of each other while Simandou, floating benignly in its sea of green mountains, lay untouched. But that is about to change.

Blocks 1 and 2 of Simandou, obtained by BSGR in a blaze of glory and then lost again, are now being developed by a joint venture between SMB, a Chinese-backed consortium, and the Guinean government. SMB says production will begin by 2025. Meanwhile, in 2011 Rio Tinto paid the Guinean government US$700 million in order to retain their hold on Blocks 3 and 4, and have gone into partnership with the Aluminium Corporation of China, Chinalco.

So it would seem that the Guinean government may after all these years profit from Simandou while China has got its hands on the world's richest deposit of iron ore. Perhaps the overall winner is the owner of Global Special Opportunities Ltd, but only that person together with a small coterie of other members of the shadow network knows who he or she is. Though one can always speculate.

The other big winners during the ebbs and flows of this tragedy seem to be the lawyers, and more business was coming their way. Despite the withdrawal of the Guinean government, the criminal proceedings in Switzerland ground inexorably on.

On 11 January 2021, in the company of his lawyer, the flamboyant Marc Bonnant, Beny Steinmetz arrived for the first day of his trial in Geneva. Instead of his habitual open-necked shirt, he was wearing a blue suit with a matching tie, and his mouth was set as he turned his tanned face away from the press photographers waiting for him. Corruption trials are a rarity in Switzerland, and this one was big news.

Taking over from the photographers outside, the court artist's sketches brought to life the excitement inside the court room, capturing Steinmetz and his fellow defendants, Frédéric Cilins – back in the dock once more – and Sandra Merloni-Horemans, whose name had appeared again and again on the documents behind the now slightly tattered-looking Deal of the Century. They were charged with the bribery of foreign public officials, and more particularly with paying at least US$8.5 million to Mamadie Touré.

The *Tribune de Genève* provided a day-by-day, blow-by-blow account of the trial, noting that 'Global Witness...covered the case in near real time, to the point of making it an emblem of corruption in the raw materials industry.'

Steinmetz's defence team trotted out the usual denials, the same arguments they had been peddling since the deal first hit the headlines: Beny Steinmetz was just an adviser to BSGR, a mere consultant who had no control and didn't make any of the decisions. 'I am not BSGR, I am not Pentler,' Steinmetz told the president of the tribunal. 'I am not making the decisions, it is BSGR.'

'He does not exercise any de facto authority,' Marc Bonnant told the tribunal. 'Beny Steinmetz had neither the legal nor the factual capacity to order corrupt payments...he is everywhere because he is nowhere, a bit like God.' But in this case God was in trouble.

The two prosecutors, Yves Bertossa and Caroline Babel Casutt, weren't having any of it. 'We know that Mamadie received an amount of around 10 million, but it's magic, it's magic corruption, via the board, managers, partners,' Bertossa told the tribunal. 'No one responsible, no culprit: BSGR is a "headless group", "moving forward on its own" with no real physical leader,' he railed. In one courtroom sketch published by the *Tribune de Genève*, the grey-suited Bertossa leans forward over his desk, hands gripping the edge of the dock, as he delivers a withering array of evidence to counter the defence's arguments. He described the Simandou deal as a 'textbook case of corruption' and an 'insidious evil that gnaws at humanity'.

On 22 January, having heard the arguments roll back and forth over the preceding two weeks, the president of the tribunal, Alexandra Banna, delivered her judgement. 'The payments [to Mamadie Touré] were the result of a one sole wish: to corrupt the Guinean president,' she said. 'Steinmetz knows all the projects of the group perfectly and is very involved in the financial aspects [...]

He is personally involved, informed, seen inside and out as the head of BSGR, the number 1 or the boss. [...] He is involved in all the important stages of the Guinean project.'

She sentenced Steinmetz to five years in prison. Cilins got three and a half, while Merloni-Horemans received a suspended sentence. Steinmetz's lawyer, Marc Bonnant, immediately announced that they would appeal 'to the Federal Court and to God if necessary'. Bonnant seems to talk a lot about God. Steinmetz has indeed filed an appeal, but it remains to be seen whether the final outcome will be decided in the Swiss Federal Court or perhaps by some more celestial body.

Meanwhile, Beny Steinmetz's website, the homepage of which trumpets his 'Career Milestones and Social Vision', makes no mention of this latest milestone in his career.

6

SLICK OPERATORS

Dan Etete's criminal career began long before his conviction in a French court for money laundering. A man with a taste for the finer things in life, his most promising caper began in April 1998, when he held one of Nigeria's top jobs, minister of petroleum, during the brutal and astonishingly corrupt dictatorship of General Sani Abacha. It began with the establishment of a company called Malabu Oil and Gas. Unlike many companies mentioned in this book, this one was not set up in a secrecy jurisdiction; its owners simply used false names.

Just a few days after the company's creation, Dan Etete used his ministerial power to award Malabu the rights to Nigeria's richest offshore oil block, lying 2,000m under the sea south of the Niger Delta. At the stroke of his pen, this newly formed company, with no employees, assets or experience, became the owner of Oil Prospecting Licence No. 245 (OPL 245), with the promise of over half a billion barrels of oil.

Only a few companies in the world possess the assets and know-how to extract oil from 2km under the sea: the oil majors like Exxon, Chevron, Total, BP, Eni and Royal Dutch Shell, which are among the biggest companies in the world. Shell first shipped oil from Nigeria in 1958. Having navigated the transition from a British colony to independence and the vagaries of the various regimes that followed, Shell knew how Nigeria worked, and it was with Shell that Malabu entered into a partnership in 2001 in order to monetize the wealth lying under the sea. This 'farmout' agreement gave Shell 40 per cent equity in the asset, and the company began an exploration of the block. And, like the seismic blasts Shell's prospectors bounced off the seabed, the shock waves created by Malabu's ownership of OPL 245 would expose the industry's complex strata of corruption.

*

Abacha's dictatorship had died with him in 1998. President Olusegun Obasanjo came to power the following year and life for Dan Etete all of a sudden began to get more complicated.

Obasanjo inherited a country in a parlous state, despite the fact that over US$300 billion of oil had been pumped out of Nigeria since the 1950s, much of it by Shell. While this natural wealth helped to fuel the booming economies of Europe and the US, Nigeria had very little to show for it. Although it was Africa's biggest economy, 70 per cent of the population – some 84 million people – were living below the poverty line.

It didn't take the new government long to sniff the whiff of corruption that hung over the awarding of a collection of oil blocks to various ministers who served under Abacha, including OPL 245; and in 2001 Malabu's, and by extension Shell's rights to the block were cancelled. Shell got the entirety of the block back in 2002, although exactly how is unclear. But their success was short-lived.

Malabu took the government to court and in 2006 the block was handed back to them. Shell countersued and so began years of suit and countersuit. Interest in commercial disputes like this is generally confined to industry insiders, but it was these court cases that shone a light, albeit a dim one, on the legal tussles surrounding OPL 245.

Global Witness puts a lot of store in the power of a hunch. This particular hunch began as a small spark that would smoulder for a few years before igniting into an investigation that has so far taken us more than a decade. An investigation that has the potential to change the face of the oil industry. The hunch belonged to one of our new staff members, Diarmid O'Sullivan. He suspected the legal wranglings over OPL 245 hid something far more interesting than a simple commercial dispute.

Diarmid came to us following a long stint as an investigative journalist. A bespectacled, bookish-looking guy of medium height, Diarmid has an infectious enthusiasm for unearthing secrets. Noting that the life of an investigator is not all glamour but often seemingly mundane, Diarmid said he found 'a real truffle-hunting pleasure in rummaging through lots of corporate documents – looking for gaps and inconsistencies'.

It was Diarmid's research into the licensing rounds of various oil blocks that brought him to what turned out to be a fateful conference in Abuja, Nigeria in September 2008. This was an early gathering of the Extractive Industries Transparency Initiative (EITI) – the international anti-corruption mechanism that we'd played a major role in creating. Nigeria had been the first country to sign up to EITI.

'I was on a panel with Basil Omiyi, the chairman of Shell in Nigeria, and I took the opportunity to ask him what was going on with OPL 245,' Diarmid told us. 'No one was admitting what everyone suspected, that Malabu Oil and Gas was probably owned by Dan Etete, and that he had awarded the block to himself when he was minister for petroleum under Abacha's dictatorship. But when I asked him, Omiyi just gave me some anodyne answer, smothering everything in foam.'

Diarmid knew he would meet Omiyi again that year in London and so he tried again, this time in a conference room in the Houses of Parliament 'full of fixers and tame diplomats'. But Diarmid didn't find out anything more from Omiyi about OPL 245. He returned to the office without any better answers: 'They talk bullshit to you. They don't lie. They go for ambiguity and evasion.'

Other work piled up at Global Witness and reluctantly we pushed OPL 245 to one side.

However, Diarmid kept a weather eye on the deal as rumours about Shell's continued interest in the block refused to be put to bed. Two years later, in December 2010, he went to another EITI board meeting: 'In a drab conference centre in a cold, unprepossessing corner of Brussels, I met a lawyer, Keith Ruddock [the general counsel for Shell Upstream]. I took him to one side and said, "You can't do the OPL deal because it's going to be dodgy." I was trying to establish whether Shell knew in advance that there was a corruption risk. But Ruddock gave me an evasive response.'

Almost immediately after talking to Diarmid, Ruddock wrote to one of his colleagues back at head office, Guus Klusener:

I was buttonholed on this by a number of revenue-trans-parency related NGOs...they had read about a possible transaction in the press and were keen to be reassured that

Chief E [Dan Etete] would not benefit from this deal. I was noncommittal on whether any deal was in prospect but indicated that Shell was indeed aware of Chief E's history and would conduct its activities accordingly.

He added, 'They were clearly unaware of the details of this proposed transaction (at least I hope so) but it is an indication of how closely this deal will be scrutinized.' How we know what Ruddock wrote comes later, but Diarmid was scathing. 'These fucking weasels know fucking well what's going on, but they just stonewall and stonewall and stonewall.'

He knew we needed to break down that wall. What broke it was the Agaev case.

Ednan Agaev, a former Soviet diplomat and intelligence officer, had been introduced to Etete as someone with good connections to Shell. Etete needed to find a buyer for OPL 245 and in late 2008 he engaged Agaev's company, International Legal Consulting (ILC) to find one. Despite the ongoing court battle with Etete, Shell were still flirting with him to regain the oil block. Then another man entered the scene. From a prominent Nigerian family, Emeka Obi, a former banker, was well versed in local conditions. Obi already had dealings with another oil major: Eni, Italy's largest company, and they already owned another block in Nigeria. Together Agaev and Obi opened negotiations with Shell, and then also with Eni some months later.

The stakes were extremely high. If Agaev and Obi pulled off the deal, their commissions would run into the tens of millions of dollars. But this job was not going to be plain sailing.

By all accounts, Dan Etete is a very difficult man to deal with. An unpredictable, unreliable, capricious and corrupt liar would seem to sum it up, and the negotiations with the two oil majors were already protracted when the proverbial straw broke the camel's back. In late 2010, Mohammed Sani Abacha, the son of the deceased Nigerian dictator, announced that he was co-owner of Malabu alongside Etete; he also told the two oil majors that if they did a deal that excluded him, he would sue. This was getting too complicated: the son of a dead dictator, the grotesquely unreliable Etete, the evident corruption behind Etete's ownership of OPL 245 and the threat of seemingly endless litigation were making the oil majors nervous, and they began looking for other solutions.

In a variation from the usual job description, Nigeria's attorney general, Mohammed Bello Adoke, began to broker an alternative deal that might just find a way through the labyrinth of litigation. Over the dying months of 2010 and into 2011, Adoke hosted numerous meetings in his office that brought together representatives of Shell, Eni, Malabu, the Nigerian government and a man called Alhaji Aliyu Abubakar, known locally as 'Mr Corruption'. The negotiations were cloaked in secrecy.

The announcement that Shell and Eni had become the proud owners of OPL 245 came in July 2011 and the companies could finally look forward to reaping the rewards from extracting the block's half a billion barrels of oil from under the sea. Dan Etete had evidently got what he wanted, but Ednan Agaev and Emeka Obi ended up with nothing. The tens of millions of dollars in commissions they had worked for had disappeared when Attorney General Adoke's parallel negotiations had prevailed. But it was Agaev and Obi who had brought Shell and Eni together in the first place, and they meant to get the money they believed they were owed.

In 2012, Agaev's International Legal Consulting (ILC) brought an arbitration case against Malabu Oil and Gas in New York's Supreme Court. ILC claimed that Malabu had breached their agreement with them: that in return for finding a buyer for the rights of OPL 245, ILC would be paid a 6 per cent commission on the price of the sale – a cool US$65 million. They claimed that they had done their job, found a buyer and were owed the money.

The documents submitted to the court became part of the public record and shone a light on how the deal had finally been done. Until then, it had been a closely guarded secret. The Italian company Eni had transferred the purchase price of US$1,092,040,000 into an escrow account in the name of the Nigerian government held at the London Wall branch of JP Morgan. Then this exact amount of money was transferred straight out again, into a depository account in the interest of Malabu Oil and Gas.

The New York court determined that because the money in question was held in the JP Morgan account in London, and not New York, the deal was a London deal. The court told Agaev that it had no jurisdiction and so he took his case to arbitration in London. This time, he lost and the US$65 million he had been hoping to get his hands on was returned to Malabu. For Agaev this was frustrating to say the least, but to us it wasn't the result of the case that mattered. 'The New York case clarifies for us what we've suspected,' Simon explained. 'The amounts of money transferred were exactly the same. The Shell/Eni consortium transfers US$1,092,040,000 into the Nigerian government's escrow account, and then the government transfers US$1,092,040,000 to Malabu, a company that had obtained the block illegally. This was a corrupt deal – a payment by Shell and Eni to Malabu.'

This view was evidently supported by the judgement of the New York court, which stated that 'it does appear that the FGN (Federal Government of Nigeria) was indeed the proverbial "straw man" holding US$1.1 billion for ultimate payment to Malabu'.

This judgement enabled us to embark on one of the longest and most in-depth investigations in our history, and it came at a particularly opportune time.

Corinna Gilfillan had joined the conflict-diamond team in London during the early 2000s and had played a significant role in getting the US behind the Kimberley Process before she began working with Simon on oil-revenue transparency. The creation of the EITI in 2002 had been an important stepping-stone in bringing transparency to the extractives sector, but we knew that as a voluntary mechanism it could only ever be part of the solution. There was every incentive for a corrupt company to keep the lid on a dirty deal and we knew we needed legislation. Corinna had established our Washington office precisely for this purpose and her first task was to lay the groundwork for a mandatory disclosure law.

'We were talking to the offices of both Republicans and Democrats and there were strong bipartisan feelings against corruption,' Corinna said. 'We drafted our own language [for a law] but we knew that under George W Bush's oil-friendly administration there would be few chances to pursue it.' But what Corinna did do was to forge strong relationships with the staff of key senators and members of Congress. Among these were Democratic senators Ben Cardin and Russ Feingold and the Republican Richard Lugar. Their dedicated support would prove crucial to the coming struggle.

Corinna was meeting with oil-company executives the whole time. 'I met with Exxon, Chevron, Shell, BP and others,' Corinna reported. 'They were *very* resistant to a disclosure law. They said that countries would kick them out; that they would be at a competitive disadvantage – every excuse, really. There was no political will in Congress for a disclosure law.' But she kept plugging away. We had allies who wanted change, like Lugar.

The breakthrough came with the Dodd–Frank Wall Street Reform and Consumer Protection Act. This legislation was introduced to bring greater regulation to the finance industry in the wake of the financial crash of 2008 and was signed into law by President Obama in 2010. With our allies in the Publish What You Pay coalition, we successfully campaigned for all oil and mining companies listed at the Securities and Exchange Commission in the US to be required to publicly declare what payments they made to governments for concessions to exploit oil, gas and minerals, on a project-by-project basis.

'Senator Lugar and I worked on the bill for several years,' Senator Ben Cardin wrote on his website. 'We had seen clear evidence that secrecy breeds corruption and that corruption can breed instability and perpetuate poverty in resource-rich countries.' This law would indeed make corruption very much harder to hide, because it obliged companies to disclose any payment over US$100,000 – peanuts in the oil world. The act captured any oil or mining company listed in the US, which effectively meant the majority of the world's oil and mining companies. The oil companies hated it and were furious.

In a last-ditch attempt to prevent Section 1504's inclusion in the law, the CEO of arguably the most powerful company in the world, Exxon's Rex Tillerson, went to Washington to meet Senator Lugar. He told Lugar that 1504 would damage the oil industry and put it at a competitive disadvantage. But Lugar stood his ground while Tillerson got 'red-faced angry', as a witness later told *The New Yorker*, although Tillerson denied it. Lugar had dispatched a research team around the world which had concluded that 'corruption was harmful to the countries concerned and harmful to US interests'. Lugar told Tillerson they would have to 'agree to disagree'. As Corinna put it, Exxon was 'really pissed off with Lugar'.

At the same time, we were working on similar legislation in Europe – the EU Accounting and Transparency Directives, virtually a mirror image of Dodd–Frank 1504. If we could capture the oil and mining companies listed in both the US and the EU, it would be the biggest blow against corruption in the oil and mining sector. Ever.

While Corinna and her team were trailing all over Capitol Hill in Washington, DC, Simon and a new teammate, Brendan O'Donnell, and their colleagues were walking the corridors of Brussels, lobbying Members of the European Parliament. Simon described the change in atmosphere since the last time we had tried to persuade them to strengthen anti-corruption laws: 'With many MEPs, if you actually got a meeting at all, they'd say, "Right, you've got ten minutes." This time, one MEP said, "Thank God you're here, Shell had 140 lobbyists here yesterday."' And that's the way the odds are stacked when you're working on anything that impacts the interests of the fossil-fuel industry.

And into all of this, OPL 245 had come along. The ability of Shell and Eni to effectively hide the payments that had secured them the block would probably not have been possible if Section 1504 or its EU equivalent had been in force at that time. As such, it was the iconic example to back up our arguments.

Catalysed by Section 1504 of Dodd–Frank, 30 other countries, including the EU member states, Canada and Norway, passed similar legislation. We had come a long way from those days in Angola when we were told, 'You'll never change the oil industry.' A global standard had been created. But although they had lost the battle globally, the oil industry could still stop it in the US. The opaque and mighty American Petroleum Institute (API) began a ten-year onslaught to prevent the implementation of Section 1504.

Brendan, a tall sardonic north Londoner of Irish descent, issued our first carefully worded challenge to Shell and Eni on 20 May 2012. Noting the details of the deal exposed by the New York case, he wrote that 'given the history of this block, both Shell and Eni need to explain what steps they took to ensure their payments did not ultimately end up in the hands of Malabu or ex-minister Etete'.

In response, Shell and Eni issued the first of what was to become a litany of denials. They denied paying any money to Malabu Oil and Gas in respect of the licence and said they dealt only with the Nigerian government. Nevertheless, I like to imagine that our press release must have caused more than a sharp intake of breath in the boardrooms of both companies. They certainly had something to hide.

We believed that the future of the OPL 245 deal rested on this point. It was now common knowledge that Dan Etete was behind Malabu, so if they knew that their payment was destined for Malabu then this meant they had engaged in a corrupt deal. The implications of that could be catastrophic for both companies, so that was the question we had to find the answer to.

'OPL 245 was an almost mythical Global Witness investigation which had been going on for years when I joined,' said Tom Mayne, who came to London from his native Manchester in 2003. With lank brown hair hanging over his forehead and pale skin, probably from too many late nights playing pubs with his band, David Cronenberg's Wife (available on Spotify!), Tom had met Global Witness staffer Laura Ribeiro at a gathering of friends in a Dalston bar. On finding out that Tom spoke Russian, Laura mentioned the possibility of volunteering for Global Witness to work on a report on Russian corruption.

Gavin Hayman took Tom under his wing, initially to investigate how an obscure shell company called RosUkrEnergo had come to control and massively profit from the pipeline that brought natural gas into Europe from Turkmenistan via Russia and the Ukraine, posing a significant threat to Europe's energy security. Following the publication of the resulting report, *It's a Gas*, Tom was approached by an industry insider appalled at what he'd read; during various subsequent conversations, Tom discovered that his new source, codenamed 'Eric', knew the failed Russian deal-maker Ednan Agaev. Eric arranged a meeting in Geneva for Tom and Diarmid to meet Agaev.

'It was a stinking-hot day and I was all suited up,' Tom said. 'Agaev was in his sixties, quite a small man. I asked him how he and Obi had got involved in OPL 245. He told me that he had top-level clearance to help Etete sell the asset, and that he had contacts at Shell. I think the idea is that Agaev is a "super-fixer".' But more important for us was that Eric alerted Tom to the existence of yet another court case.

*

Similarly cut out of the income loop, Agaev's partner, Emeka Obi, brought his own case against Malabu. This case was heard by Lady Justice Gloster at the High Court of Justice's Commercial Court in London, a specialist court that deals with business disputes. Especially those 'where a large amount is at stake'. Without Eric, it's unlikely we would have heard about the case or managed to get hold of the transcripts from it. At his desk in Buchanan House, Tom immersed himself in hundreds and hundreds of pages of them. They made fascinating reading. 'Dan Etete was on the stand and was making no sense. His lawyer had to sit there and listen to his client's charge sheet being read out to him. Someone should write a play about it, it was comedy gold,' Tom said, smiling at the thought of it.

Through the winter and spring of 2012 and 2013, Lady Justice Gloster heard the labyrinthine story of how Emeka Obi and his business partner Ednan Agaev sought to sell OPL 245 to Shell and Eni. Reading the court transcripts, it sounds like Etete put on a good show as he lied, contradicted himself and, perhaps rather ironically, described the case as a fraudulent scheme to do him out of US$200 million. Often verging on farce, Etete's testimony required the court to decamp to Paris because he had been refused entry to the UK for previously lying on a visa form about his 2007 conviction for money laundering. Reading the judge's comments about Etete, I almost felt sorry for those executives in Shell and Eni who had had to negotiate with him. But most important of all, this case laid out in detail the outcomes of the negotiations brokered by Attorney General Mohammed Adoke that eventually saw the sale of OPL 245 to Shell and Eni.

Taken at face value, the Nigerian government agreed to act as a middleman. Shell and Eni would pay the government, and then the government would transfer the money to Malabu. That way the oil majors could say they had come to a deal with the government. What the government did with the money afterwards was up to them. In the judge's words:

> *What was not in dispute, however, was that, after the inter-vention of the Attorney-General of the FGN, Malabu, ultimately, on 29 April 2011, disposed (to use a neutral word) of the OPL Assets, in return for the receipt of the sum*

of $1,092,040,000. This transaction was effected by the execution of three inter-related [resolution] agreements as between two or more of variously Malabu, the FGN, NAE [Nigeria Agip Exploration, a subsidiary of Eni] and the two Shell companies, SNEPCO and SNUD, respectively.

What Adoke had proposed was that rather than paying the agreed price into the Federation Account at the Ministry of Finance as required under the Nigerian constitution, one of the resolution agreements required a subsidiary of Shell to pay a signature bonus (an up-front payment for a new oil deal) of US$207 million into an escrow account held at JP Morgan in London in the name of the Federal Government of Nigeria. At the same time, NAE would transfer the mouthwatering US$1,092,040,000 into the same account.

A second agreement would direct the Nigerian government to transfer the US$1,092,040,000 into the coffers of Malabu Oil and Gas. Under the third agreement, Malabu would relinquish all its rights to OPL 245 to Shell and Eni. The three companies would all get what they wanted, bringing an end to years of legal disputes. Or so they had hoped. Instead, it resulted in the New York arbitration case brought by Agaev, which put the details of the deal in the public domain. Even then they might never have come to light had it not been for Diarmid's truffle hunting. In an interview with the *Economist*, Tom described the deal as a 'safe-sex transaction', with the government acting as a 'condom' between the buyers and seller.

'This case was tailor-made to illustrate the problem we were dealing with,' said Simon, referring to our efforts to get strong anti-corruption laws in the US and Europe. 'If the laws we wanted had existed in 2011 when Shell and Eni paid that US$1.1 billion, it would have immediately been public information rather than a shady backroom transaction. As it was, there was little chance that anyone would find out what they'd done.'

The case was extraordinary not just because it had thrown a light on how the OPL 245 deal had been put together, but also because Lady Gloster had ruled in favour of Emeka Obi's claim against Malabu and awarded him US$110 million. It was short of the US$200 million he had been asking for, but it was still an awful lot of money. 'The UK courts have been used to divvy up the loot from a highly suspicious and possibly illegal oil deal,' Simon said. 'It's like the court helping a couple of squabbling bank robbers divvy up the spoils.'

We had anticipated this and had already submitted a complaint to the Metropolitan Police Proceeds of Corruption Unit (POCU) to freeze Obi's money, but POCU were blocked by the Crown Prosecution Service (CPS). 'Even though there has been plenty of time to intervene, and an abundance of evidence showing the corrupt nature of this deal,' Simon said. So the UK released US$110 million and wired it to Obi's account at LGT Bank Schweiz in Geneva.

In 2013, after a decade of carrying out some of our most sophisticated investigations, Tom moved on from Global Witness. At the High Court when Lady Gloster's judgement was read out, Tom handed over the baton to Barnaby Pace, who has been devoted to the case ever since. And as our team was evolving, we were also bringing in a group of people who would prove to be essential allies in the quest to see justice done in the case of OPL 245.

Rake-thin, long-haired and with a smoker's cough, Nick Hildyard is a quiet legend in the NGO world. A founding editor of the *Ecologist* magazine, he went on to co-found a tiny research and advocacy organization, the Corner House. Nick's intellect, passion and anger at injustice sear the air when he speaks. But far more worrying for anyone at the wrong end of his research, he'd already proved he could hold the powerful to account.

When in 2006 Prime Minister Tony Blair called off a Serious Fraud Office investigation into corruption surrounding British arms giant BAE Systems' notorious Al Yamamah arms deal with Saudi Arabia, Nick was appalled by this political interference in a criminal investigation. The Corner House teamed up with the Campaign Against Arms Trade and mounted a legal challenge to reopen the case, a 'David against Goliath' effort. They lost, but the case propelled the issue even further into public consciousness. What would happen if Nick's strategy with BAE was adapted to another corruption case: OPL 245?

The Corner House had been working on another Nigerian corruption scandal with a whistleblower called Dotun Oloko, which linked the UK's Department for International Development

(DFID) with investments into companies connected to James Ibori, the super-corrupt former governor of Nigeria's oil-rich Delta State. Dotun's unequal struggle against forces so much more powerful than him had been aided both by the Corner House and an Italian organization called Re:Common, led by Antonio Tricarico. This trio had formed a powerful bond and it was in 2012 that Dotun asked whether they should do something about OPL 245. Nick contacted Simon and shortly afterwards, along with Antonio and Barnaby, they met in London.

Corruption is one of the hardest crimes to track because it is by its nature carried out in secret. Its protagonists, or the smart ones anyway, deliberately construct labyrinthine structures to conceal it, and this complexity makes it difficult and expensive to prosecute. That's why so many corruption cases never come to court and why so many of those that do are subject to failure. But Etete, Obi and Agaev weren't that smart. Their double dealing and greed had led them to the New York Supreme Court and the Commercial Court in London, and those hundreds of pages of court records, painstakingly studied by Tom and Barnaby, laid out how the deal was done. Shell and Eni didn't come out of this looking too bright, either. When Nick saw the evidence he was in no doubt what to do. 'Pushing complaints and getting the bastards into court is a new tactic,' Nick said, describing his experience putting together complaints to the police in the hope that they would catalyse an investigation. 'Seizing assets is what really hurts criminals. Getting them to court, getting them convicted and seizing their bloody assets.'

'You've got to think like a lawyer,' Nick explained. He isn't one himself but by this time had been working this way for almost 20 years. 'You're limited on where you can point the finger. You've got to put together the information you've got and put it into a form that says to the police, "You've got to investigate it." You have to ask yourself, how would that letter look to a judge if you took out a judicial review? These are the things that go through my mind when I make a complaint.'

Nick's first complaint was to the Metropolitan Police Proceeds of Corruption Unit (POCU), calling for the freezing of the funds held in the JP Morgan escrow account in London. The complaint fell on fertile ground.

POCU already had a weather eye on OPL 245. 'It was a back-burner case, sitting on our Case Management System,' I was told by former head of POCU Jonathan Benton. Following receipt of our complaint, though, Benton put it on the main hob. People thought he was mad, letting these eccentric anti-corruption campaigners through the door, but he told us he was certain 'that OPL 245 was a disgusting, awful bit of corruption'. Benton knew about the JP Morgan account. 'When the escrow-account money started moving from JP Morgan we could watch it – effectively live. You don't get anything better than that as an intelligence tool,' he said.

POCU's investigation amassed 40,000 documents relating to OPL 245 and had taken Benton to Nigeria many times. 'I was on a mission to force the Nigerians, diplomatically, to deal with Dan Etete,' Benton told me. He soon figured out that one of the central characters was Nigeria's attorney general, Mohammed Adoke. 'He was the fixer on the Nigerian side...we had traced money transfers to his brother.'

Benton had a great relationship with Nigeria's anti-corruption unit, the Economic and Financial Crimes Commission (EFCC), and described its founding chairman, former police officer Nuhu Ribadu, as 'as genuine as they come'. Dotun agreed and had told Nick that despite the corruption at the top of the political system in Nigeria, the EFCC had carried on investigating OPL 245 behind the scenes.

But Benton had a less favourable impression of the EFCC's then head, Ibrahim Lamorde. 'Adoke wanted to come and see me privately,' he said, but as his role was 'rather unique', he couldn't do that. He was a senior police officer but spent time in the Foreign Office with people from other arms of government dealing with a range of sensitive issues: 'A private meeting with a country's attorney general who is himself the subject of an investigation could open a whole can of political worms.' Benton wanted to avoid that. Then Adoke began playing dirty tricks. Jonathan Benton found himself literally hijacked.

On a trip to Abuja, he needed to go to a meeting but he'd already let the High Commission's car go for the day. 'Protocol demanded that I only travel in an armoured vehicle and Lamorde offered his EFCC car,' Benton said. 'The route to my meeting seemed strange to me and I realized I was being taken to the Ministry of Justice.' He called the high commissioner to alert him to what was happening while he was still en route. So despite his best efforts, Benton ended up in a private meeting in Adoke's office. 'I got out my notebook and I wrote everything down. It's all in my book.' When Benton told me this I smiled as I thought that despite all the advances in technology, it's great that when the chips are down a Scotland Yard detective still gets out the trusty notebook.

Benton said Adoke was worried. 'He wanted to meet detectives to see who was going to get nicked. When you've met interesting people, as a cop, for 25 years, you get to be a pretty good judge of character.' Benton could tell that Adoke was up against the ropes.

But POCU's case was foundering. We never found out the whole story. Jonathan Benton was tight-lipped but one of our sources, a police officer frustrated by the case's stagnation, told us that by acting as a conduit for the funds between Shell, Eni and Malabu, the Nigerian government had effectively legitimized the deal, 'pouring Holy Water on it'. Re:Common's Antonio took the resistance he subsequently saw from UK authorities as a positive sign, at least, because it showed we were on the right track.

Nevertheless, disappointed in the lack of progress in the UK, we turned our attentions to Eni's home town of Milan. It was the obvious place to submit another complaint. Antonio had previously got to know Milan's chief prosecutor, Francesco Greco. Antonio approached him to brief him on OPL 245, and Greco suggested we contact one of his colleagues, a man who would go on to play one of the key roles in the OPL 245 saga.

Fabio de Pasquale had already built a reputation for prosecuting the most powerful of criminals, and this in a country where the obituary columns provided a stark reminder of the risks involved for those who did. Could a small group of NGOs convince a hard-bitten public prosecutor to devote the extensive resources required to investigate this case among all the others that crossed his desk? A veteran of two corruption trials of former prime ministers, including Silvio Berlusconi, he was certainly not afraid of the public eye – and prosecuting the top executives of Italy's largest company in which the government owned a 30 per cent stake would certainly be a trial in the public eye.

Well-practiced at his craft, Nick and the team wrote our second complaint relating to OPL 245 and submitted it to de Pasquale's office. There was nothing else to do but wait to see whether he would take it up.

Some weeks later in the London office, Simon tapped me on the shoulder and ushered me outside onto a darkening Portsoken Street. 'Fabio's taken up the case,' he told me breathlessly. He was almost quivering with excitement.

Getting the Milan public prosecutor to accept a one-billion-dollar international corruption case – one of the biggest ever tried anywhere – had been a success long fought for. We and our allies had, between us, devoted less than ten people and a comparatively tiny budget to investigating the massive deal that was OPL 245, but now we were able to hand over much of the work and responsibility to the authorities whose job these cases are. But we had no plans to stop there. We kept investigating on our own and went on to file a complaint in the Netherlands, where Shell are headquartered, and Switzerland, where some of the money ended up. Things began to move fast.

Like a group of toreadors, Global Witness and its allies had been goading the Shell and Eni bull, jabbing the sharp banderillas of embarrassing evidence into their thick corporate hides. A favourite setting for this pursuit was Eni's AGM, held at its offices in Rome. In 2013, acting as a proxy for the owner of one share in Eni, Simon attended their annual general meeting with just as much right as any of the company's biggest shareholders to pose questions to the company's CEO. Democracy in action in one of the most unlikely settings.

It was the following year, at the 2014 AGM, that we knew that Eni was becoming seriously rattled. In March the company's CEO Paolo Scaroni was convicted over an unrelated pollution case and sentenced to three years in prison. He was replaced by his No. 2, Claudio Descalzi. You would have thought that Descalzi's debut AGM would be both a wonderful opportunity to stamp his leadership on Italy's largest company and a chance to demonstrate it was turning over a new leaf. Instead, he simply didn't show up.

'Eni's offices in Rome are in a tower block in a landscaped park. It's a 400–500-m walk from the metro to the room where the shareholders go in,' Simon reported. Having arrived early, Simon,

Barnaby, Nick, Dotun, Antonio and his colleague Elena were sitting in the park. 'We had submitted the questions we wanted to ask beforehand, in writing, but we got no response,' Simon said. 'What we did have were the email addresses of the board, so while we were waiting, using Barnaby's mobile hotspot in the park outside, we emailed every member. We later heard that they were all in one room together when all their phones were going "ping ping ping" at the same time and they opened their messages, and it was us! It was hilarious.'

But at this point our long-planned strategy nearly went awry. When the team went to Eni's building, they were refused entry. Although we had used a specialist company to become the proud owners of an Eni share, something had gone wrong. The team remonstrated with the gatekeepers and were told there was a problem with the share. 'The company we had used made a mistake and they wouldn't let us in,' Simon said. 'So we start heading out again. By coincidence Beppe Grillo, the leader of Italy's Five Star Movement, was there and as we're ejected, there's a press throng outside in the park. Eni's PR guy seemed to panic at the thought of a bunch of disgruntled NGOs with access to half the Italian press corps outside.'

And the PR guy rushed out. 'He offered a meeting with their corporate social-responsibility people,' Antonio said. 'But Simon said no, we don't spend time talking to CSR people – we need to talk to the legal counsel, the people in charge of the operation.' Simon continued, 'He then told us that we could come to the meeting but not ask a question because the share was not in order. Luckily Antonio and Elena owned their own share and were able to ask questions anyway. Then the PR guy said to come back at 5pm.' It seemed that we had got our meeting, but with whom?

'The AGM adjourned for lunch. The food was delicious, and you can walk around and meet the company's top leadership and the major shareholders, but we stood out like a nasty disease in the corner,' Simon said. The team left the AGM to go to a café and came back at the appointed time. 'We were whisked up to Eni's boardroom on the 12th floor.' With views over the park and the city beyond, the room was dominated by the large conference table, empty except for a Dictaphone Barnaby had got permission to use to record the meeting.

'We found half of Eni's senior management in the room,' Antonio said. Eni's chief counsel, Massimo Mantovani, led the meeting. 'The company's No. 3, Roberto Casula, was there too.'

'Altogether there were five or six people, including two or three CSR people,' Simon said. 'They started to say everything was fine, by the books. Mantovani said we appreciate your concerns, etc. But they completely misjudged us – they should have concluded that we knew what we were talking about, and they did look nonplussed at what we knew.

'… and then Mantovani starts to lose control of the meeting and Casula goes off on one, saying "I'm tired. I'm tired, I'm fucking sick and tired. I have never been corrupt in my life." You could almost see Mantovani kicking him under the table,' Simon grinned. The CSR people looked mortified by the management's eruption.

'We knew that at meetings like this you should only ask questions that you already know the answer to,' Antonio said, and Antonio had a killer question. He had heard the recording of a wiretapped phone conversation ordered by another prosecutor in a completely separate case. The call was between a man called Luigi Bisignani and another man, apparently a senior figure in Eni's ranks. We suspected we knew who that other man was. This was our trump card.

In Italy, mention of Luigi Bisignani's name evokes the same reaction as Al Capone's in the US, and it is not a name that the new boss of Italy's largest company can afford to be associated with. Following a career in journalism, Bisignani served as a press officer in the Treasury and the Ministry of Public Works during the scandal-hit regime of Prime Minister Giulio Andreotti, and he was no stranger to scandal himself. Convicted of misuse of party funds in the nineties, Bisignani has been named in numerous corruption investigations and was exposed as a member of the same illegal P2 Masonic lodge as the Mafia-linked banker Roberto Calvi, whose body was discovered hanging from Blackfriars Bridge in June 1982. So how is it that such a man as Bisignani became a supreme political lobbyist and was rumoured to be one of Italy's most powerful men, with an office down the corridor from the CEO in Eni's offices and another next to Silvio Berlusconi, Italy's former far-right prime minister and host of the 'bunga bunga' sex parties, who was himself at the centre of a series of corruption investigations?

The wiretap recording captures Bisignani telling the other man how to construct the OPL 245 deal. Who could this other man be, a man senior enough in Eni to be able to structure a corrupt deal of the scale of OPL 245? The outgoing CEO, Paolo Scaroni, had publicly denied that it was him. Could it in fact have been Scaroni's No. 2 – now the company's No. 1 – Claudio Descalzi?

That a man with no formal role whatsoever at Eni was possibly telling the company's No. 2 how to structure a corrupt deal would take a lot of explaining and was, for anyone, a bastard of a question to ask on the day of Descalzi's first AGM, even though he wasn't there.

But Antonio asked it. Mantovani strenuously denied that the other man was Descalzi, and said that if Descalzi was there he would deny it himself. But Nick kept up the pressure, asking what due diligence had they done before appointing Descalzi to the top job. 'We ended up really grilling them,' Nick said. 'Did you, Massimo, in your capacity as Eni's chief counsel, put it to Mr Descalzi whether or not he was on that call with Mr Bisignani?' We kept repeating the question and the mood of the Eni staff became increasingly heated.

Then Antonio overheard Mantovani whisper to his colleagues in Italian, 'They think it's Christmas', before snapping in English that we didn't have the right to prosecute them. We said we did have the right to ask questions. The conversation picked up by Barnaby's Dictaphone dissolves into a barely discernible maelstrom of denials and accusations from Eni's senior personnel as different people shout over each other, with our team pressing our questions into the opposition, enraging them even more.

'We had asked why Claudio wasn't at the AGM and they told us he was very busy,' Simon said. 'Their answer was absolutely absurd.' For the incoming CEO of Italy's biggest company to miss his inaugural AGM was nothing short of extraordinary. Simon, Nick and Antonio concluded that it was probably because he was intimately involved in the deal: 'Our questions to him at the AGM could put him in a place where he had to either lie about the relationship with Bisignani, or admit it. He would be condemned either way.'

Checkmate.

Suddenly Mantovani got up and left the room, closely followed by Casula, a neat, bespectacled man with a goatee who had gone apoplectic again. As he left, he pointed at Barnaby's Dictaphone, saying we didn't have permission to use it; and the crescendo of shouting increased as Barnaby's calm voice pressed the point that we were recording because we didn't want to misquote them. Casula demanded the tape, which he wasn't going to get.

'They all walked out, leaving the embarrassed-looking CSR people to guard us and escort us out of the building. It was pure theatre,' Simon said.

Nick echoed Simon's description of events. 'The recording is hysterical. It was really good fun, a really good day's work. Later they called and said they wanted to do a joint press release,' said Nick. 'We said fuck off.'

Our close alliance received a blow when the courageous whistle-blower, our colleague Dotun, after years of struggle at immense personal and financial cost, decided he needed to step away. We had achieved much together and this was a real loss, but fate was still smiling on us.

Olanrewaju Suraju – Lanre to his friends – emerged from the student protests he led in his youth to found the Human and Environmental Development Agenda (HEDA), to work on good governance, transparency, environmental sustainability and social justice. 'It's my passion,' he told me. 'The discovery of oil has been more of a curse for Nigeria than a blessing. Before oil, in the 1950s and 1960s, Nigeria had a thriving economy. We had a currency stronger than the US dollar. You could go to university for free, with fully subsidized accommodation plus a three-course meal,' he said. 'Oil was presented to the people as the height of achievement for the country, and they abandoned everything else. Forty-three years ago, Nigeria was a leading world producer of palm oil, but now we're nowhere. We have gone from a safe environment to complete environmental degradation. We are one of world's worst polluters from gas flaring. Fifty per cent of the population live below the poverty line. We are ruled by puppets put in office, compromised political leaders in provinces. People can't do farming as a consequence of oil.'

HEDA was the only national NGO tracking OPL 245 and it wasn't long before Lanre joined our team.

Meanwhile the Italian prosecutors were unearthing a corruption plot that spread its tentacles far wider than the cosy cabal of Shell,

Eni and Malabu, reaching all the way into the upper echelons of the Nigerian government.

The US$1.1 billion paid by the oil majors hadn't hung around in the JP Morgan escrow account in London for long. US$801.5 million was transferred to two Etete-owned companies, Malabu Oil and Gas and another shell company, Rocky Top Resources. Keeping around US$300 million for himself, Etete transferred the remaining US$520 million to the reclusive, and in most people's view, equally corrupt, billionaire Alhaji Aliyu Abubakar. Of this, Abubakar kept US$54.4 million and, in an operation the logistics of which make one gasp, converted the remaining US$466 million into cash in both US dollars and Nigerian naira at local bureau de change offices. This cash – an amount that would weigh five tonnes if it was in $100 bills – was, according to the Italian prosecutors, 'intended for payment to President Jonathan, members of the government, and other Nigerian public officials'. These, of course, included the attorney general himself, Mohammed Adoke.

Despite it being a freezing morning, Shell felt the heat on a sunny February day in 2016 when 50 officers from the Italian financial police, together with their Dutch colleagues, entered the company's historic Renaissance-style headquarters in The Hague. The raid lasted all day and most of the night. Of particular interest were the executive offices, including those of Simon Henry, Malcolm Brinded and Shell's CEO, Ben van Beurden. He hadn't been involved in the OPL 245 deal, but he was about to inherit the aftermath.

When Van Beurden answered a call that evening from Simon Henry, Shell's chief financial officer, he was unaware that his phone was already being tapped by the Dutch police and that the tapes of his calls would subsequently be leaked to the press. And us.

'Don't volunteer any information that is not requested,' Van Beurden told Henry. This information lockdown evidently applied to their own shareholders too. 'The last thing you want of course is some sort of request to issue a stock-exchange release…There is nothing to be said other than that we are being asked to provide information.' This was an understatement: the police left Shell's offices with 90,000 documents.

Shell's statement to the press extolled their ethical values:

*We can confirm that representatives of the Dutch Fiscal
Intelligence and Investigation Service (FIOD) and the Dutch
Public Prosecutor recently visited Shell at its headquarters in
The Hague. The visit was related to OPL 245, an offshore
block in Nigeria that was the subject of a series of long-
standing disputes with the Federal Government of Nigeria.
Shell is cooperating with the authorities and is looking into
the allegations, which it takes seriously.*

*Shell attaches the greatest importance to business integ-
rity. It's one of our core values and is a central tenet of the
Business Principles that govern the way we do business.*

But behind the scenes the beleaguered CEO told Henry, 'There was
apparently some loose chatter…particularly the people that we hired
from MI6 [who] must have said things like, "Well, yeah, you know,
I wonder who gets a payoff here"…I haven't seen them, but apparently it was judged to be, y'know, just pub talk in emails, which was
stupid, but nevertheless, is there.'

It certainly was.

Throughout the nine years since Shell and Eni had got their hands
on OPL 245, throughout the burgeoning law-enforcement investigations in the UK, Italy, Switzerland and The Hague, there had been
one constant: Shell and Eni repeatedly rejected the escalating allegations of corruption and denied that they had negotiated directly
with Malabu Oil and Gas. They stuck to the story that they had
simply paid the Federal Government of Nigeria for the rights to the
block. But just how much Shell actually knew would soon become
a lot clearer.

In early 2017, details of the Milan prosecutor's file were leaked,
and among the gems it contained were a trove of emails and transcripts of wiretaps – manna from heaven for investigators like us.
Barnaby, Nick and Antonio began to go through the emails, which
dated back to 2009. If you're into anti-corruption work, as we are,
you will understand the excitement we felt at seeing the inner workings of Shell's strategy exposed, laying bare the real story behind
OPL 245.

Playing a leading role in the negotiations with Etete were
two Shell employees and former spies, John Copleston and Guy

Colegate, who the Milan public prosecutor said 'used to work for MI6'. In one email, Copleston himself said he had done 'two tours as UK Intelligence Rep in Nigeria', and it was these emails, feeding intelligence from their meetings back to their bosses in The Hague, that exposed that Shell not only knew they were dealing with Etete but were actively courting him, that the deal was corrupt, that it involved the president of Nigeria and – crucially – that this knowledge went right to the top of Shell.

'Saw my Delta man,' wrote Copleston, concealing his source's identity in true spy style in a January 2009 email to two of Shell's most senior Africa executives. 'He spoke to Mrs E this morning. She says E claims he will only get 300m we offering —rest goes in paying people off.' Putting two and two together, we believe 'E' stands for Etete.

In October the same year, Copleston and Shell's vice president for sub-Saharan Africa, Peter Robinson, met with Etete in Abuja – a man, we need to remember, who was convicted of money laundering just a couple of years before. 'We are getting along very well personally – lunch and lots of iced champagne,' Copleston wrote. A few months later, Guy Colegate, Shell's man on the ground, wrote: 'Etete can smell the money...If at nearly 70 years old he does turn his nose up at nearly $1.2 bill he is completely certifiable... But I think he knows it's his for the taking.' This email from March 2010 was forwarded to Shell's then CEO Peter Voser. Malcolm Brinded, Shell's head of upstream – effectively the second-most senior man in the company – sent the draft deal to Voser saying, 'Your formal endorsement is appropriate given the history and the political/business principles issues involved.' Which was a delicate way of putting it.

In May 2010, Nigeria's ailing president Umaru Yar'Adua died and was replaced by the vice president, Goodluck Jonathan, an old friend of Etete's and, according to Colegate, a former tutor to Etete's children. Jonathan was contesting the 2011 presidential election and needed funds. In a briefing to senior colleagues at Shell, Guy Colegate wrote: 'In Abuja it is still a case of all politics and no government...Jockeying for ministerial position remains intense, with many aspirants offering substantial sums to purchase their way into office...With an election only 10 months away the need to build war chests for campaigning is strong.'

On 15 July 2010, Colegate met with Etete in Paris and reported back the next day to Peter Robinson:

> Long meeting in Paris – salient points
>
> Etete claims he has and has shown (though not copied) a letter from president reiterating Malabu's 100% equity/contract award.
>
> This letter clearly an attempt to deliver significant revenues to GLJ as part of any transaction.
>
> Our source says this letter 'has really damaged deal' as Etete now 'uncontrollable' – he stated deal was almost there on a proposed 50/50 split with RDS [Royal Dutch Shell]. I made no comment.
>
> Italians look like they may abandon the whole thing as they realize there will be no RDS agreement on this basis and the letter has torpedoed reasonable discussion with the chief.

It was around this time that Malcolm Brinded had entered into talks with Eni, after they had been brought in by Malabu's fixer, Emeka Obi. Ahead of a meeting with his Eni counterpart, Brinded was briefed by Peter Robinson that 'the president is motivated to see 245 closed quickly – driven by expectations about the proceeds that Malabu will receive and political contributions that will flow as a consequence'.

This email could not leave Brinded in any doubt that the deal was corrupt, and that money from it would likely flow to Nigeria's top political leadership. But rather than walking away from the deal and notifying the authorities as a responsible company should, they continued with the negotiations. 'What's really interesting about the former MI6 guys,' Nick said, 'is that not once did they reflect on corruption, the law, etc. They're looking at which political leaders are building up a war chest – they are grooming those politicians.'

On the day that the deal was finally signed, 14 April 2011, Peter Robinson proudly emailed his colleagues. 'Malabu initialled all agreements,' he wrote. 'Compliments to our legal team who have done a brilliant job.' The deal had finally been done, and doubtless a few more bottles of iced champagne were sunk in Abuja, Milan, Paris and The Hague.

All this information confirmed what we had long been saying: Shell knew. Which seemed like a good name for a report.

Shell Knew was published on 10 April 2017, six years almost to the day since Shell and Eni had inked the deal, and it was going to be a long day for Barnaby. On BBC Radio 4's flagship *Today* programme, Barnaby rammed home the report's message that the fifth-biggest company in the world had been routinely lying to law enforcement, the press, the public and its own shareholders, and that the corruption was not just tolerated but was known about at the highest levels of the company.

The piece ran throughout the day and was covered by news outlets across the world. By the time Barnaby appeared on the BBC *Ten O'Clock News* over 14 hours later, Shell's defence had crumbled and they admitted what we had known all along. It fell to Andy Norman, the company's vice president for global media relations, to break the news: 'Over time, it became clear to us that Etete was involved in Malabu and that the only way to resolve the impasse through a negotiated settlement was to engage with Etete and Malabu, whether we liked it or not.'

On 20 December 2017, magistrate Giuseppina Barbara ruled in Milan that Eni and Shell, together with various key individuals, should go to trial. The present and past CEOs of Eni, Paolo Scaroni and Claudio Descalzi headed the list. Roberto Casula, Eni's No. 3 and the man who had lost his cool under our questioning in Rome, plus several other senior Eni executives, were on the stand with their bosses. Luigi Bisignani was also on the list.

They were joined by Shell's No. 2, Malcolm Brinded; the man who inked the deal, Peter Robinson; and the two former spies, Copleston and Colegate; as well as the middlemen Agaev, Obi and Obi's sidekick, Di Nardo. And of course no such list would be complete without the inclusion of Etete himself and the man who divvied up the spoils, Nigeria's Mr Corruption, Alhaji Aliyu Abubakar.

Barnaby was a regular fixture at the trial, which began in September 2018 in Milan's Mussolini-era Palace of Justice, an imposing grey stone block of a building designed by one of Il Duce's favourite Fascist architects, its twin neoclassical columns dividing the four-storey-high glazed walls towering above the entrance. He constantly reported back to us in the office and live-tweeted proceedings to a dedicated and highly engaged group of followers, many of them based in Nigeria.

The case was centred around the Milan public prosecutor's allegations that US$520 million from the OPL 245 deal was converted into cash and intended to be paid to Nigerian president Goodluck Jonathan and other Nigerian government officials, with further allegations that money was also channelled to Eni and Shell executives as kickbacks.

'You've seen all the documents and then it's like *The Lord of the Rings* – you've read the book then all of these people are there talking about it – it has a filmic quality,' Barnaby told me. 'It's a very grand courthouse but inside chunks of plaster are falling from the walls and the ceiling, and there's exposed wiring everywhere... There are huge cages, big enough for 50 people... Antonio Secci, Dan Etete's lawyer, looks like an army sergeant in a tight suit and he'd sit in the cage because there were not enough seats. He seemed to sit there as an act of preference.'

Things started not to go Shell and Eni's way right from the start. Emeka Obi, the man whose successful claim in London's Commercial Court to take a US$110 million slice of Malabu's US$1.1 billion had unwittingly disgorged the inner workings of the OPL 245 deal into our hands in the first place, and another middleman, Gianluca Di Nardo, had elected to go for a fast-track trial in order to receive a reduced sentence. They were convicted of international corruption related to OPL 245 and sentenced to four years in jail. The court ordered the seizure of US$98.4 million from Obi and more than 21 million Swiss francs (US$21.9 million) from Di Nardo. In her reasoning, the judge said that 'The management of oil companies Eni and Shell...were fully aware of the fact that part of the $1.092 billion paid would have been used to compensate Nigerian public officials who had a role in this matter and who were circling their prey like hungry sharks...It was not mere connivance, but a conscious adhesion to a predatory project damaging the Nigerian state.' As Barnaby told the press, this was a decision that would 'send shivers down the corporate spines of the oil industry'.

It was a judgement that could bring little comfort to Brinded, Descalzi and their co-defendants but Shell and Eni put on a brave face and issued the usual denials. 'Based on our review of the Prosecutor of Milan's file and all of the information and facts available to us, we do not believe that there is a basis to convict Shell or any of its former employees of alleged offences,' Shell told the press, while Eni maintained that it had done nothing wrong, reiterating that it had dealt directly with the Nigerian government.

Meanwhile Nigeria's anti-corruption unit, the Economic and Financial Crimes Commission, had been investigating the circumstances around the OPL 245 deal and had issued arrest warrants for Etete, the former attorney general Adoke and an Eni official. Seven months later, in November 2019, Adoke was arrested by Interpol in Dubai, where he'd arrived for a medical appointment. Just two months before, he'd published his reminiscences of his time as Nigeria's attorney general. *Burden of Service* apparently provides a stout defence of his role with regards to the OPL 245 deal. You can buy it on Amazon, but you really shouldn't.

On 21 July 2020, Milan's public prosecutor laid out his recommended sentences for the accused:

> *Agaev and Falcioni six years; Bisignani six years; Colegate, Copleston and Robinson six years and eight months; Armanna and Pagano six years and eight months; Brinded seven years and four months; Casula seven years and four months; Scaroni and Descalzi eight years.*
>
> *For Etete...we ask for the highest penalty...For his misconduct, that was driven by absolute and relentless hunger for money; for being the main vehicle, or the only vehicle, of corruption of Public Officials, namely Jonathan, Adoke and Diezani, through his money launderer Alhaji Abubakar Aliyu, we ask a penalty of 10 years.*

But, for now at least, these recommendations are rather academic. I don't know who was more surprised – us and our allies or the defendants in the dock – when on 17 March 2021 the three judges, dutifully wearing their pandemic masks, trooped into the empty courtroom to deliver their verdict. It took them less than a minute to acquit all the defendants, saying there was no case to answer. With that, they turned on their heels and trooped out again.

The news made the headlines across the world, but if the defend-ants were not guilty, who was? Matthew Page, an associate fellow at the Chatham House Africa Programme, told Reuters, 'This is a huge blow for natural-resource governance and transparency in Nigeria... The OPL 245 deal has been a multilayered tale of corruption and malfeasance and international complicity that's been going on for two decades.'

Presumably the two middlemen, Emeka Obi and Gianluca Di Nardo, had seen the writing on the wall when they opted for a fast-track trial with the chance of a reduced sentence. However, in the light of the acquittals, these sentences have since been quashed, and the order freezing around US$120 million of their assets was lifted, but as I write, it's not clear whether the Swiss authorities will act on it.

Although they cited 'lack of certain proof' of corruption as the main factor in their decision, the judges also were in no doubt that something was awry, noting that the vast money flows generated by the deal were 'circumstantial evidence of the generically illicit nature of the payments derived from the proceeds' of OPL 245. However, they concluded that 'it is not acceptable to [assume] that a large part of this sum in cash, if not all, ended up [with the] Nigerian public officials who made the illicit agreements possible'.

Meanwhile the Dutch investigation into the OPL 245 deal contin-ues, while the Nigerian government, which had lost US$1.1 billion to a criminal cabal, vowed to 'continue to hold those responsible for the OPL 245 fraud accountable'. And so will we. 'Today's verdict does not mark the final word in this scandal for Shell and Eni,' Barnaby told the press. And indeed it doesn't: in early June 2021 the OPL 245 case promptly became even more convoluted than it already was when the public prosecutor of Brescia announced it had placed the Milan main prosecutors of the case, Fabio de Pasquale and Sergio Spadaro, under investigation for withholding evidence that would have been helpful to Eni's defence. Their boss, Francesco Greco, the highly respected head of the Milan Public Prosecutor's Office, backed his colleagues and promptly got targeted by the same investigation. Based on these allegations, the Italian Justice Ministry ordered its own administrative inquiry into the case. The prosecu-tors made no public response to this move, but the following month both they and the Nigerian government appealed the acquittal verdict against Shell, Eni and all the individual defendants, with the appeal likely to come to court in early 2022.

This is the real world – the world we live in. This initial verdict on the OPL 245 case was certainly disappointing, but we really shouldn't have been surprised. More than anything, the Italian verdict showed just how difficult it is to curb corruption in this most corrupt of industries. The judges didn't question that US$1.1 billion was paid by Shell and Eni into an escrow account at JP Morgan in London, most of which almost immediately squirrelled its way into the bank accounts of Dan Etete, a convicted money launderer, with a chunk of it continuing its journey into the hands of Alhaji Aliyu Abubakar, Nigeria's 'Mr Corruption'.

The message that the judges gave prosecutors and anti-corruption organizations like ours that day was, essentially, that if you're not actually in the room when a corrupt deal is being done, then you're not going to achieve a conviction. Perhaps more disturbingly, the subsequent investigation into the prosecutors themselves may show that if you dare to mount a prosecution against companies as powerful as Shell and Eni, you may end up in the crosshairs yourself. If so, it's a pretty clear message – perhaps the perfect example of the shadow network at play?

But maybe the joke is on Shell and Eni after all. Their rights to explore OPL 245 expired in May 2021 and the Nigerian government is not willing to issue any oil mining licence while prosecutions continue in Nigeria and elsewhere. So while the oil companies may have prevailed in court, for now at least, their Holy Grail is lying undisturbed, 2,000m under the sea.

Corruption is not a victimless crime. In May 2018, Nigeria, one of the two wealthiest African countries, overtook India as home to the greatest number of people living in extreme poverty. According to the Brookings Institution, a prestigious Washington-based think tank, 80 per cent of the Nigerian population – that's 87 million people – live on less than two dollars a day.

Not a drop of oil has been extracted from the OPL 245 block.

7

NO SAFE HAVENS

LONDON – PARIS – NEW YORK

On a cool June day in 2010, a private jet out of Latvia touched down at Farnborough Airport in Hampshire. Its occupant, a man in his mid-thirties, was met on the tarmac by border officials and arrested. Within days he had claimed political asylum. His name was Maxim Bakiyev.

Just two months previously, Kurmanbek Bakiyev, the president of the former Soviet state of Kyrgyzstan, had fled the country following a people's revolution. According to the new government, in the two years before his hurried departure he and his son had embezzled well over a billion dollars of state funds that had flowed through the country's largest bank, the Asia Universal Bank (AUB), into a web of companies registered in the UK, New Zealand and elsewhere. From these companies, the money was channelled into further companies until these multiple streams, like a river delta, were virtually impossible to trace back to the source.

Time was when fugitives from justice would hole up in Spain or some country in Africa or South America without an extradition treaty with the jurisdiction they'd committed their crime in. Things are easier now. You just get the shadow network to pull its strings and you don't need to be a fugitive at all.

Maxim Bakiyev was a pathfinder to the next phase in our work to tackle corruption. The outrageous spending habits of the sleazy kleptocrats I covered in Chapter 4 are just part of the story. It's one thing to use corruptly obtained funds to buy the odd mansion or yacht, but what do you do if you want to get serious money out of the country you stole it from and into a place where it's secure, where you can spend it at will and where it's pleasant to live? And how do you keep the hounds of law enforcement off the scent?

The Colombian drug lord Pablo Escobar had fleets of small boats and planes transporting hundreds of millions of dollars in cash to the US and various Caribbean islands, and even then he had too much to move and had to bury bales of the stuff all over the Colombian countryside. But that's clumsy. One of the best ways to do it comes down to a simple question. What is the most expensive fixed asset you can buy?

Ellie Nichol joined Global Witness from Oxfam and has worked on some of our most challenging campaigns. She is softly spoken – always a challenge for me as I've been half-deaf for years – and has a methodical approach to campaigning, very different to my 'Let's just go do it and see what happens' style.

She cut her teeth on the Cambodia beat. The investigations she steered laid bare the nepotistic stranglehold on the country's economy by companies controlled by the ruling family of the super-corrupt dictator Hun Sen. She went on to work on our Afghanistan campaign and one of my more surreal experiences at Global Witness was arriving with Ellie and fellow campaigner Juman Kubba at the barricaded entrance to the headquarters of the International Security Assistance Force (ISAF), the NATO-led military coalition in Kabul. As dusk fell, Ellie, Juman and I were guided through a labyrinth of high-blast walls into the inner sanctum, where we had been invited to dinner by the US Army's larger-than-life Brigadier General H R McMaster, in charge of the coalition's anti-corruption Task Force Shafafiyat. We called it Task Force Faffalot. Shaven-headed, brash, with a booming voice and looking far too much like Robert Duvall's helicopter-cavalry commander in *Apocalypse Now*, McMaster was rather surprisingly an amazingly insightful guy, and one who pushed boundaries. Sitting around the laminated table with his intelligence chiefs and eating bland processed food – all shipped in from the States – the likes of which I hadn't had inflicted on me since school dinners, we watched with amusement the alarm on his colleagues' faces as he said we could have access to all their intelligence on corruption. He evidently got sat on because it never materialized, but it was exciting at the time. That he had some integrity and brains was demonstrated when some years later he resigned as Donald Trump's national security adviser.

Returning to work after a year's maternity leave, Ellie came up with a strategy in support of our corruption campaign. 'I've identified this gap in our work,' she told us. 'Many of the cultural centres where the criminals chose to spend the proceeds of crime are actually on our doorstep in London and Paris, plus the US. That's always been one of the most outrageous and relatable sides of global corruption stories.' On top of that, having just returned to her role, she admitted she was attracted by pursuing an idea that involved a lot less travel than her normal work.

'I tend to break things down into component chunks when I'm thinking about problems,' Ellie said. 'What are the primary ways in which the rich and corrupt spend their money? And what are the most important? What are the tasty stories that we can bring out to tell the narrative and construct a campaign around? And what are the policy opportunities that we have in the UK, the US and France?'

What Ellie came up with, through chatting with the Global Witness team and also various journalists and our allies at Transparency International, was a way to bring corruption stories from far-off places right to our own doorstep. 'One of the things that people have always known about, and that has been reported in the papers for a long time, is the fact that loads of dodgy characters have been choosing to buy up large tracts of property in London,' she said. 'Everyone knows this, but no one has really proven it, or dug beneath it and painted a bigger picture of what's happening and where it's happening, or what the solution is, or what action can be taken.'

Ellie had put her finger on one of the elephants in the room and it was a very big elephant. We were not just talking about people who want to spend a few million on a big house, but those super-crooks – often the family members of a head of state or senior politician – who want to channel the hundreds of millions if not billions of dollars they've extracted from their own countries into more convenient locations. In a 2014 *Financial Times* article, Cynthia O'Murchu put a figure to just one aspect of it: £122 billion of UK property was owned by offshore companies. Some of this will be legitimate, but how much isn't?

*

Just as her campaign brainchild was getting off the ground, Ellie
became pregnant with her second child and she and her boss,
Anthea Lawson, began interviewing for maternity cover. One of the
candidates was Chido Dunn, a young Australian lawyer. Unexcited
by her first foray into commercial law at one of the big London law
firms, she had a brief stint at the Foreign and Commonwealth Office
tackling weapons of war. Chido was scouring job ads when she
came across ours, looking for someone to focus on property. 'Hey, I
don't really know anything about property,' she said cheerfully, but
applied anyway.

A walking advertisement for the healthy outdoor Australian lifestyle, Chido is blonde, charming and smart as a whip. Her desire to
chase things down rabbit holes would be put to very good use and
those first few months of 2015 were going to be a campaigning whirl.

London had long been popular with oligarchs from the former
Soviet Union, the source of their wealth often mired in secrecy. They
seemed to be a good place to start. Chido and Ellie approached
Tom Mayne, our Russian-speaking anti-folk-music star who had
played such an important role on the OPL 245 investigation. They
asked Tom if he could identify cases to work on. Cases where money
laundered into the UK was used to buy high-end property. Tom
didn't hesitate. He had unfinished business from an investigation
he had carried out in Kyrgyzstan three years before, into Maxim
Bakiyev, the former president's son. The man who had touched
down at Farnborough Airport five years before.

LONDON, 2012

It was in 2012 that Tom had got interested in the Bakiyevs. Maxim
Bakiyev's literal and metaphorical flight to the UK had its roots in
the political conflagration that tore his country apart in 2010 and
in the vast sums of state funds that had been funnelled out of the
country through the Asia Universal Bank – and that's what Tom had
been tracking down. He had managed to obtain a wealth of documents, including a list of bank transfers from the Asia Universal
Bank, taken from the SWIFT international bank-payments system.

Most of these transfers were probably quite legal. But perhaps, among the thousands of companies listed there, there was some clue as to where those hundreds of millions of dollars had gone.

We knew that the companies we were interested in would likely have nominee directors: people who managed the company for the real owner, whose identity would be hidden. So the only way to delve into what had happened would be to look for patterns; some clues linking various different companies together, or something that showed that they were operating according to an overall plan.

Sitting in our Holborn office, Tom hunched over his desk and checked and cross-checked the information from the documents he'd picked up. Trawling through the publicly available records at Companies House, something caught Tom's eye. One Yuri Voznyak, the director of a company called Velcona Ltd that featured in the SWIFT document, had travelled to London to attend a general meeting on the day of the company's registration, 23 April 2008, at Suite 2, 23–24 Great James Street. It was a long trip. Yuri was listed as a resident of Kaluga, a town about 200km outside Moscow.

According to Companies House records, Yuri wasn't the only Russian who attended meetings in Suite 2 on that day. Ekatarina Bobrova, another Kaluga resident, was recorded as having attended the general meeting of her new company, Mediton Ltd. Pavel Kuznetsov, who lived a little closer to Moscow, was also there for Nedox Ltd. Did these three people – all of them directors of three apparently completely separate companies – really travel all the way from Russia to London for a routine meeting at the same address on the same day?

Tom probed deeper. The founding director of Velcona was listed as Joahna Alcindor, based out of the Seychelles; Nedox's founder, Cinthia Julie Alcindor, was also Seychelles-based, as was Mediton's initial director, Elisana Labonte. The company secretary of Mediton and Nedox was listed as Eurodata Ltd, also based in the Seychelles. Velcona's company secretary was United Services Ltd in Belize. All three companies were registered on 23 April 2008. Nineteen months later, having presumably served their purpose, Mediton and Nedox were dissolved on the same day, 3 November 2009; Velcona followed a month later. These close links alone didn't prove anything, but they were signposts that Tom was probably on the right track as he peeled through the layers of something very fishy.

According to the SWIFT documents, from June 2008 until the Kyrgyz uprising in April 2010, US$699 million was transferred into the accounts of Yuri's company Velcona, while US$700 million was transferred out again. If you're investigating money laundering, as Tom was, this is a red flag because it looked like what it was: Velcona wasn't trading anything – it was a dormant company – so somebody was simply moving money around the place. Another red flag was rather more profound: Yuri Voznyak had died three years before he made the trip to London.

Tom's subsequent investigation exposed the scale of the fraud at Asia Universal Bank. No one knows how much money was moved out of Kyrgyzstan in the final days of President Bakiyev's rule, but the SWIFT documents alone put it at well over a billion dollars.

'It is so easy to set up a company with hidden ownership in the UK that even a dead man can do it.' Not a line from a Zombie thriller but the opening sentence of *Grave Secrecy*, the report Tom and Anthea put together documenting the results of Tom's Kyrgyzstan investigation. The report was an important plank in our campaign to show how the UK played a key role in facilitating money laundering and therefore in facilitating organized crime such as terrorism, narco-trafficking and straightforward theft. Tom left Global Witness shortly after the publication of *Grave Secrecy* to become a freelance consultant, but it wasn't his swansong. It wasn't long before we needed to call on his expertise again, and he had some unfinished business to deal with.

LONDON, 2015

'In Kyrgyzstan there was a lot of talk from the authorities that Maxim Bakiyev had moved to the UK and claimed asylum,' Tom said. 'That he had this house somewhere just outside London. But we didn't have the address. For years I was thinking, I need to find this address, I just want to go and look at the house.'

Tom had managed to get his hands on a loan agreement between Maxim Bakiyev and Boris Berezovsky, the Russian oligarch and opponent of Vladimir Putin who was later found hanged in a bathroom on his estate in Ascot, just outside London. Tom described his source as someone 'who [knew] Boris...Boris's world and the Russian world very well.' He said, 'I think Maxim Bakiyev had loaned Boris some money and Boris put his Rolls-Royce up as collateral if the loan didn't get repaid. The document detailed this weird loan agreement. I think it was £20 million, something like that, that Maxim, who was well-off at that stage, was loaning to Boris, whose wealth decreased after becoming an enemy of Putin.'

But it wasn't the details of this loan that interested Tom. What did was that the document listed a partial address for Maxim Bakiyev, including the first half of a postcode: KT20. Could this be the house Tom had long been thinking about? KT20 placed the house somewhere around the upmarket leafy commuter towns of Reigate and Banstead in the Surrey countryside, around 25 miles south of London. Towns I knew well from my childhood, and which seemed unlikely places to house the fugitive son of an ex-dictator. But to identify the actual road the house was on, Tom needed the second half of the postcode.

He started searching various property databases. 'Rightmove has quite a nice thing,' Tom said, referring to the UK's largest online real-estate portal, 'which gives you the properties purchased in the last five years over a million pounds.' Because Tom had a partial postcode, he was able to narrow the search. 'But it was still a needle in a haystack. I bought details of various high-priced properties built or bought within the time frame from the UK Land Registry, at £3 a pop, hoping to find Bakiyev's name on it, or a company that I know would link to him. I bought maybe five or ten of these, but it wasn't working.' Tom had drawn a blank. Undeterred, he kept rootling around for information, and then some luck came his way. The US authorities brought an extradition case against Maxim Bakiyev for insider trading on the New York Stock Exchange.

'That case fell through,' Tom said. 'But it did give us his address in the court documents. This has allowed us to get the Land Registry record.' And with that we got a company name. The house had been purchased in August 2010 for £3.5 million by a company called Limium Partners Limited, registered in Belize on 28 June 2010, just a couple of weeks after Bakiyev had arrived in the UK. But Belize is a notorious secrecy jurisdiction that doesn't even list the shareholders of companies registered there. From these records, it wasn't possible to identify who actually owned Limium.

To double-check his assumptions, Tom indulged in one of his investigative tricks. He folded a blank piece of paper, put it into a plain envelope and had it couriered to what he suspected was Bakiyev's Surrey home. The courier's receipt came back. It was signed 'Bakiyev'.

Score one point to Tom.

And Bakiyev had made another mistake. 'He'd used a company which was registered at the same address as all the other companies we looked at in the *Grave Secrecy* case,' Tom said. 'The company that bought the house is registered in the same place by the same company service provider, International Corporate Services (ILS), in Belize.' It was a great bit of evidence that pointed towards his whole financial empire being connected with the money-laundering bank in the Kyrgyz Republic.

The opacity that cloaks the financial sector means that organizations like ours can rarely find all the answers, but we can make educated assumptions. In *Blood Red Carpet*, the short report we published summarizing Tom's detective work into Bakiyev's Surrey house, we noted:

> It may of course be a coincidence that Bakiyev Jr. lives in a mansion owned by an anonymous company that is registered at the same Belize address as companies involved in an alleged Kyrgyz money-laundering scandal. However, Global Witness believes that it is more likely that Limium's beneficial owner is Bakiyev Jr., and as such that some of the money the Kyrgyz authorities claim Bakiyev Jr. stole may in fact have been used to buy Bakiyev Jr.'s country idyll. Indeed, if the money used to purchase the Surrey mansion did not come from one of the various alleged corruption scandals that Bakiyev Jr. and his family have been associated with, then where did it come from?

So Tom got his wish to visit and photograph Bakiyev's house, a twin-gabled mock-Tudor mansion separated from the road by wide iron gates. He made the journey several times, the most memorable one being when he accompanied a film crew from the Kyrgyz service of Radio Free Europe. 'I went with this intrepid Kyrgyz reporter who was asking a lot of neighbours about what they know about this fellow living in this house,' Tom said. 'He really wanted to go up the drive and deliver a letter, but I think Bakiyev must have seen what was happening and shut the gate. He pressed a button and the gate closed. Then his nanny came out and the reporter had a quick word with her and in the end the reporter just posted the letter. Not through the front door, but through the letterbox which is attached to the gate.' It was the closest Tom got to Maxim Bakiyev: 'He was definitely at home and definitely would have seen that a film crew was outside.'

None of Bakiyev's neighbours wanted to be filmed, but they had heard various rumours about their mysterious neighbour. 'Often they hadn't got the country right,' Tom told me. 'They called it Russia or Kazakhstan – but they'd heard that some fellow was in this house, from a strange place.'

Tom followed the reporter into the local pub and showed the guy behind the bar a photo of Bakiyev. 'Oh yes, he comes in all the time. Gets a pint and sits by himself,' Tom paraphrased the barman. I tried to imagine what it was like being part of a corrupt all-powerful ruling family, fleeing a people's revolution and then nursing a pint in a local pub in Banstead. It was probably rather boring and lonely but far less stressful. Until we came along, anyway.

Maxim Bakiyev was granted political asylum in the UK, starkly illustrating that there is a two-tier system: if you have a lot of money, regardless of how you made it, you will be welcomed with open arms. While a fugitive member of Kyrgyzstan's former ruling family, accused of numerous crimes including corruption and money laundering, was living in a gilded cage in the leafy lanes of Surrey, countless other migrants and refugees, whether simply seeking better lives or fleeing from conflict and persecution, are routinely locked up in the UK's inhumane detention centres.

Thanks to Tom, Ellie's new campaign had hit its first target. It had not only positively identified the £3.5 million mansion in the heart of the Surrey countryside but also highlighted a critical flaw in the UK regulations to keep crooked money out of the property sector. While estate agents are required to carry out due diligence on the seller of a property, they aren't required to carry out any checks on the buyer. So as long as you have the cash, anyone can buy into the UK property market with impunity.

But tracking down Bakiyev was child's play compared to what came next.

'Transparency International are the nerds of the anti-corruption world,' Rachel Davies told me. As Transparency International UK's head of advocacy, I guess she should know. Around the time that Ellie began conceiving our campaign on property in late 2013, TI UK was on the same track. A much bigger organization than Global Witness, with chapters all over the world, TI's reach and expertise was critical to success in this campaign.

TI UK began analysing different players in the shadow network: accountancy, the legal sector, the property sector. 'These are meant to be the gatekeepers that make sure that anti-money-laundering rules are followed,' Rachel told me.

In early March 2015, the same month that *Blood Red Carpet* hit the news stands, TI UK's report on London property was released and caused a sensation. *Corruption on your Doorstep: How Corrupt Capital is Used to Buy Property in the UK* showed that a minimum of 36,342 London properties were registered in offshore tax havens. It highlighted that 75 per cent of properties whose owners were being investigated for corruption were registered offshore – 38 per cent of them in the British Virgin Islands (BVI). In fact, a staggering £3.8 billion of UK property was bought by BVI companies in 2011 alone.

'The report resonated with people,' Rachel said. 'It really resonated with me – someone in her thirties who was just unable to get on the property ladder. I was thinking, why is it that we have a society where it's easier for corrupt individuals to buy up property than it is for an anti-corruption campaigner like me?'

From this point on Global Witness and Transparency International worked in close collaboration on the property campaign to optimize our complementary campaigning skills and political reach. A key element of this was Global Witness's deep-dive investigative skills, and we were onto a new lead – a case that could make all the difference.

On 24 February 2015, an inmate in Vienna's grim Josefstadt prison was found hanging in the bathroom of his solitary-confinement cell. His death was officially ruled a suicide, but rumours still abound that the prisoner was murdered. Whatever the truth, a cursory glance at his life suggests that few people would mourn him. This was no ordinary criminal.

Rakhat Aliyev was the former head of the KNB, the successor to the KGB in the former Soviet state of Kazakhstan, as well as being the boss of the tax police and the country's ambassador to Austria. He was also the son-in-law of the country's dictator, President Nursultan Nazarbayev, and his marriage to Dariga Nazarbayeva had certainly not hindered his meteoric rise to power and wealth. During his tenure as the country's feared secret-police chief, Aliyev had built a vast business empire with interests in oil, telecoms and banking; with his wife he owned Khabar, Kazakhstan's main TV station, and he earned the nickname 'Sugar' for the 10 per cent stake he held in one of the world's largest sugar brokers.

But things fell apart. Rakhat Aliyev's wife divorced him in 2007 and he was accused of a raft of crimes, including kidnapping, torture, fraud and money laundering. He moved to Malta for a while and finally handed himself in to the Austrian authorities, who had issued an arrest warrant, accusing him of the murder of two officials of the Kazhak state bank, Nurbank, in which he was a shareholder.

Torture and murder are beyond our pay grade, but was Aliyev as bad as he had been painted? Were the accusations of money laundering true? If so, could some of that money have made its way to London?

Exposing Maxim Bakiyev's bolthole in London's commuter belt had ruffled some feathers, but we needed to pluck the whole bird if we were going to prevent the UK from continuing to be the haven of choice for some of the most insalubrious characters out there. Help came from an unlikely quarter – the most famous detective in history...

Although not himself the most famous detective in history, Tom Mayne was, nevertheless, a very good one. He was doing some consultancy work with a small US-based organization, the Eurasia Democracy Initiative, led by Peter Zalmayev. He was scouring bundles of documents when he came across several focusing on Rakhat Aliyev. Tom had heard the name before. In fact, he had met the man while researching the mining industry in Kazakhstan, the focus of our 2010 report *Risky Business*.

It was a stifling hot day when Tom and Diarmid O'Sullivan took the elevator up to Aliyev's office in Vienna, sweating in the suits they'd put on for the occasion. 'He had these two big burly bodyguards. He was chain smoking, obviously very nervous,' Tom said. 'President Nazarbayev's corruption was self-evident to him, but he was very keen to show that he was not part of the system, even though he totally was. His empire had been built when he was deputy head of the tax police and head of the KNB, the state security service,' he continued. 'Many people said that he was misappropriating businesses and building up companies, taking over other people's companies and threatening people, but now he was this supposed democrat.'

With these memories in his mind, it was not surprising that finding Aliyev's name in Peter Zalmayev's documents struck a chord with Tom. 'I found that Rakhat Aliyev, or someone close to him, owned this £140 million chunk of land on Baker Street. I knew that two of the people involved with the network of companies owning this property were connected to Aliyev.'

Tom also knew that Ellie and Chido were on the lookout for a big story; and with his campaigner's nose he knew that this could be it. Baker Street in the heart of London is a prime piece of real estate, and proving that a large chunk of it had been bought with money laundered by a corrupt secret police chief from Kazakhstan would be news in itself. 'The first stage was very simple,' Tom said. 'You had these guys who definitely could be shown to have worked for Rakhat Aliyev. The complexity was trying to get to the bottom of the corporate chain.'

Tom, Ellie and Chido pored over the floor plans of the Baker Street property, Abbey House, an iconic Art Deco building that had been built for the Abbey National Building Society in the 1920s. The main building had been torn down and replaced by a block of luxury flats, but its original Portland-stone frontage topped by a magnificent clock tower survived – just a façade, like the companies that owned it.

Sherlock Holmes's comfortable apartment where, high on morphine, he solved some of his most complex cases, was situated at 221b Baker Street, an address that never existed. But if it had, it would have been smack in the middle of Abbey House, which was at 219–229 Baker Street. In fact, as soon as Abbey House was built in

the 1920s, mail began arriving there addressed to Sherlock Homes
– so much mail that they needed to hire a full-time staff member to
answer it all. We know the media like a hook to hang a story on,
and if the Kazakh secret-police chief had laundered money to buy
Sherlock Holmes's apartment that would definitely be a nice one.

As winter slowly gave way to the spring of 2015, Tom sat at
his kitchen table in north London poring over the documents.
Occasionally, dressed in the long black overcoat he habitually wore,
he'd get the Tube and make for the British Library, where he'd sip
herbal tea and browse through company databases. Painstakingly he
set out to disassemble the mind-numbingly complex puzzle created to
conceal the true owners of 219–229 Baker Street. He discovered that
between 2008 and 2010, a network of linked companies had gone on
a shopping spree, acquiring £147 million of London property.

In April 2008, Parkview Estates Management Limited purchased
an imposing red-brick Queen Anne-style mansion in Highgate for
£9.3 million. Its high hedges shielded the house, with its seven
bedrooms and indoor swimming pool, from the quiet residential
street. In April 2013, the ownership of the mansion passed to a
Panamanian company, the Villa Magna Foundation. A year after
Parkview bought the mansion, another company, Greatex Limited,
purchased the freehold of a different property in Baker Street,
but within six months sold it on for a £1.12 million gross profit.
Greatex also bought the leases of two properties near Hyde Park,
subsequently selling one of them, worth £1 million, to a company
registered in Jersey, also in April 2013. In March 2010, yet another
company, Dynamic Estates Limited, came up with the big money,
shelling out £98.475 million for the main Baker Street property,
which included Abbey House.

Dynamic and Parkview were linked, Tom discovered. Both were
wholly owned subsidiaries of a company called Farmont. In turn,
Farmont and Greatex were also linked, both owned by yet another
company registered in the British Virgin Islands.

The next task for Tom was to try to unearth the identities of the
real people behind these companies, and that was a job of pure
detective work. He called up old contacts to unlock their memories, and scoured press articles that followed Aliyev's trail – from
Kazakhstan to Austria and beyond. He studied hundreds of pages

of court records and testimony, and gradually the fog that obscured the companies began to lift as if stirred by the wind, allowing tantalizing glimpses of people, names and places. The lynchpin of the network became visible in Malta.

On 16 February 2012, while on the run from the mounting charges against him in Kazakhstan, Rakhat Aliyev answered questions put to him by the Austrian public prosecutor via the Maltese Magistrates Court. Aliyev admitted owning a German metallurgy factory called Metallwerke Bender Rheinland GmbH and its Austrian parent company, Armoreal Trading GmbH. This testimony was reinforced by the fact that Armoreal covered the immodest €20,000 hotel bill racked up by Aliyev and his father-in-law, President Nazarbayev, during a week-long stay in Austria in 2006.

Acting on a hunch, Tom trawled through German and Austrian company registries to see what he could find about these companies. It was a good hunch. Aliyev's second wife, Elnara Shorazova, was a director of Armoreal and also acted as its liquidator when it was dissolved in 2010. Meanwhile her father was a director of Metallwerke between 2007 and 2010. But the trail was only just beginning.

The managing director of Metallwerke from August 2005 to February 2007 was one Massimiliano Dall'Osso, an Italian citizen who also sat on the board of directors of Armoreal with Shorazova, Aliyev's second wife. Ferreting through yet more company registries, Tom identified that Dall'Osso was also a director of Farmont, Dynamic and Parkview, the companies that had bought the London properties we were interested in. Tom, like all good investigators, didn't leap to any conclusions, although it was tempting. Instead, like the fictional resident of one of these properties, he kept on probing.

We wrote to Dall'Osso asking him who owned these companies; but, despite having served as a managing director of Metallwerke, he denied knowing who the owner was. In response to our questions, he also said: 'At no time was Mr Aliyev the UBO [ultimate beneficial owner] of [Farmont, Dynamic and Parkview].' Thus unequivocal denial was conceivable. Just. Despite his proven links to Aliyev and his wife, via Armoreal and Metallwerke, Dall'Osso could feasibly be representing some other wealthy client. The trail continued.

In his testimony to the Maltese court, Aliyev had also named another company, AV Maximus Holding, as belonging to him. News reports in *Malta Today* mentioned a company with a very similar name, AV Maximus SA, as being part of Aliyev's network. One of the directors of AV Maximus SA was a Frenchman, Bernard Enry, who served on the board for 11 years from May 2003 to June 2014. Enry was also a director of Villa Magna, the Panamanian company that had taken over the Highgate mansion. We wrote to Enry.

His lawyers replied, saying that 'Rakhat Aliyev never was the ultimate beneficial owner of the Villa Magna Foundation. Confidentiality owed to Villa Magna's [*sic*] means that Mr Enry cannot tell you who the actual beneficial owner is.' We wrote to Enry again, probing possible links between the various AV Maximus companies. His lawyers wrote to say that Enry was not aware of any 'Maximus' companies which may have been registered outside of Switzerland. They did not respond to our allegation that Enry had known or associated with Aliyev and/or Shorazova.

What we had so far was not definitive, but it did show that Dall'Osso and Enry were involved in property companies that could be connected to Aliyev and Shorazova and had not denied knowing or working with either of them. The links didn't stop there. Greatex Limited, the UK company that had bought and sold the smaller Baker Street property and taken the leases on another two near Hyde Park, was registered on 4 December 2007. Two days later, a company with a similar name, Greatex (Suisse) SA, was registered in Geneva. Its president was Nurali Aliyev, Aliyev's eldest son. He was just 22 years old. In November 2007 a Kazakh citizen, Mukhamed Ali Kurmanbayev, was appointed a director of Greatex (Suisse) SA. Four months later, he also became a director of Greatex Limited in the UK. He listed his address as 36 Rue de Monthoux, Geneva.

Another Greatex company, the Greatex Trade and Investment Corp., was registered in 2007 in the BVI. Its registration in this secrecy jurisdiction meant that Tom couldn't identify its shareholders and directors, but by looking through their accounts he found that this company wholly owned Greatex Limited and was, from 2010 to 2011, the ultimate controlling party of Farmont. A search of the UK's Companies House showed that Kurmanbayev was also a director of Farmont and Dynamic, the company that spent

£98.5 million on Abbey House in Baker Street. When Kurmanbayev resigned those directorships, he was replaced by Dall'Osso.

The blanket of secrecy surrounding BVI-registered companies meant we couldn't prove links between the owners of Greatex (Suisse) SA and Greatex Limited. But we could make some assumptions. The companies had similar names, they were registered at near enough the same time and shared a director: Kurmanbayev. Aliyev's son Nurali was the president of Greatex (Suisse), so it wasn't too wild an assumption that a member of the Aliyev family might be behind Greatex Limited and, ergo, the property it owns.

We wrote to Kurmanbayev. Via his lawyers he too denied that Rakhat Aliyev was the beneficial owner of the companies: 'Our client never had any relationship, whether professional or personal with Rakhat Aliyev, either directly or through intermediaries. Nor has our client ever met with or had any professional or personal relationship with Rakhat Aliyev's widow, Elnara Shorazova.'

In a subsequent letter they went a little further, confirming that Nurali Aliyev was the president of Greatex (Suisse) SA. They added:

> In about May 2007, Rakhat Aliyev was suspected of being involved in the murder of two individuals. It is evidently clear from all public domain reports that thereafter he was ostracized from his family. [...] Our client did not join Greatex until November 2007. It is worth noting that when our client joined Greatex, his principal condition for accepting the position was that Rakhat Aliyev was not involved in the business and he would not be required to deal with him, whether directly or indirectly. [...] Furthermore, at no time whatsoever was our client on notice that any of his instructions were from Rakhat Aliyev, nor that any of the transactions to which our client was a party involved any criminal acts, including money-laundering.

And that was about as far as we could get. Confused? You're meant to be. In fact, they're banking on it. Rakhat Aliyev and members of his family were certainly linked to all these companies, but everyone we had approached unequivocally denied that he was their beneficial owner. So who was?

*

Meanwhile, Chido was grappling with another factor in this already complex investigation. 'We were very aware that Rakhat Aliyev had many enemies in Kazakhstan,' she said. 'And that it was hugely likely, although we didn't know for sure, that somehow the information had made its way to us because somebody wanted us to know about it.'

She was referring to a critical part of an investigator's role. We depend on sources to bring us information, but we need to try to divine why someone is giving it to us. Is it because they have an axe to grind with the person they're snitching on? Or maybe they're in some commercial competition with them? Or could they simply be doing the right thing? Chido went on: 'We had to really balance what we were looking at, but even if it served the interests of someone else it doesn't mean it wasn't true. But we had to be really careful about that. And we had to be really mindful of the fact that something could be a forgery.'

Tom had been given an Interpol document among the stash of papers from Peter Zamayev. It showed that some of the people involved in the properties were being investigated for money laundering. Chido gave the document to a contact of ours with experience of Interpol notices, who said it looked like the real thing – which, according to Chido, 'certainly made our very nervous lawyers slightly less nervous'.

Meanwhile the pressure on the investigative team was increasing. We had heard from Peter Zamayev that the Nazarbayevs, presumably Aliyev's first wife Dariga and son Nurali, had received a tip-off that they were under investigation, which meant trouble, and they were looking to sell the properties. If that happened, there would be no story and they would get away with it. We were racing against the clock.

Our focus so far had been on Rakhat Aliyev, an assumption we'd reached because known associates of his were definitely linked to the properties we were looking at. But Chido had taken a pragmatic view. We didn't know for sure that Aliyev was directly connected and – given that he was dead – we couldn't ask him. But we knew that the Baker Street story was strong enough to be one of the keys that would unlock political policy on the property issue. We were working right up to the line, but the night before the report we'd been putting together was to be published, and after all the painstaking legal checks had been completed, Tom was looking at a document in German. He gave it to a friend of his, a native German speaker, and she spotted an anomaly. The document revealed that one of the key managers of the property, who used to work for Aliyev, was now working for Dariga Nazarbayeva, his ex-wife. 'This significantly changed things,' Tom told me. 'It suggested the guy had swapped sides and therefore the properties could be hers.'

'But what we said still stood up,' Chido said. 'There was so much intrigue in this because there were so many different vested interests…what we said in the report was that these properties could all be linked to Kazakhstan's first family.'

Benson Beard, of estate agents Bective Leslie Marsh, was probably full of curiosity as he waited at the door of the five-storey, five-bedroom house in Chelsea to greet a potential buyer. The meeting had been arranged by Tom Ward, a fixer for a wealthy Russian client interested in a high-end London property. And at a cool £15.75 million, houses don't come much more high-end than this.

The sleek Mercedes limousine pulled up and disgorged a larger-than-life portly Russian in his fifties and an undeniably hot blonde probably still in her twenties. An SUV behind them contained a tough-looking shaven-headed man who kept close to his boss. Benson opened the stately door of the house and ushered Boris and his mistress into the large, opulent hallway, dominated by a huge gilt mirror.

Benson suggested they go to the fifth floor and then walk their way back down through the house. Thrilled by the idea of having their own lift, Nastya said, 'Why look any further?' Boris laughed and rolled his eyes resignedly. 'I shouldn't have brought her here, now it's not my decision!' he joked in his booming, heavily accented voice. Benson must have been excited at the prospect of a quick sale, as his firm stood to make £315,000 in commission if it went through.

'I love it,' Boris said. 'But it's not that simple.' He went on to explain that he was a healthcare minister and ran the procurement of all the drugs in Russia. His salary was meagre but, he confided, 'You know how it is. From every contact, a little bit I put in my pocket…Stolen funds. Money. It's by way of compensation.' Boris emphasized that there was no way he could be linked to the transaction. 'The money for this comes out of the Russian government budget.'

'Don't talk to me about where it comes from,' Benson broke in. 'I don't need to know.'

Boris thought for a moment. 'The Russian government won't find my name on this?'

'Absolutely not.' Benson reassured him that because his client was the seller, he didn't need to know anything about the buyer's finances.

'Have you done this sort of thing before?' Boris enquired.

Benson looked non-committal for a moment. 'Probably.'

Ten days later they met again and Benson had done his homework. He had identified a lawyer to help Boris. All he needed to do was to set up a company to do the purchase: that way, Boris's name would never appear on the Land Registry documents.

Unfortunately for Benson and a number of other London estate agents visited by Boris and his squeeze, he was the victim of an undercover sting. Boris Borisovich was an anti-corruption campaigner and the glamorous Nastya an award-winning Ukrainian anti-corruption journalist called Natalie Sedletska.

From Russia with Cash was screened by Channel 4 in early July 2015 to rave reviews. As with *Candid Camera*, the viewer watches with a kind of delicious dread as the unwitting estate agents listen to Boris's tales of corruption, and then go ahead and tell him that they can find ways around the rules. It was utterly damning. As a result, Benson Beard was expelled from the Royal Institute of Chartered Surveyors for failing in his professional obligation to report potential money laundering to his company or the police. He remains an associate director of Bective Leslie Marsh.

'Together with TI and Boris, we were a dream-team triumvirate,' Chido said. TI had better connections with the government than we did, and they brought her along to every meeting. This, together with Boris's information and our own, made us an almost unstoppable force.

On 22 July 2015, shortly after *From Russia With Cash* went out, our report *Mystery on Baker Street* was published – just four months after Chido and Tom received the first tip-off. To investigate an issue of this complexity, write it up and get it through our stringent legal checks in this time frame was little short of a miracle.

Global Witness is a member of BOND, a coalition of organizations tackling poverty, inequality and injustice, and as part of their anti-corruption group Chido met with one of Prime Minister David Cameron's special advisers (Spads) at No. 10 Downing Street. Chido talked him through our findings and the need for there to be a public register of property ownership. Not the companies that owned properties but, critically, the people *behind* those companies. A few days later, as she stood looking out of the office window, Chido received a call from Downing Street. 'The prime minister is making a speech in Singapore tomorrow morning. Watch it.'

Standing behind the lectern at the Lee Kuan Yew School of Public Policy on his Britain Means Business tour, Cameron got the pleasantries out of the way and came to the thorny issue of corruption. 'Bad for business and bad for the economy,' he said. 'We know that some high-value properties – particularly in London – are being bought by people overseas through anonymous shell companies, some of them with plundered or laundered cash. Just last week, there were allegations of links between a former Kazakh secret-police chief and a London property portfolio worth nearly £150 million.'

In the space of four months, Ellie, Chido and Tom, with our allies at TI and Boris, had brought this new issue to the top of the international political agenda. Not just in the UK, but internationally. So how was Cameron going to tackle this?

'As a first step, I have asked the Land Registry to publish this autumn data on which foreign companies own which land and property titles in England and Wales. This will apply to around 100,000 titles held on the Land Register and will show for the first time the full set of titles owned by foreign companies.' Cameron added to this commitment by pledging to host an anti-corruption summit in 2016, then concluded with a snappy slogan: 'London is not a place to stash your dodgy cash.'

David Cameron's Anti-Corruption Summit slated for May 2016 was given extra impetus by the release of the Panama Papers a month before. As Cameron prepared to welcome world leaders, policymakers and anti-corruption organizations to London, temperatures were raised when he was overheard telling the Queen that countries like Afghanistan and Nigeria were 'fantastically corrupt'. True enough, perhaps. But it missed the point of why the summit was being held at all: because London is the place to stash your dodgy cash because London is also fantastically corrupt. Corruption is a truly globalized industry.

For Chido, it was a disappointment. 'The summit didn't amount to as much as we'd hoped, but it was useful in the sense that it reframed corruption as not something that is "done over there", but something that's done in the UK and other places, and that needed to happen.'

Matthew Hancock, minister for the Cabinet Office at the time, told the BBC about Cameron's plans: 'It does not matter where in the world your company is registered; if you own property in London or sell things to government, as part of government procurement, then you have to declare the beneficial ownership – in other words, the ultimate ownership of the company.' This was an amazing win for our NGO coalition and other anti-corruption NGOs and journalists. But then came an unexpected setback.

'We had this political headwind and political agency behind this big announcement, and then a couple of weeks afterwards we had Brexit,' Ellie said. 'It was an incredible lesson as a campaigner. You're riding the waves when they're good, but you need to be prepared for headwinds to start blowing against you pretty quickly – and you should always be thinking about what your Plan B is. What do you do when within the space of a couple of weeks the key political backer – who happened to be the prime minister – resigned, and the UK had voted to become much more isolationist in its approach?'

We and TI UK went into overdrive to keep the pledge to create the property register on the table.

'In 2017 we heard rumours that this policy was about to be quietly dropped by the government,' TI's Rachel Davies told me. She met with another Global Witness campaigner, Naomi Hirst, for breakfast in a café near London's Borough Market. 'We were throwing every idea we could down on paper. We knew we needed to throw everything we could at this. Absolutely everything. Because if we didn't, there was such a real risk it was just going to get dropped.'

Global Witness and TI UK cornered ministers at party conferences, collared MPs and pursued civil servants. 'We were pushing,

pushing, pushing, pushing, trying to keep the pressure on, trying to send the message to the government: "You won't be able to quietly drop this."' What Rachel described highlights the intensity of NGO advocacy. We succeeded for a time, but then there was a General Election, a new prime minister and a new Cabinet. 'And we had to do it all over again,' Rachel said.

It was November 2019 and a critical event was getting ever closer. 'The Queen's Speech is coming up. How do we make sure it gets in the Queen's Speech and it doesn't drop off the agenda?' Rachel said. 'We contacted loads of private-sector firms that we knew on the TI side of things, asking them to write letters to the minister or to No. 10. We got Conservatives in the House of Lords to write to No. 10.'

Together we succeeded in holding the Boris Johnson government to Cameron's original pledge. But then another curveball came in the form of Covid-19, which completely subsumed parliamentary business. We hope that the pledge will survive into the next parliamentary session, but we're not complacent about that.

On 29 May 2019, a ten-bedroom mansion in The Bishops Avenue, Hampstead – one of London's most expensive streets – was hit by an Unexplained Wealth Order (UWO) secured by the UK's National Crime Agency (NCA). The house on what's known as 'Billionaires' Row' was the home of Nurali Aliyev and his family. A second UWO was issued against another exclusive home in Denewood Road, just a 20-minute walk away on the other side of Highgate Golf Club. This was the £9.3 million mansion we had identified in *Mystery on Baker Street*, owned by the Panamanian Villa Magna Foundation. The final UWO was secured against a super-luxury Chelsea flat estimated to be worth £40 million. The NCA issued a simultaneous 'freezing order' to prevent the properties, together worth £80 million, from being sold or transferred.

Unexplained Wealth Orders are a new tool in the UK's anti-corruption arsenal, giving law-enforcement agencies the power to investigate and seize assets they suspect have been purchased with the proceeds of organized crime, fraud and money laundering. TI UK had played a major role in bringing these laws about and this was only the second time they had been put to the test. According to the NCA's press release, 'Three Unexplained Wealth Orders have been secured as part of a National Crime Agency investigation into

London property linked to a politically exposed person believed to be involved in serious crime.' They were on the trail of the hundreds of millions of dollars they suspected were looted by Rakhat Aliyev who had 'been involved in...bribery, corruption, blackmail, conspiracy to defraud, forgery and money laundering,' according to an investigator quoted on the BBC, who continued: 'I also believe that members of his family, including Nurali Aliyev, have been involved in money laundering.'

Nurali Aliyev and his mother, Dariga Nazarbayeva, needed a good lawyer. Predictably, they found succour at our old friends Mishcon de Reya. Mishcon instructed Clare Montgomery QC to get the UWOs overturned, and they prevailed. It seemed that Nurali and Dariga had also found themselves a good judge, from their perspective anyway. In a judgement that bore painful similarities to Lady Justice Gloster's divvying up the spoils between the two criminal fixers in the OPL 245 case, Mrs Justice Lang wrote that 'notwithstanding his criminality, Rakhat Aliyev had been a successful businessman' – noting that Dariga's wealth stemmed in part from a company she had received her 'formal interest' in as part of her divorce settlement from Aliyev in 2007.

Mrs Justice Lang's judgement went on to outline Nurali's remarkably extensive business accomplishments as listed on LinkedIn. When he found spare time from his duties as the deputy mayor of Kazakhstan's capital, Astana, he focused on an impressive array of chairmanships. She included his stratospheric success in Nurbank, reputedly owned by his father: 'From March 2006–July 2010, he was a director at Nurbank, located in Almaty, Kazakhstan. He was initially appointed as Deputy Chairman from March 2006–April 2007, before becoming Chairman of the Board in April 2007 (when 22 years old).'

Thus Mrs Justice Lang reached the conclusion that Nurali was sufficiently independent of his parents by 2008 to purchase 33 The Bishops Avenue for himself, and with that she discharged the UWOs. Mrs Justice Lang wasn't the first judge to have a credulous faith in the extraordinary entrepreneurial skills of the scions of dictators. 'Surely the criminality negates any kind of business success?' Tom Mayne said, disgusted. 'Notwithstanding his criminality, Jeff Skilling was a successful CEO at Enron? Notwithstanding his criminality, Harvey Weinstein was a successful ladies' man?'

The NCA appealed, but the appeal failed.

In November 2020, an investigation by *The Times* and *Source Material*, an investigative journalism outfit led by our old friend and former Global Witness investigator Leigh Baldwin, confirmed that the Baker Street properties were indeed owned by Dariga Nazarbayeva and her son Nurali.

It is of course possible that Rakhat Aliyev's ex-wife and his son are innocent of any crime. We don't know the scale of Nurali's business acumen when at the age of 22 he became the president of Greatex (Suisse), a company that shortly afterwards acquired a £100-million property in the heart of London. Perhaps his mother, the daughter of President Nazarbayev and apparently worth around US$600 million, is indeed a successful businesswoman in her own right. The cases of state looting and corruption that Global Witness has investigated over the years are littered with ultra-rich ruling families and senior politicians of notoriously corrupt states who claim that they have quite independently built fantastically successful business empires. The use of companies set up in secrecy jurisdictions, a practice actively defended by the likes of Mishcon de Reya, makes it very hard to disprove. We needed to turn our attention to another facet of the shadow network: those that made possible such anonymous incorporation.

Rosie Sharpe had been with us since she volunteered in our Bickerton Road days in the early 2000s. After initially working on Cambodia, she began working on tackling the secret beneficial ownership of companies. 'So we started to think about an undercover investigation,' Rosie said. 'We were inspired by the work of Jason Sharman, an Australian academic.'

Sharman and two fellow academics, Michael Findley and Daniel Nielson, had posed as consultants wanting to create new companies. They had approached 3,700 company-registration agents in 182 countries to test their appetite for corruption risk and their compliance with the international standards set by the Financial Action Task Force (FATF). Some of their enquiries were designed to appear to come from low-risk countries like Norway, others from notoriously corrupt countries in Africa or the former Soviet Union. In some cases, they deliberately raised red flags suggesting terrorist links. The results of their survey made interesting reading.

Forty-eight per cent of the formation agents did not ask for proper identification in compliance with FATF standards, and around half of these didn't ask for any documentation at all. Agents based in OECD countries performed worse than the usual suspects from the Caribbean tax havens and the Channel Islands. One American formation agent stated that they feared the company could be used as a front for terrorism, but said they'd consider doing the job for a fee of US$5,000 per month.

Rosie knew a good idea when she saw one; but while this academic exercise had been hugely valuable in illustrating the scale of the problem, it didn't identify any of the companies or individuals involved. We needed to replicate something like this but to do it our way. We started by sending an undercover investigator to a couple of company-formation agents, but the results were disappointing.

'It's very unusual to go to meet a company service provider; they do their business online,' Rosie explained to me. 'You just type "shell company offshore" into Google and you get loads of companies that will set up your own shell company in a matter of minutes. So it's slightly weird for them to have someone actually knock on their door. If you do, you tend to meet a person who isn't super-qualified and doesn't really know how to answer the questions that are being posed to them. When you watch the secret film footage, the main thing you feel is sympathy for this poor person being asked all these awkward questions like, "Is it okay if we open a company and use it to launder some money?" They just don't know what to reply,' Rosie smiled.

Rob Palmer elaborated further: 'But then on the last day the investigator went to a law firm, and it was so clear. They sat around this polished, posh, giant wooden table. Lawyers in suits who had this smirk on their faces. This is what we need to do – we need to go after the lawyers. They're the ones who really understand what they're being asked to do.'

Rosie and Rob wanted to go undercover to expose the lawyers who facilitated corruption. I was sceptical about whether this would work. If you are a corrupt politician looking to get dirty money into the US, you don't just google lawyers, give them a Gmail address and turn up unknown on their doorstep. Rosie was worried too: 'It might be just a complete waste of time and money.' Rosie and Rob convened a meeting of senior staff and when we were all crowded into that meeting room, they did an impressive job of selling the idea. I was dubious about whether it would work, and the potential legal risks were pretty dizzying. But we were also keen and gave the go-ahead despite our doubts. Would it work or not? There was only one way to find out.

Rosie's team had decided to focus on a prestigious location in a highly regulated country. If the system was rotten in one of these places, then it was likely to be completely putrid elsewhere. We settled on New York. We chose it not only because it was one of the world's great financial centres, and one where we knew that many corrupt people bought property, but also because in New York we could take a secret camera into a private space perfectly legally. So now we knew where. The next question was, who was going to do it, and how?

Like Ellie, Rosie is extremely methodical and she wanted our investigator to be as well briefed as possible. 'Obviously, you can't script something precisely, but we've tried to think up all the possible questions that we could ask. And we've invented two personas for this. One is: "I'm an adviser to an African minister, who's getting to the end of his political life and he's made quite a bit of money. Bribery is such a dirty word, but he'd like to bring the money into the US and enjoy the fruits of his labour and his retirement,"' Rosie said.

The second story was that the investigator poses as a consultant working for a Russian oil company that wants to pump money into various US politicians' election campaigns. We test-ran this by emailing a few lawyers to gauge their interest, but this didn't get anywhere. 'Every single lawyer came back with exactly the same message: "What you're proposing is completely illegal. We can never help."'

So we needed to come up with an adviser to an African minister.

In the summer of 2014, a tall man in a white linen suit, a dapper white hat and a pair of rather incongruous Birkenstock's pushed open the door of an office building on Lexington Avenue, Manhattan, just a block away from the Chrysler Building. He walked directly across the lobby to the reception desk, where he was asked for his photo ID. He blustered, frantically searching his pockets and muttering to himself in his strong German accent – but it was no good, he had left his ID behind at his hotel. Instead, he proffered a business card which identified him as Ralph Kayser, an adviser to the minister of mines in a mineral-rich country in West Africa. His tanned, lined face, topped by a mop of unruly iron-grey hair, had seen a thousand African suns and gave credence to his story, and he was undoubtedly quite charming. Satisfied, the receptionist directed him to the elevator. As he was whisked skywards, Ralph Kayser mentally ran through the checklist of things he had to cover.

The elevator doors slid open silently and he found himself in the reception area of top New York law firm Sullivan & Worcester. Ushered into a small meeting room, Ralph, a rather hesitant and bumbling man, haphazardly dumped a handful of things – his keys, mobile phone, some coins and other paraphernalia – onto the conference table next to him. He was fussy about where he sat. He had sensitive eyes, he told the people he was meeting, so he couldn't sit facing a window looking into the summer Manhattan sun. He couldn't sit with his back to the window either, because he suffered from vertigo. Ralph Kayser could be irritating, but he remained charming.

James Silkenat had enjoyed an illustrious legal career. He gained his law degree at the New York University School of Law, became law professor at Georgetown University, then a partner at Sullivan & Worcester and by the time he met Ralph Kayser he was also the president of the American Bar Association. He sat opposite Ralph, his own thatch of silver hair almost equal to Ralph's mop. His colleague, Hugh Finnegan, sat to Ralph's right, and they both adopted a sincere-looking 'we're ready to listen' stance.

Ralph introduced his advisory role for the African minister and explained how his boss needed to get some money into the United States. A lot of money.

'Companies are eager to get hold of rare earths or other minerals. And so they pay some special money for it. I wouldn't name it bribe. I would say "facilitation money",' Ralph told them. He told them it was all legal. And now his boss wanted to enjoy the fruits of his successful career and was looking to buy a New York townhouse, a jet and a yacht. 'But,' Ralph stressed, 'his name must not be connected to the purchases. If his name appeared in connection with buying some real estate and the other rich-man's trappings it would be, to say the least, very embarrassing.'

'Right. 'Cause...presumably his salary in, wherever it is, would not cover the kinds of acquisitions we're talking about?' Silkenat asked.

'For sure. It's the salary of a teacher here [in New York],' Ralph responded. 'And so how can we make sure that he is being able to buy property here and to live a nice life, but his name being out?'

'Right. Any guesses as to how much money we're talking about for the brownstone and the other items?' Silkenat asked.

'For the brownstone...between 5 and 20 million; it depends where. Let's say, about US$10 million. For a second-hand Gulfstream I could imagine 10, 20 million. A yacht would be at least, if you're talking about an Abramovich yacht, this dimension, would be around 200, 300 million. So I would start, let's say with around 50 million coming here, [but it's] not a one-off,' Ralph said in his heavily accented English.

Silkenat looked thoughtful as his colleague Finnegan outlined just how Ralph's client could bring his money into the US and keep his name out of it. He could set up a series of anonymously owned companies based in multiple jurisdictions, which would create an almost unnavigable labyrinth.

'So Company A is owned by Company B, which is owned jointly by Company C and D, and your party owns all of or the majority of the shares of C and D,' Silkenat weighed in.

'So we, we create several companies?' Ralph asked, trying to understand this idea.

'Yes,' Finnegan responded.

'All in New York or different states?'

'Well. Like I said, at some point, probably pretty quickly, you'd go offshore.'

Silkenat and Finnegan had laid out a roadmap of how Ralph Kayser's client could launder the money he had stolen into the United States. The minute secret camera that was among the paraphernalia Ralph Kayser had carelessly dumped on the table at the beginning of the conversation had captured every word, with James Silkenat in shot throughout.

The meeting with Silkenat and Finnegan was the fourteenth meeting that Ralph Kayser had during those first two weeks of June, and it was the last one. We had learned enough. His questions had been designed to raise suspicions that Ralph's client was not kosher and that he was trying to launder the proceeds of crime. Although Silkenat and Finnegan had clearly explained how Mr Kayser could launder money, they were the only firm who said that they would need to check no crime had been committed; and who said that if they suspected that one had they would be obliged to report it. But, as the meeting drew to a close, the two lawyers were not short of enthusiasm.

'I'm happy to chat whenever it's possible to move the ball forward on this,' Silkenat told Ralph.

In another meeting, John H Jankoff of Jankoff & Gabe PC advised Ralph, 'The first problem you have is you can't bring the money into the US because the United States has an anti-corruption act. So you have to move the money to a neutral site, like the Cayman Islands, the Isle of Man, whatever. The money goes there, then…you set up a corporation [that] says I would like to buy a brownstone in New York.'

His partner, Lawrence M Gabe, was evidently a cautious man. He asked Ralph for his phone number, saying, 'I'm certainly not putting this in emails.'

'Sending an email with just an outline would be fine, as well, so it's…'

'I don't like emails,' Jankoff interjected.

'You don't like emails?' Ralph asked.

'That's how you catch people,' was Gabe's succinct response.

Meanwhile in his book-lined office at Henderson & Koplik LLP, Marc Koplik, shaven-headed and resplendent in wide blue braces and a blue polka-dot tie, oozed privilege as he told Ralph, 'They don't send the lawyers to jail, because we run the country.'

Only one firm out of the 14 Ralph met refused to play ball. Jeffrey Herrmann warned that 'under the Foreign Corrupt Practices Act bribing foreign officials is illegal' and dismissed Ralph with a terse, 'This ain't for me. My standards are higher.'

Ralph Kayser had back-up in New York in the shape of Rob Palmer. 'We were holed up in this little apartment in Hell's Kitchen, and Ralph would go out every day. He's just got such a wonderful manner, slightly cheeky. And he's in some ways so implausible that it's hard to believe that he would be an undercover person. He went out every day in this white linen suit, with Birkenstock's, to go meet these lawyers, and he must have just come across as this guy who says that he hangs around Africa and knows all these people, and wants to move dodgy money into the US. And I could totally see that Ralph could be someone who could be engaged in those types of behaviour.'

Every day when Ralph returned home from work, he and Rob would go through the footage. Noting where the lawyers had implicated themselves the most, learning lessons for the next meeting, and making sure the film was backed up.

When he got back from New York, Rob left nothing out. He was particularly impressed by the way the lawyers navigated these perilous waters. 'Like, "I'm not gonna outright say I'm going to break the law for you. But I'm going to heavily suggest and wink, nudge." That's the way these games are played,' Rob said. 'What is so extraordinary was that these lawyers are prepared to say this stuff to someone they've only just met, who they didn't know anything about? Can you imagine if you were someone who was really in this world, and had all these links and all these relationships, how far you could go?'

What Ralph and the team had obtained in New York was far more than we could have hoped for. Our communications team wanted to make our significant investment in this investigation pay, and they began foraging around for the best media partner for the exposé.

Charmian meanwhile had become the public face of our campaign to pressure governments to bring in public registers of companies, to throw a spanner in the works of corrupt deals like Simandou (see chapter 5) and OPL 245, and the complex company structures that enabled criminals to buy up property empires worth hundreds of millions of pounds in London. They all depended on the almost impenetrable labyrinth created by layer upon layer of secretly owned companies.

Charmian had been introduced by an old Global Witness friend, the author Misha Glenny, to Bruno Giussani, the European director of TED, and she was invited to speak on the need to end anonymous companies. Her 2013 talk at TEDGlobal in Edinburgh was viewed over 2.6 million times and it led to the award of the prestigious US$1 million TED Prize in 2014, building a powerful head of steam to the campaign.

Meanwhile our comms team had begun to build a crucial new relationship with the makers of the primetime CBS news magazine show *60 Minutes*, who were enthusiastic to screen Ralph Kayser's amazing escapades. We had all the material, but we also had a problem. Because we named and shamed rich and powerful crooks, we were well used to navigating legal risk – but the risk was now of a different order. This investigation had targeted some of New York's top lawyers.

More than a year was to pass, but on 31 January 2016 *60 Minutes* broadcast *Anonymous* and Ralph Kayser's secret film footage was beamed across America. The story about anonymously owned companies being used to launder money into the US reached policy-makers and households alike.

The day after the report aired, two members of the House of Representatives, Peter King and Carolyn Maloney, both members of the Financial Services Committee, cited the story when they introduced legislation that 'takes aim at the phenomenon of anonymously owned companies, which have in the past been used as financial vehicles for criminal enterprises and terrorism.' Maloney told a press conference that the *60 Minutes* piece was 'explosive' and 'scandalous'.

Working with over a hundred allies, members of the Financial Accountability and Corporate Transparency (FACT) Coalition, we kept the pressure on Congress. The Corporate Transparency Act was finally passed by the House of Representatives on 22 October 2019. After a year of nailbiting delays, on 11 December 2020 the US Senate passed the annual National Defense Authorization Act, which that year included the Corporate Transparency Act. *Fortune* magazine noted that

> *A multiyear undercover investigation conducted by Global Witness along with extensive reports published by the* New York Times *have exposed the criminal enterprises that anonymous shell companies enable. In every state, more information is required to get a library card than to form a secret company, and the U.S. is the largest incorporator of companies in the world. The passage of the legislation will be a substantial blow to those who have long abused the secrecy provided by our financial system.*

Our old friends at Mishcon, seemingly more concerned with their clients' interests than with tackling the global evils of 'criminal enterprises and terrorism' that so concerned Carolyn Maloney, had instead been spending their time mounting what they proudly called an 'assiduous' campaign against these moves. Under the lead of Mischcon partner Filippo Noseda, they launched a 'Legal challenge to Common Reporting Standard (CRS) and Beneficial Ownership (BO) registers' and lodged a formal complaint with the UK's information commissioner under the new EU General Data Protection Regulation (GDPR).

Marc Koplik's boast that lawyers don't go to jail didn't stop the New York Supreme Court Appellate Division from at least issuing him and John H Jankoff a public censure for their advice to our investigator, saying about Koplik that 'He counseled a client to engage in conduct he knew was illegal or fraudulent and suggested to the client that lawyers in the United States can act with impunity.'

Six years after the sting, on 29 April 2020, the American Bar Association's Standing Committee on Ethics and Professional Responsibility issued its own censure in its Formal Opinion 491. Referencing the sting on both Jankoff and Koplik, the opinion was drily titled 'Obligations Under Rule 1.2(d) to Avoid Counseling or Assisting in a Crime or Fraud in Non-Litigation Settings'.

James Silkenat is no longer a partner at Sullivan & Worcester. Among his other activities, he now sits on the board of directors of the World Justice Project, an NGO established to promote the rule of law. Its website notes that 'Effective rule of law reduces corruption, combats poverty and disease, and protects people from injustices large and small. It is the foundation for communities of justice, opportunity, and peace – underpinning development, accountable government, and respect for fundamental rights.'

8

RESISTANCE: THE FRONTLINES, 2012–2020

At first I thought I was fighting to save rubber trees, then I thought I was fighting to save the Amazon rainforest. Now I realize I am fighting for humanity.

Chico Mendes

CARDAMOM MOUNTAINS, CAMBODIA, 26 APRIL 2012

'And then we look behind us and we see two motorcycles coming, the sun glaring behind them. It was a very surreal image; these two shadowy figures coming towards us on motorcycles. And I see something poking up from behind their backs and you can tell they are guns – AK47s. There was a soldier on one bike, and a soldier and a military police officer on the second one.' Olesia Plokhii and Phorn Bopha will never forget that day, and neither will I.

The two journalists with the *Cambodia Daily* newspaper were accompanying renowned forest activist Chut Wutty on an investigation in the remote Cardamom Mountains. On the third day, Wutty stopped his 4x4 at a remote forest settlement to look at the harvesting of the critically endangered 'yellow vine', *Coscinium fenestratum*, a creeper used in traditional medicine and rumoured to be an ingredient in the narcotics trade. As the journalists took photographs, the people there grew hostile. Bopha translated what she heard of the conversation: 'What are you doing here? Why are you taking photos? You're not supposed to be here.' Wutty said it was time to go, urging the two women to return to the car. But some of the men blocked the car door, preventing them from leaving. Then they were forced to hand over two of their three cameras.

'They had guns and the situation had gone from scary to very scary and we realized that this could get bad very quickly,' Olesia told me. 'It's not a good feeling; we're in the middle of nowhere and we barely have reception on our cell phones.' As the temperatures rose, Wutty got frustrated and physically pushed away whoever was at the door and trying to open it. But that guy fought back and grabbed Wutty's shirt. 'It kind of happened in slow motion,' Olesia continued. 'I saw the buttons fly off and I saw Wutty's tattoo, a tiger on his chest. And then he said, "Get in." But the car wouldn't start, and our hearts stopped. The car is quite old, but it hadn't ever not started the entire trip, and that is the moment that it chose not to start. I think I must have taken the last photo ever taken on Wutty's camera, of him speaking to these guys outside of the car.' Plokhii flipped the camera over and took out the SD card before that camera too was confiscated. Then came the final altercation.

Wutty told Olesia to get out of the car and lift the hood to start it, while he and Bopha remained inside. 'There was a wild argument happening between Wutty and the military police officer who stood in front of the car,' Olesia said. 'Wutty told me to try to start the car by putting two wires together. I had no idea what I was doing but he directed me in a way that worked, and I heard the engine start.' Wutty shouted, 'Get in, get in, get in,' and Olesia ran from the front of the car to the passenger side door, and then she heard shots. 'I don't remember how many shots there were, but there were at least two. I ducked and was mortified and horrified. But at the same time, I didn't have a chance to feel those emotions. I was running completely on adrenalin by this point. I said to Bopha, "Let's go, let's go." And she got out of the car and the two of us ran across the road into the forest. We ran maybe 40 feet or 50 feet and crouched down in the forest looking at the car. We checked ourselves to see whether we had been shot. But we didn't see any blood on ourselves. We didn't feel any pain. I just said, "I'm okay, I'm okay. Are you okay?"'

Olesia continued, 'Then Bopha said, "We'll die in the forest." And I realized she was right.' The thoughts raced through Olesia's brain. 'We're in complete wilderness. We have no food, we're completely unprepared, we will die. We have a better chance of going back to these people with guns and our friend, who's likely now been shot.' So after about two minutes Olesia and Bopha emerged from the forest back onto the road.

'Things were very quiet at the scene. And as I went towards the car, I saw a body lying flat on the ground with legs extended. And I realized that that's the military police officer who had been standing near the car,' Olesia said. 'I wasn't happy to see him on the ground but a part of me was relieved, because it meant that maybe the shots I heard were related to him and not Wutty. We went towards the car. This guy looked pretty dead. I looked at his face and it was kind of green at that point. The life had left his face. That was very scary. But my concern was Wutty. So I went towards the driver's door and he seemed to be sitting there the way that he was the last time I saw him. He looked okay, but he was clearly not conscious. And so I looked for a gunshot wound and I saw a small puncture in his knee, his left knee. And there was a hole where the pants are. And there was some blood; I wouldn't say it was gushing. I had never seen a gunshot wound, but it looked like a gunshot wound. But totally survivable.'

Not really knowing what to do, Olesia rifled through her pack to get her EpiPen, meant to be used on someone suffering a life-threatening allergic reaction. 'I just stuck it in his leg, just hoping that it would bring him back to life. But there was nothing. Then I did a closer scan of his body and that revealed a gushing wound in his stomach.' What became clear in the days after the murder was that Wutty had been shot at multiple times; there were bullet holes in the window and in the frame of the vehicle. 'But I think he was only shot one time, and the bullet went through the knee and into an artery in his abdomen,' Olesia said. 'I think he was killed instantaneously.'

The military policeman lying lifeless by the car had been shot by one of his own colleagues. In the immediate aftermath of the killing, another military policeman arrived and became distraught at finding his dead friend and he lunged at Bopha but was restrained. The men shouted at one another and Bopha heard one of them say, 'Let's move the car into the forest and just kill them both.' But by then curious villagers were gathering and a group of regular police showed up and the two journalists were safe. Within a week, Olesia Plokhii left the country, justly afraid for her own security. Phorn Bopha continued her career as a journalist in Cambodia, winning a prestigious award for her courage.

The Cambodian government enquiry into Wutty's killing was opened and closed within three days, the murder blamed on the military policeman lying conveniently dead in front of Wutty's car. Further investigation was prohibited. Cambodia's dictatorial prime minister Hun Sen had created a country where environmental activists and journalists can be gunned down at will, with little or no chance that the intellectual authors – those who had actually ordered the killings – would ever face justice. The terror this creates is just the right environment to be able to hand out valuable business concessions to your friends and family without too many awkward questions.

Global Witness had documented this phenomenon for years. Our reports, such as *Cambodia's Family Trees* and *Country for Sale,* were a constant thorn in the side of the Cambodian government. Kem Lay, a highly popular social commentator, was interviewed by Sok Khemara on Voice of America Khmer, on 8 July 2016, the day after the release of our latest report, *Hostile Takeover.*

VOA: 'A lot of people have been surprised by the release of the Global Witness report criticizing Prime Minister Hun Sen and his relatives for their control of more than 100 companies, and their alleged "hostile takeover" of the Cambodian economy. How serious are the allegations in this report?'

KL: 'I read this latest report, and I read the previous [Global Witness] report from 2007 called *Family Trees*...[it includes] case studies, contracts and images that are realistic. And there is also another [Global Witness] report about logging companies, which was released in February 2009...and talks about a "Country for Sale". This means that [Cambodia's ruling elites] created companies for real-estate bidding, including for buildings, state lands, economic land concessions, mining concessions and other public real-estate interests. And for this report, *Hostile Takeover*, we are very certain of its reliability...However, the findings are still considered "understated". This means that this report only shows what is already there on the table, and if we compare it to the pond, we only see just a few fish that are jumping above the water surface. But it is possible that there are still plenty of other fish underneath.'

Two days later, Kem Ley was gunned down as he took his regular morning coffee at a Caltex gas station in central Phnom Penh. Tens of thousands of Cambodians thronged the streets for his funeral, a public display of grief that shook the corrupt regime of Hun Sen. International press coverage linked the killing to Kem Ley's mention of our report. This episode was a stark reminder that while an international organization can get away with criticizing the super-corrupt, it is the extraordinarily courageous critics on the ground who bear the real risks.

A former soldier called Oeuth Ang was quickly arrested, saying that he killed Kem Ley over a gambling debt – an explanation that drew widespread derision. After a half-day trial in 2017, he was convicted of murder and sentenced to life in prison. But I don't doubt that the real architects of Kem Lay's murder have never been brought to justice.

Just weeks after Wutty's murder, a 14-year-old girl was shot and killed by military police in northeast Cambodia during a land dispute between her community and a rubber-plantation company. Within a few months a journalist investigating timber cartels was found brutally murdered in the boot of his car. Neither of those cases was investigated by the authorities. State-sanctioned and state-tolerated murders are not rare and not confined to Cambodia. But Wutty's murder was different. He was kin.

I was leaning against a desk chatting to a few colleagues in our Holborn office when the news about Wutty's killing came in. It was like a body blow. Wutty used to work for us when we had an investigation team based in Phnom Penh. We had to close that office due to physical threats to our staff and Wutty went on to found his own organization, the Natural Resource Protection Group, and became the country's foremost environmentalist. To lose a colleague at all is a tragedy, but it doesn't get any worse than losing one to murder.

Megan MacInnes and Josie Cohen of our land team were addressing a meeting at the World Bank in Washington when they heard the news. Megan had worked closely with Wutty in Cambodia and her voice cracked with emotion as she told the audience, who we were pushing to tackle land-grabbing, what had happened. They shifted uncomfortably in their seats. 'This is the moment that will always stand out,' Josie wrote. 'It highlights so perfectly the huge gulf between those employed in offices around the world to work on land policy and those fighting on the frontlines to protect our land and forests.'

The question was: how could we narrow that gulf?

*

Much of our work, and much of this book, has focused on the lengths warlords, corrupt politicians, rebel armies and companies will go to – and the depths of criminality they resort to – in order to get their hands on valuable natural resources like timber, diamonds, iron ore and oil. But the most valuable natural resource of all is land. Everything we produce and everything we eat requires land. In the Western world, citizens' rights to land are protected by reams of law, but in much of the developing world it is cowboy country. The 21st-century scramble to control vast areas of land is every bit as brutal as the colonial expansion of the past 600 years or so. The assault on indigenous people in Latin America today is no different than the 19th-century genocide of Native Americans in what is now the US.

The rights of indigenous and tribal peoples are enshrined in international law and are recognized in the United Nations Declaration on the Rights of Indigenous Peoples (UNDRIP), which was adopted by the UN General Assembly in 2007. One of the key provisions is the right to Free, Prior and Informed Consent (FPIC). This enables indigenous peoples 'to give or withhold consent to a project that may affect them or their territories'. Among the plethora of international laws and rights that are routinely ignored by governments all over the world, the failure by governments to uphold FPIC ranks high. The implications are deadly.

The people who live in the forests that are being felled for timber, or cleared to make way for soy and palm oil plantations or cattle ranching, or the people who live on land designated for a mine or for oil exploration – all of them are simply collateral damage. They are terrorized, murdered and criminalized. Chut Wutty was just one of countless people who try to defend their land. But he was the first person I knew personally who had been murdered for doing so.

My first feeling was powerlessness. The second was anger. I decided there and then that Wutty must not have died in vain. We needed to criminalize the true criminals. Not just those who terrorize whole communities and throw them off their land, but the companies at whose behest this is done and the financiers behind them.

As the traffic roared along Holborn below, a bunch of us sat in the office and brainstormed: me, Mike Davis, Megan, Josie, Oliver Courtney, Fiona Napier, who ran our environmental campaigns, and Gavin, our campaigns director. 'We all know that the killing of activists like Wutty has been going on for years. Remember Chico Mendes,' I said, referring to the Brazilian union leader and environmentalist who was gunned down by loggers in 1988 and whose death had reinforced his iconic status in the environmental movement. 'We know this shit happens, but how many people are actually killed?'

I aired an idea to document the killings of environmental activists around the world. Not just to compile a bunch of statistics, but to use it as a powerful tool to reinforce our land team's objective to tackle land-grabbing. The idea took. Fiona Napier assumed control of the project and brought in Billy Kyte to start researching the grim cases we would need to put together. Billy, tall, dark-haired and rebellious, had started at Global Witness following a stint with Peace Brigades International (PBI) in Mexico, where he and other volunteers acted as human shields, physically accompanying at-risk human-rights and environmental activists wherever they went. He knew what it was like on the frontlines.

Together with a hired consultant, this new team put together our first briefing on the killings of land and environmental defenders. Because we were starting from scratch, it took the form of a survey. We spoke with over 30 organizations, ranging from national and international environmental and human-rights NGOs right through to the United Nations. We wanted to collate different experiences and statistics to present as near to complete a picture as possible. And we only had two months in which to do it because we had identified an international deadline that we simply couldn't afford to miss: Rio+20.

The upcoming United Nations Conference on Sustainable Development was to mark the progress – or rather the lack of it – made in the 20 years since the much-vaunted non-event that the Rio Earth Summit turned out to be. Scheduled to take place in Rio de Janeiro in June 2012, it would bring together heads of state, governments, intergovernmental and civil-society organizations and the world's press. Just the audience we needed to reach to raise the crisis of these murders.

Hidden Crisis was published less than two months after Wutty's murder. The report's cover featured a photograph of a rough wooden cross hammered into the sandy soil of Equateur Province in the Democratic Republic of Congo. It bore the crudely painted name of 70-year-old Moloma Tuka, together with the date he died, 3 May 2011: the day after he had been beaten up by police called in by a logging company, Siforco, to suppress protests against them in the village of Yalisika. His fellow villagers were also beaten, women and children were raped and several people arrested.

The report's 15 pages documented that a minimum of 711 activists had been killed around the world over the past decade. One person per week, every week, for ten years had been slain as they investigated or protested against mining operations, land-grabs for agribusiness, hydro-dams and logging. And the numbers were on the rise: 106 people were killed in 2011, twice the number murdered in 2009.

The report was a rush job. It was far from perfect, and we knew it vastly under-reported the true number of killings, but it was the first time that the killings of land and environmental defenders, country by country, had been documented in this way. And it wasn't just a bunch of numbers; we knew the name of every victim, and it touched a public nerve.

Billy arrived at Rio+20 by himself. Although he was already a veteran of the frontlines of human rights, he was a novice at a meeting like this, which was probably his strongest suit. It's hard to describe the sheer scale and general dysfunctionality of conferences like these if you haven't been to one. Presided over by UN Secretary-General Ban Ki-moon, it drew in over 100 heads of state and 50,000 participants and probably produced more hot air than climate change, but there was valuable work we could do here. 'It was huge, different types of tents everywhere, lots of side events,' Billy said. 'It can be quite overwhelming; you don't know where to start.' But Billy is savvy.

He made for the media tent, where he got talking to someone employed to liaise with the press. Billy pitched the report to him, highlighting that year after year more than half of the killings took place in Brazil. 'Typical Brazilian,' Billy said fondly. 'He became so emotionally involved in the subject.' This press-liaison officer leaked Billy the contact details of every single international journalist there – more than 1,000 of them. 'That was the first stroke of luck I had there.' The second wasn't long in coming.

In some rare downtime, Billy was sitting in the media tent watching a football match on the TV when he saw the UN high commissioner for human rights, Navi Pillay, walk past. Billy dashed out, gave her the report and pressed her to raise the issue at the conference. As a back-up, Billy also primed a journalist, Fabíola Ortiz of the Inter Press Service, with some questions to ask Pillay at her post-speech press conference. It may not sound like much, but to get an issue raised at a forum like this by a top UN official can catapult it into the limelight. 'I have just now met the representative from Global Witness,' Pillay told the press conference. 'He gave me the figures and of course it is shocking…because more and more I can see that as people learn their rights they are going to be protesting against the appropriation and illegal use of their lands.'

The report had got to the top of the UN system – it was a good start for a new campaign.

PERU, 2014–2015

We were crowded cheek by jowl on two benches as we felt the chopper's engine straining to lift her off the apron at Pucallpa's tiny airport. We'd already ditched most of our spare clothes and equipment, but we were still overweight. The pilots looked concerned, but finally the old Bell Huey juddered a couple of metres above the ground and then, nose down, gathered speed as she headed down the runway and finally lifted into the sky.

We left the outskirts of Pucallpa behind and flew low over the canopy of the Amazon rainforest stretching away to the horizon, like a green sea. Sitting by one window was Alex Soros, George Soros's second-youngest son, who had bankrolled the trip that had been organized at our behest. The other window seats were occupied by the photographers among us: Robert Curran, a half-Peruvian half-American Miami-based photographer, two journalists from the Peruvian press, David Hill from the *Guardian*, Tom Berwick of the Rainforest Foundation US and a Peruvian lawyer called Margot. Sandwiched between them were my colleague Chris Moye, me and Michael Vachon, officially George Soros's head of communications but in reality a sort of consigliere. Every inch the tough-talking New Yorker, Michael doesn't suffer fools gladly. But right now he was silent, because he really doesn't like helicopters.

We were here to document the situation in a remote Amazonian village at the forefront of the war on land and environmental defenders. Saweto, located in the dense rainforest in eastern Peru just 20km from the Brazilian border, is a seven-day boat ride from the provincial capital, Pucallpa. Its people are the Ashéninka, whose territory spans both sides of the border. Seven months earlier, four of their leaders, Edwin Chota, Leoncio Quinticima, Jorge Ríos and Francisco Pinedo, had been on their way to meet fellow Ashéninka across the border in Brazil to discuss the problem of illegal logging carried out by gangs linked to narco-trafficking. They never arrived.

The dismembered bodies of Chota and his friends were found in the forest they had been trying to protect. But – unusually – their lonely murders made international headlines because Edwin Chota was a highly accomplished campaigner and journalists had taken interest. Previously both Chota and Jorge Ríos had been profiled in *National Geographic* for their work tackling illegal logging and narco-trafficking.

'En route some illegal loggers just shot them.' Chris Moye had joined us from our alma mater, EIA. Tall, black-bearded and laconic, half-Brazilian, half-English, Chris is a thoughtful, dedicated and passionate campaigner. 'The killing was a massive deal,' he said. 'Chota had been a thorn in their side for 10 years or more. He knew how to document the illegal logging and offered all of that informa-tion as a formal complaint to Peru's Forest Inspection Agency. It was that that really sparked the conception and the idea to kill him. They knew what they were doing was high risk and they had reported the numerous death threats they had received to the government, but no one had acted in their defence.'

News of the killings exploded throughout the world, including in a 2014 *New York Times* editorial.

Our trip to Saweto grew out of a chance meeting I had in New York in September 2014 with David Kaimowitz of the Ford Foundation in a corridor in UN headquarters, where we were both advocating for the UN to do far more to prevent the destruction of the world's forests. David and I had known each other for years. Ford was one of our most important funders and David was passionate about the plight of land and environmental defenders. And he came up with a great idea. The 2014 international climate-change talks, COP20, were being hosted by Peru. 'Why don't you put out a report on these killings and hold Peru's feet to the fire ahead of the meeting?' he suggested. It was a brilliant piece of strategic thinking. By then it was widely accepted that the world needed to stop the destruction of its forests if we were to successfully tackle climate change. It was also becoming widely accepted that the people who live in and depend on the forests are its best protectors.

Edwin Chota's community at Saweto were fighting to obtain legal rights to their land to protect it from illegal logging, and there, as in many places, the organized crime gangs behind the destruction of the forests were the same as those growing and smuggling coca. If Peru, the host of the biggest climate-change conference, could not protect the rights of its own people, then any climate commitments they might make would be meaningless.

We didn't have much time because, as we had learned over the years, to have any hope of making an impact at a major international event like the UNFCCC we needed to be on the road, armed with our evidence, around three weeks beforehand. That gave us just two months. I chatted to Chris Moye to see if he could do it. He looked thoughtful, and then nodded. 'Hey man, why not?' I have often wondered how someone so laid-back managed to turn out as much work as he does, but he does. The result, *Peru's Deadly Environment*, was published in mid-November.

The report's findings were glaring. Peru was the second-most dangerous country in Latin America in which to be a land and environmental defender, and the fourth-most dangerous in the world. At least 57 defenders had been murdered there since 2002. If the Peruvian government was serious about tackling climate change, then it needed to get serious about tackling this issue. Forests are a carbon sink; they absorb around a third of the CO_2 emissions from fossil fuels every year – around 2.6 billion tons of it. But when they're cut down, the carbon they contain is released into the atmosphere: annual CO_2 emissions from deforestation exceed that of all the cars and lorries in the world. As the *Guardian* put it: 'Deforestation of the vast Peruvian Amazon – which accounts for about half of the country's carbon emissions – almost doubled in 2012 as farmers, miners and illegal loggers pushed deeper into the forest.'

World Human Rights Day took place during the meeting. Thousands of demonstrators, including hundreds of indigenous people, resplendent in their feathered headdresses, faces painted with traditional rich red designs, took to the streets of Lima demanding that the government live up to its national and international obligations and defend the defenders. Our report hit home and the pressure was building.

I first met Diana Ríos on a freezing winter's day in a café in Manhattan. In line with the strategy of raising the plight of Peru's defenders, we had nominated her for the Alex Soros Foundation's Award for Environmental and Human Rights Activism, an award Alex had conceived following Chut Wutty's murder. Diana was unmistakeable with her long black hair and her face daubed with red paint, her head disappearing into the hood of a vast quilted jacket that had been bought for her. Following the murder of her father, Jorge, she had tentatively stepped into his shoes and was becoming a new champion of her community's struggle.

Not only was this the first time she had left her country, but it was also only a few months since she had first left Saweto at all. It was a testament to her courage that she took the vast skyscrapers of New York, the biting cold, the traffic and the crowds in her stride. She had not heard of institutions like the World Bank or the UN, but she was taking on the world. With the Soros press machine at her disposal, she did interview after interview with the international media. She toured numerous congressional offices in Washington, accompanied by expert staff from the Soros organization. 'When this disgusting crime was brought to my attention, I decided to give the third ASF award in their honor,' Alex told *Forbes* magazine.

It was against this background that a bunch of us were crowded into that old, overloaded helicopter skimming the canopy of the Amazon towards Diana's home. Mile after mile of dense forest unrolled beneath us, broken only by the occasional clearing with a few huts and the brown waters of the meandering Alto Tamaya River. My eyes were hungrily absorbing what I saw, and everything I was seeing was at risk, and my anger was building. Then I had something else to think about.

We hit heavy weather. The huge sky was dotted with isolated bursts of cloud and although the pilot navigated as best he could between them, the weather became so violent that the helicopter started shaking. 'The pilot told me and Tom that he thought it was only 50/50 that we would make it,' Chris said. 'He didn't know if he should turn back or carry on.' We carried on, with most of us in blissful ignorance of the danger we were in. Michael Vachon was up front where the shaking was worst and he definitely looked worried. For me, I just felt that hanging suspended from the whirring rotor blades seemed a whole lot less stable than being supported by wings, and I didn't fancy plummeting through the trees to crash unseen in the depths of the forest.

But finally we approached a bare, grass-covered hill rising from the forest canopy. Full of curiosity, we looked down towards the scattering of timber and palm-frond huts and the upturned faces of the small crowd that loomed ever closer as we gently touched down and disgorged from the chopper. It was an amazing feeling. I had never before been anywhere this remote. No roads. Some 160km to the nearest town. Just forest and river. The village chief welcomed us – a dark-skinned man with shortish black hair, he was wearing a white robe with vertical gold and black stripes that reached the ground. He held a bow as tall as he was in front of him, and in his other hand a two-pronged fishing spear. To his right, a boy just over half the height of his father and dressed in a simple brown robe held a bow and two long arrows twice as tall as he was. Alex was undoubtedly the guest of honour and they welcomed him as one.

He was wreathed in smiles as they led us to the village school, which doubled as a community building. Unlike the rest of the buildings, which consisted of a wooden platform measuring around eight metres by five topped with just two walls and a roof woven from palm fronds, the school was a well-made wooden classroom, brightly painted in blue with three blackboards and good solid desks and chairs. Education was revered here.

The villagers drifted into the room in dribs and drabs. The women with their long black hair, many wearing naturally dyed dark robes of blue and deep reddish-brown, most carrying a couple of very young children and followed by a horde of older boys and girls. The men wore either the traditional robes or simple shorts and T-shirts.

Alex had raised the community's struggle to obtain title for their land in the international press, but knew that visiting Saweto and meeting various Peruvian ministers would help gain this issue more prominence where it was needed most. In that simple schoolroom, villager after villager stood up to speak. The community's new president, Ergilia Rengifo, the widow of Jorge Ríos and Diana's mother, told us that the physical threats to the community persisted and that the narco-traffickers 'even threaten the police with death'. Another community member, Guillermo Arévalo, complained that the police had still not acted to clamp down on illegal logging around Saweto.

It became clear that a narco/timber Mafia was in operation here. Trees were illegally felled and floated downriver to the sawmills in Pucallpa. There the authorities turned a blind eye as the mills used forged permits disguising the wood's illegal origin. The state institutions were at best hopelessly uncoordinated and at worst complicit. Meanwhile every night the engines of loggers' boats could be heard moving down the river past the village. The shadow network was at work.

Despite all the publicity, the community were standing alone, sharing their remote territory with the armed gangs who had murdered some of their number and who continued to make threats. Alex, casually dressed in jeans, blue shirt and baseball cap, spoke about his commitment to their cause. All the while the cameras clicked and whirred.

Then the villagers offered us cups of their traditional alcoholic drink, masato. It's best to down a few of them before you learn how they make it. 'The villagers chew up some corn,' Chris told me gleefully. 'Then they spit out the liquid that results from the chewing into a bucket, and that ferments and turns into alcohol.' It made us forget the helicopter ride.

When the meeting broke up, we followed a slippery, muddy track down to the main village, where Diana's family lived. The same stilt-and-platform houses nestled among the trees; pots and pans hung on the walls close to the cooking fire, chickens roamed everywhere and each house had one or two dogs – in order, so I was told, to keep the jaguars at bay. That will make the midnight pee interesting, I thought.

The houses were connected to each other by muddy paths that wound through the forest. Just beyond the village we could see the brown Alto Tamayo River between the trees. On the other side, we could see the police post that had been established following the murders of Edwin Chota and his colleagues but was now long deserted, leaving the villagers to their fate. Stacked outside were the trunks of some illegally logged trees, seized and now abandoned.

We sat on the platform of Diana's home with her and her family, eating simple food and drinking more masato. We talked late into the night before bedding down on thin mattresses on the floor of another community building. I was looking forward to the night, to the silence or whatever noises the forest would bring, and was soon asleep. But in the early hours I was jolted awake by the sound of loud disco music thud-thudding away. I was bemused; there was no electricity here. If I had known the source I wouldn't have got back to sleep so easily.

In the morning I asked Diana about the music. She looked me directly in the eye as she said, 'It comes from a boat moored at the next village,' and pointed in the direction where the music had come from. 'The village is only 150m away but it's out of sight behind the trees and a bend in the river. It belongs to the narco-traffickers. The music was a signal because you, Alex and the other foreigners are here in Saweto. They want you to know that they know.'

Chris, Alex and I questioned the villagers further and found out that the killers of Edwin Chota and his companions lived in that village, and the full horror of what it means to be a defender began to dawn on me. It's not just that you stand a good chance of being tortured and killed for standing up for your way of life, but in remote communities like this, days away from any help, every second, every minute, every hour of your life is spent in fear. I looked at Diana, diminutive in size but seething with a strength and determination to stand up to the terrible odds she and her people were facing.

Back in Pucallpa, this time with Diana, we met with Ucayali's governor. We wanted to get him to commit to protect the community.

Manuel Gambini was one of those super-affable, very well-groomed and eager-to-please people, a type that I had met many times before and didn't trust one bit. Tall with well-cut brown hair, Ralph Lauren polo shirt, smart slacks and loafers, he looked every inch the preppie, out of place in this frontier town. But on the campaign trail just six months earlier, this former coca farmer was reported to be one of seven gubernatorial candidates across Peru's 24 states under active investigation for drug trafficking and related crimes. He also owned a sawmill.

Together with the cohort of journalists, Diana, Chris, Alex and I crowded into his office on the main street. Diana, wearing a dun-coloured homespun gown, her face daubed with traditional red designs, told Gambini about the problems her community faced. Despite the inequality of their positions, she was undaunted, fixing him with her stare as she spoke. Then Alex and I explained why we were there, making it plain that international and not uninfluential eyes were watching what happened here.

Then it was Gambini's turn and he told us everything we wanted to hear. If someone tells me everything I want to hear, I get very suspicious. Chris translated to Alex and me as Gambini claimed credit for any progress there was and blamed the central government for anything that was wrong. 'The regional government wants to protect forests and local communities, but the problem is with the central government. They don't provide enough resources and there's no political will,' he told us. 'It's essential that the national government protects forests by working with indigenous communities.'

At one point he began extolling the virtues of planting palm-oil plantations, drawing a quick rebuke from Alex. He and I had travelled with his father in Indonesia and had seen the havoc wreaked by palm-oil plantations on the forests there and the people who depended on them. Diana raised herself to her full height of only 5 feet and again made an eloquent pitch, asking what the progress was on Saweto's land title. Gambini responded that it would go through its last stage soon. This at least was some specific information.

I left the meeting feeling like I'd been massaged with a sheepskin glove but hadn't got anything out of it. Gambini had been charming and helpful; he'd even given Alex and me a present, a carved wooden statuette of a bare-chested fisherman carrying a massive Amazon catfish on his shoulder. We'd seen them for sale in the tourist shops in town and I had resisted the temptation, but it's rude to turn down a present.

Back in Lima we began a round of meetings to put pressure on the government to grant land titles to indigenous communities, and to Saweto in particular. One of the most important was with the

US ambassador. After standing in the sun for ages, growing hotter and hotter as we negotiated the excruciating security controls common to every US embassy – ten times worse than any airport – we were finally led into a large meeting room where we basked in the excellent air conditioning. Ambassador Brian A Nichols was very welcoming and was supported by around five or six embassy staff as he described the United States' efforts to support the Peruvian government and introduced what turned out to be one of those rather silly intractable issues used by people who don't want to take action. The US had offered six helicopters to the Peruvian government to help them tackle narco-trafficking, illegal logging and other crimes taking place in the vast forests. But the government had said they couldn't afford to insure the craft or fill them with fuel. However, as one staffer there said, 'Peru has $66 billion in reserves. Despite a fiscal crisis, Peru is not poor.'

Then a heavy-set guy with a shaved head leaned forward across the conference table and fixed us with his stare. He introduced himself as a counter-narcotics agent from the Drug Enforcement Administration (DEA). Wow, I thought, he looks just like Hank, the DEA agent in *Breaking Bad*. He listened closely as we described our visit to Saweto and our meeting with Governor Gambini. At that he raised his eyebrows and said conspiratorially, 'I am not at liberty to divulge any information we might possess, but you will read in press reports that the governor of Ucayali has been linked to the drugs trade. I would not discourage you from believing those reports.'

Saweto officially received title to 88,000 hectares of land on 30 January 2015. It had taken them and their supporters over a decade to achieve. We shall never know, but I think the balance was tipped by the brutal murders of Edwin Chota, Jorge Ríos, Leoncio Quinticima and Francisco Pinedo and the international outcry they engendered. Diana's recognition by the Alex Soros Foundation and her championing of their campaign had borne fruit. The support of the Rainforest Foundation US and Margot, their tireless lawyer, had proved invaluable to them. Our visit, our report and David Kaimowitz's idea had all helped raise the pressure on the Peruvian government. But in these cases, the story is never really over. The real tragedy is that it seems someone has to get killed for their problems to be noticed, and that is far too high a price to pay.

*

Following his first foray at Rio+20, Billy had formed a small team to work on putting together annual reports on the killings of defenders. Through 2013 and 2014, Brazil topped the league in overall killings; but the highest kill rate per capita was in Honduras. We needed to know why.

It was in 2015 that Billy arrived in San Pedro Sula, which carried the chilling record as the most dangerous city in the world outside of a war zone. Waiting for a meeting in a hotel foyer, Billy watched the presenter on the TV blaring away in the corner reel off the city's daily death toll: two young girls raped, five people shot dead and three beheaded. It wasn't yet noon.

While in Honduras, Billy was to have his first meeting with one of the most iconic figureheads of the defenders' movement. A member of the Lenca indigenous group, Berta Cáceres came with an awesome reputation. While still a student, she co-founded the Civic Council of Popular and Indigenous Organizations of Honduras (COPINH). Since then, in addition to being a wife and a mother of four, her life had been devoted to campaigns against illegal logging and agribusiness plantations, but it was answering a request from the Lenca people of Rio Blanco, who were opposing the construction of the Agua Zarca hydro-electric dam on the Gualcarque River, that brought her international recognition.

'We met for the first time late at night on a petrol-station forecourt and ended up sharing a hamburger,' Billy explained to me when he began to realize the level of threat she was under. 'We chatted for a couple of hours. She had a kind of driver/security person who was waiting in the wings near us, and she would look over her shoulder a lot. You could tell that this is someone who's lived under extreme pressure. She was very open and honest, and she talked about the challenges that she had with her own family, about what to do with them given that she's received so many threats. She had sent one of her daughters to university in Argentina because she didn't want her to be around.'

Berta had good reason to be cautious. Killings and other attacks on COPINH members had been ongoing for years, which is why the courage she had to continue her work was all the more remarkable. Just 17 months earlier, COPINH member Tomàs García and his

17-year-old son, Allan, were taking part in a peaceful protest at the dam site at Rio Blanco when the Honduran military opened fire. Tomàs died instantly. Allan was hit several times but survived. The following year, William Jacobo Rodríguez was killed. His 15-year-old brother was tortured to death, his body thrown into a river. Other COPINH members were subject to repeated threats and attacks because of their opposition to the Agua Zarca dam. María Santos Domínguez had a finger hacked off by a machete wielded by one of eight people who had attacked her.

Berta herself had received dozens of death threats but none had been investigated by the police. These killings, attacks and threats were not a series of random events. In June 2016 the *Guardian* reported that two US-trained elite units had been given a hit list containing dozens of names of social and environmental activists with orders to wipe them all out. According to their source, a first sergeant in the National Inter-Agency Security Force (FUSINA), Berta's name was on it.

The Agua Zarca dam was destined to produce electricity that would be consumed in faraway cities, while the Lenca people faced the loss not only of the land the dam would be built on but also their entire way of life. The Gualcarque River was the source of their water but was sacred to them too. The crops they grew, the wild animals they hunted and the natural plants they gathered were essential for both food and medicine. Agua Zarca became a battleground between company profits and a people's way of life.

The campaign Berta led, the protests and the legal actions she brought, drew more and more attention to the problems associated with the dam and it was notching up some significant successes. One of the world's biggest dam builders, Chinese-owned Sinohydro, pulled out, together with the World Bank's International Finance Corporation (IFC). That left just the Honduran company constructing the dam, Desarrollos Energéticos, SA, better known as DESA. The remaining financial backers included the Dutch development bank FMO, its Finish equivalent, Finnfund, and the Central American Bank for Economic Integration. But as COPINH's campaign successes mounted up, so did the threats and attacks against them.

Billy visited Honduras twice in 2015 and both times Berta connected Billy to key contacts and helped him learn about the dire situation facing defenders in Honduras. On the second trip Billy was accompanied by Chris Moye and a photojournalist called Giles Clarke, who had generously and somewhat courageously volunteered to document the investigation. They travelled to Rio Blanco to witness a COPINH protest at the dam site. 'It was hellishly hot when we went down there,' Billy said. 'We could see the private security guards and heavily armed soldiers on the other side of the river defending the dam construction site. One of the people there was a light-skinned Honduran who was obviously orchestrating the activities of the army and private security guards.' It would be several years before Billy found out who this man was. One of Giles's photos captured the scene: the soldiers carrying their heavy weaponry looking down from the high ground on the opposite bank; it was an image filled with menace.

A few months after Billy had first met her, Berta was catapulted to international prominence. On 20 April 2015, she was awarded the Goldman Prize, the Oscar of the environmental world. Billy went to San Francisco for the awards ceremony and met Berta in her swanky hotel room as she was preparing to take the stage. 'She was having her hair done by stylists in this huge suite, you know, fruit bowls in the corner and all that,' Billy said. 'Unfazed, she was still taking phone calls from indigenous leaders back in Honduras. You would have thought that someone like that might be a bit overwhelmed by those kinds of surroundings, but she took it in her stride. She knew that this was a means to an end. She knew that the kind of frills and whistles were over the top, but for her to get an audience of that size, and to put across the message, this needed to be done.'

It was a big day for us too. We released our latest report, *How Many More?*, on the same day. The report's depressing headline was that 116 land and environmental defenders had been killed during 2014, an average of two people per week. The numbers were climbing. Piggybacking on the international coverage of the Goldman Prize, our Washington office organized an event to launch our report there, not least to give more prominence to Berta's cause.

I sat next to Berta on the panel, together with an old ally, Bennett Freeman, a former US deputy assistant secretary of state for democracy, together with a senior State Department official and Joel Simon of the Committee to Protect Journalists. Berta spoke passionately about the situation in Honduras and summed up the death threats she had received – 33, by that time. By uncanny coincidence – or perhaps not – President Hernández of Honduras was giving a speech in an upstairs room of the same building. We considered gate-crashing and in hindsight I wish we had. Back in Honduras Berta's now global campaign was more than ruffling a few feathers.

Douglas Giovanny Bustillo, a former US-trained lieutenant in the Honduran Army's 5th Battalion, became head of security for DESA in 2006. He worked alongside Sergio Ramón Rodríguez Orellana, DESA's manager of social, environment and communications affairs, who ran a network of informants reporting back on Berta and COPINH. When he wasn't spying on COPINH, Bustillo was organizing attacks on them in close cooperation with the armed forces, including the one where Tomás García and his son were shot. The offending soldier's criminal defence was paid for by DESA. It was only after he left his job in June 2015 that Bustillo was approached by one of DESA's senior executives to organize an altogether more ambitious plan: the assassination of Berta Cáceres.

His first task was to put together a hit squad. Henrry Javier Hernández, alias 'Comandante', a former sergeant in the 15th Battalion, was to lead it, and was tasked with selecting his fellow hitmen. He brought in Elvin Heriberto Rápalo Orellana, alias 'Chelito' or 'Comanche', rumoured to have carried out various murders, and Edilson Atilio Duarte Meza. The final member of the team was Óscar Aroldo Torres Velásquez, alias 'Coca'.

The attack was planned for 5 or 6 February 2016 in Berta's hometown of La Esperanza, and she and COPINH's offices were put under increased surveillance by the hit squad. Bustillo alone made 147 calls from Esperanza during January and February, and it was Bustillo who asked Major Mariano Díaz Chávez, a US-trained Special Forces officer and head of intelligence of the army's 1st Battalion, to provide the gun. This was duly handed to Henrry Hernández on 5 February. But the killers had problems with their vehicle and also discovered that Berta was not alone. At the last minute, the operation was aborted.

Bustillo returned to La Esperanza on 22, 27 and 28 February and gathered enough information to report back to a senior DESA executive on Berta's and COPINH's planned activities for 2 March. On 1 March, DESA's Sergio Rodríguez texted a WhatsApp group comprising two other DESA executives and its head of security: 'A group of approximately 15 persons went to Esperanza for a radio training'. They knew where Berta would be, and when. The stage was set.

The team met up in the town of La Ceiba on the morning of 2 March and travelled to La Esperanza, arriving shortly before 4pm – when, according to their mobile-phone data, Henrry Hernández called Bustillo. The frequency of calls escalated during the afternoon as the assassins communicated with each other and various third parties.

At 11.25pm, Berta sent a WhatsApp message to a friend. 'Well, wherever you are, I hope you're well. Truly. Be careful please, okay? Kisses.' She can only just have pressed send when two men kicked open the back door of her house. Gustavo Castro Soto, a Mexican activist who was staying with Berta, heard her call out, 'Who's there?' The next thing he knew there was someone in front of him pointing a gun. He just had time to hear six shots from Berta's room before he too was hit. Shot in the ear and left arm, he fell to the ground. As soon as the killers left, Gustavo staggered to Berta's room. She asked him to call for help, but quickly died. A horrified Gustavo nevertheless did as his friend had told him. 'This is Gustavo. They just killed Berta. I'm wounded.' He had survived only by playing dead.

It was a cold and damp March morning when I left the office to grab a sandwich. I was returning along Portsoken Street when I saw Billy, Chris Moye and Alice Harrison huddled outside the main entrance, cigarettes cupped in Billy's and Chris's hands. 'Berta's been shot,' Billy said simply. I joined them in a stunned silence as the drizzle fell.

Sitting next to me on the panel in Washington, she had been very open about the fact that it was quite likely she would be murdered. And now, despite all the publicity COPINH's campaign against the Agua Zarca dam had raised, and despite her international prominence, the killers had been emboldened enough to go ahead and murder her anyway. But it was not really surprising. One of our key findings as we documented the depressing litany of killings worldwide was that most of these murders were never investigated. Prosecution rates globally were in single digits; and even then they were usually only the trigger men, not the architects of the killings.

Global Witness couldn't investigate a murder, but we could expose the rotten system – the shadow network that made Honduras the deadliest place on Earth per capita to be a defender.

This dire situation had stemmed from the 2009 coup and the succession of right-wing governments that had followed. Declaring Honduras 'open for business', companies with links to senior politicians snapped up mining concessions and vast agribusiness plantations and won corrupt tenders to build hydro-electric dams. The US trumpeted investment into Honduras's extractive sector and the country received a large chunk of the US$750 million foreign aid that it ploughed into Central America. The big development banks followed suit, with investments flowing in from the International Finance Corporation and the Inter-American Development Bank. For the people whose land was being stolen from them, the levels of violence had escalated. We decided to lift the lid on the whole stinking cauldron.

Throughout 2016 Billy and his colleague Ben Leather carried out several field investigations in Honduras. They linked up with local civil-society groups and travelled into remote and dangerous regions, and began to build a picture of the corruption and the escalating levels of violence that went with it: the three Tolupan indigenous leaders shot dead peacefully protesting against the mining and logging trucks crossing their territory; Concepción Gutiérrez, threatened with violence for refusing to sell her land to a mining company owned by well-connected businessman Lenir Pérez; and Ana Miriam and her sister-in-law Rosaura, who were beaten for opposing the Los Encinos hydro-electric project controlled by the husband of the president of the ruling National Party, Gladis Aurora López.

'We put together various case studies documenting the investments of numerous high-profile public figures that were linked to a lot of the cases,' Billy said. 'There was a complete lack of consultation of indigenous people for many of the projects, which led to protests in the first place, which then led to further attacks and threats and ultimately killings of activists.' A deadly spiral. 'And we tried to join the dots in terms of which state officials were connected with which companies, and which victims were suffering from the attacks.'

Billy and Ben returned to Honduras in January 2017 to launch *Honduras – The Deadliest Place to Defend the Planet.* 'One of the main objectives of the report was to show solidarity with the people who had helped us put it together, so we needed to launch it in Honduras. 'Patrick, we have to be alongside these brave activists,' Billy told me. The decision to launch in-country wasn't taken lightly; to expose the architects of this problem in a country with little rule of law and immersed in extreme violence was risky. But I agreed with Billy and Ben's rationale and I signed off the high-risk trip authorization, though not without qualms.

The day they arrived in Tegucigalpa, the capital of Honduras, they sent out a press release and were deluged. A stream of interviews culminated with Billy and colleagues from a Honduran indigenous-rights organization, the Movimiento Independiente Indígena Lenca de La Paz (MILPAH), arriving to take part in Honduras's flagship current-affairs TV programme. *Frente a Frente*, which means 'face-off', sets up two opposing sides to discuss a particular issue. Its entire 7am to 9am slot was devoted to our report. 'They had us face-off against a government representative, someone from the private sector, and a so-called environmentalist who was far away from being an environmentalist – someone the government brought in,' Billy told us all in the pub after his trip. 'What was fantastic was that the TV cameras zoomed in on the report, literally page by page. We had a diagram in the middle that showed the different links between high-profile government officials, companies, victims and the attacks themselves. And the presenter would talk the audience through every single stage of the diagram and investigation.' For us, it was a win-win situation. But it almost wasn't.

The last 15 minutes of the programme were devoted to a phone-in. Billy had been told beforehand that the presenter and the channel itself were pro-government, and he was expecting a stitch-up. 'The first person to call up was the environment minister,' Billy said. 'He railed against the report itself and accused me of staining the honour of the Honduran people. Then at the end of his rant, he said, "As soon as you leave the TV studios, we're going to arrest you."'

This wasn't funny. What was even less funny was that at that moment Ben was in a taxi on his way to a meeting with that same minister. His phone rang. It was the UN. 'Turn back,' they told him.

'The minister has just threatened your colleague live on air and they're going to arrest him.'

Ben ordered the taxi around and met up with the UN, and together they made their way to the TV studios. By this time Billy was in the toilets on the phone to his appointed emergency contact at Global Witness, Alice Harrison, and she immediately alerted me. Then Ben called Billy and told him to wait for them. Billy told us, 'Then they came in and took me out, and there's the UN with flak jackets, the whole thing…and a scrum of Honduran journalists asking me what was going on. The good thing was that I was able to use the situation as a platform to talk about the report.'

Then he and Ben were bundled into a UN car and taken straight to the office of the UN high commissioner for human rights. Despite the fact that the report had slammed the US for bankrolling the Honduran government, the US ambassador was really helpful and pulled a few strings. The situation eased.

In discussion with me and Alice, Billy and Ben decided to go ahead with their final day's meetings. They had arranged to meet another group of activists in the ultra-violent city of San Pedro Sula, in the north of the country. It was again a high-risk strategy and they decided to avail themselves of help from an unlikely source. Honduras had recently embarked on a programme to protect human-rights activists; sometimes they would provide private security guards, or CCTV for their offices and houses. 'We thought it might be a good idea to test this protection mechanism ourselves,' Billy said, 'as a way to try and embolden this protection mechanism and to show to local activists that it can be used.' And they needed all the help they could get. The report had accused Gladis López, the head of the ruling National Party in Congress, of links to an illegal hydro-dam project owned by her husband. Following Billy's TV appearance, she held a press conference of her own and announced that she would launch a case of defamation against Billy, Ben and Global Witness. She added that she hoped that they would be arrested.

In consultation with the UN and the US Embassy, Billy and Ben were met at San Pedro Sula's airport by an armed Honduran detail together with US plainclothes security. 'I don't know if they were the CIA or who they were, and I don't know if they were suspicious of these Honduran security guards who were sent for protection or not,' Billy said. 'But we were chaperoned from the airport to our hotel by a combination of private security and US spooks. So bizarrely we ended up getting protection from the part of the Honduran state which had to do with human rights against another part of the Honduran state that had threatened me live on air with arrest.'

Billy and Ben's final press conference went ahead, and we all sighed with relief as they finally arrived safely back in the UK. They had made their mark. Honduras's corrupt elite had been exposed in all their ugly glory and international attention was focused on the corruption and violence so prevalent there.

We upped our advocacy efforts and in Washington I met with our old friend Tim Rieser. He too had met Berta and was outraged at her murder. 'It's a tragic reminder that even those who achieve international acclaim are in mortal danger if they challenge powerful interests in a country like Honduras, where anyone can get away with murder,' he said. A new poster adorned the already crowded walls of his small office, a larger-than-life poster of Berta's face. Tim was already on the case. His boss, US senator Patrick Leahy, a senior and influential member of the Senate Appropriations Committee, called on President Hernández to find and punish those responsible for 'this despicable crime'. Until then he was refusing to authorize the release of US funds for military aid to Honduras, and that would hit them where it hurts.

COPINH demanded an independent investigation into Berta's assassination, a request turned down by the Honduran government. As a result, the International Advisory Group of Experts (GAIPE) comprising five leading human-rights lawyers was formed by COPINH and several leading international justice organizations. GAIPE carried out four visits to Honduras, interviewed over 30 people and finally gained access to a fraction of the mobile-phone data in government hands. Their investigation exposed that the harassment and murder of COPINH members had been a well-resourced and coordinated programme carried out over a period of years by senior DESA executives, in league with state security forces and prosecutors. In the immediate aftermath of the murder these same people sought to cover up the facts and misrepresent the assassination as a crime of passion, with confidential information about the status of the investigation flowing freely between law-enforcement authorities and the company.

The investigation also highlighted that DESA didn't have the funds to construct the dam it had tendered for. It was its close relationship with the government that had enabled it to leverage international funding for the project and it was this funding, among others, that helped finance DESA's war against COPINH. GAIPE's analysis, based on evidence and using the neutral language of law, was a chilling exposé of the cold mechanics of a hit. This time international reaction was too strong to ignore.

In December 2019, the four members of the hit squad, plus three others, were each sentenced to 34 years for Berta's murder, plus another 16 years for the attempted murder of Gustavo Castro Soto. The former Special Forces officers Douglas Bustillo and Mariano Díaz Chávez, plus DESA's social, environment and communications manager, Sergio Ramón Rodríguez, each got 30 years. Billy was pretty certain he had seen Bustillo before: the light-skinned Honduran he, Chris and Giles had seen on the other side of the river during the protest at the dam site in 2015. It's chilling to look at Giles Clarke's photographs of that day, especially the long-lens shot of the heavily armed soldiers looking down from the hill with murder on their minds.

On the second anniversary of Berta's murder, DESA's executive president, Roberto David Castillo Mejía, a West Point-trained military intelligence officer, was arrested at San Pedro Sula airport as he tried to leave the country. He was charged with being the 'intellectual author' of Berta's assassination and the shooting of Gustavo Castro Soto.

After years of delays during which his defence team threw up obstacle after obstacle, Castillo's trial finally began on 6 April 2021. 'Our struggle for justice was never about the hitmen. It's always been about wanting to prosecute and jail the decision-makers – those who ordered and paid for her murder,' one of Cáceres's daughters, Bertita Zúñiga, told the *Guardian*.

The trial lasted one day short of three months and Bertita got her wish. On 5 July 2021, Castillo, DESA's former boss – the malevolent spider at the centre of a web of greed, murder and terror – was led into the High Court in Tegucigalpa and convicted of being a co-conspirator in Berta's assassination.

Together with COPINH, Berta's family is also suing FMO, the Dutch development bank that co-financed the Agua Zarca dam.

Six years earlier, in an unrelated case, Brendan O'Donnell applied to the City of London for planning permission to demolish St Paul's Cathedral. The reason he gave was that he wanted to search for precious metals that might lie underneath Wren's 17th-century masterpiece. Brendan, who later joined Global Witness and worked with Simon on corruption in the oil and mining industry, was then a campaigner with the humanitarian-aid organization ActionAid. The headline-grabbing stunt was a stroke of genius and focused international attention on the struggle of the Kondh tribe in India's Orissa state to prevent Vedanta Resources, a British mining company, from destroying their sacred mountain, Niyamgiri, which sits on a rich reserve of bauxite, the principal ore of aluminium. The tribe believes Niyamgiri is home to their god, Niyam Raja.

ActionAid's point was well made: are the way of life, culture and religion of a remote tribe any less important than our own? In 1991, Larry Summers, then chief economist of the World Bank, evidently thought so. In a now infamous memo, he wrote: '"Dirty" Industries: Just between you and me, shouldn't the World Bank be encouraging MORE migration of the dirty industries to the LDCs [Least Developed Countries]? I can think of three reasons.'

Summers went on to outline that foregone earnings due to pollution-related problems were much cheaper in countries with the lowest wages, and that pollution-related deaths were of less concern in countries that already had a high infant-mortality rate. 'I think the economic logic behind dumping a load of toxic waste in the lowest wage country is impeccable and we should face up to that,' he wrote. The furore the leaking of Summer's memo caused didn't stop him from becoming a senior adviser to presidents Clinton and Obama.

Summer's views still manifest themselves in realpolitik. Companies that want to access valuable natural resources – and land in particular – can get away with things in the world's remotest and poorest regions much more easily than they can in the rich world. The corruption they engage in and the violence they tolerate, or even sanction, are far harder to track down in isolated territories where the local people lack the means to communicate what's happening to them, and where the power and forces of the state, bribed into pleasant acquiescence, ruthlessly support their new corporate masters.

Land and environmental defenders are on the frontline of what is often a real shooting war. They are paying the price for the cheap palm oil, iron ore, beef or oil that are ripped from their land and exported to global markets. This is where the shadow network holds sway, but the extraordinarily courageous and self-sacrificial struggle mounted by people like Berta Cáceres and Edwin Chota, against forces so much more powerful than they were, is beginning to turn the tables. It is a struggle that highlights the worst evils of the shadow network and puts a lie to any notion that corruption is a victimless crime. Berta and Edwin paid the ultimate price, but we're all paying something.

According to a 2013 report sponsored by the UN Environment Programme, the externalized environmental costs of key industrial sectors like agriculture, forestry, fisheries, mining, oil and gas exploration, construction and others are in the region of an eye-watering US$7.3 trillion per year. In a salient example, it is estimated that the environmental costs of the beef industry in Brazil, which is responsible for around 80 per cent of the deforestation in that country, are around 18 times more than the total revenue it generates.

The report concluded that almost no company on Earth would be profitable if they were forced to pay the true environmental costs of their operations. Put another way, this is a bill picked up by the taxpayer and the planet, not the companies that run it up. The impacts on the Earth are obvious to anyone who reads about species extinction, climate change and the implications for the world's poorest and most vulnerable people.

I don't think the threats against defenders are going to diminish anytime soon, because the tentacles of resource colonialism continue to probe the world's remotest places in an endless search for more land, more minerals, more timber. But there's a lot we all can do. The relentless attacks on peoples and communities in some of the world's remotest regions now make international headlines. They didn't use to. They bring into sharp focus the raw impact of agribusiness, oil, mining and other industries on the lives of ordinary people. And, by default, they highlight our role as consumers of the resources these people are paying the ultimate price for.

Global Witness is part of a network of organizations across the world that have joined forces to defend the defenders, with our research a valuable contribution to the work. Together we have seen momentum on this issue grow, raising concerns in the corridors of power about the impacts of 'development' on the planet and its most vulnerable people.

In March 2018, I joined the UN Environment Programme's launch of its Environmental Rights Initiative at the Palais des Nations in Geneva. In 2019, the UN General Assembly recognized 'the contribution of environmental human-rights defenders to the enjoyment of human rights, environmental protection and sustainable development', and condemned the violence against defenders, calling upon member states to act.

By the time this book is published there should be new European laws in place that force companies to disclose social and environmental harms in their supply chains, the result of intense lobbying by us and around a hundred other organizations. That is just a beginning.

We will continue to add to the amazing work done by indigenous and national and international organizations who work tirelessly to protect and fight for the rights of defenders, by documenting the attacks and criminalization of defenders and publicizing them as well as we can. We'll seek the prosecution of the hitmen who kill defenders, and even more importantly, of those who give the orders. And we all need to bear witness to this assault – this war – on the people who the planet can least afford to lose. Those people who, to the core of their being, genuinely understand how humanity can – and must – live in harmony with the environment.

These people are not simply the collateral damage in a war of exploitation. They are one of our few hopes of survival. Their wisdom and experience are things from which the rest of humanity must learn if we are to survive, and the core of the message is a simple one. Ignoring these people is like sitting at the top of a very tall tree and sawing off the branch you're sitting on because you think it'll make a profit.

EPILOGUE

Over a quarter of a century has passed since three young idealists cooked up a seemingly bonkers plan to put an end to the Khmer Rouge. It was a leap into the dark with the slimmest chances of success. In October 1995, a year after we had received that first £18,000 grant from Novib, I remember being genuinely surprised that Global Witness was still in existence, but it had turned out to be our time. We had embarked on those first few campaigns mainly on gut feeling. We hadn't known that an apparently separate bunch of issues were all connected by a network. That discovery only dawned upon us slowly when the same names, the same lawyers and the same companies began to appear in unrelated investigations.

Companies with something to hide and organized-crime groups share the need for the shadow network. They depend on it to smooth over the interfaces between what's illegal and legal; what's morally acceptable and unacceptable. Like an electrical relay, it makes the connections in the circuit that enables the dark side of business operations, such as corruption, to run through our society like an electric current: silent, invisible, powerful and, sometimes, deadly.

Misha Glenny put it another way in his bestselling book *McMafia*, where he said that 'Global Witness has successfully highlighted that organized crime is not about sinister corporations planning to take over the world. It is about a complex interplay between the regulated and unregulated global economy which defies simple solutions'. We hadn't thought of it like that, but then again Misha is cleverer than we are.

Our first investigation had, genuinely rather surprisingly, been successful and exposed the US$10–20 million per month that the Khmer Rouge were earning from their timber trade with Thailand. The real shock though was that the governments of both Cambodia and Thailand were complicit in helping them do it. We had shown that the prime ministers of both countries were directly implicated and very likely personally profiting from it. This deadly business had been carried out far away from prying eyes, profiting from the war that was itself thriving from the trade, a deadly perpetual-motion machine prolonging the suffering of one of the most abused populations on Earth.

The revelation that diamonds, an international symbol of glamour and success, were soaked in blood put the issue of conflict resources firmly on the map. It hadn't been there before. The governments and companies that collaborated to profit from some of the late 20th century's most brutal wars were thrust into the limelight. 'The diamond wars were the secret of the diamond trade until, quite suddenly, they were not,' Matthew Hart wrote in his book *Diamond: A Journey to the Heart of an Obsession.* 'It seemed to happen in an instant, as if a curtain had been ripped aside and there was the diamond business spattered in blood. Its accuser was a little-known group called Global Witness.'

We were just as surprised as anyone else and probably felt that the diamond-industry official interviewed by Nick Shaxson in his book *Poisoned Wells* was nearer to the mark when he said, 'Global Witness is just a bunch of well-intentioned hooligans.' Well, if we could wind people up as well as helping to propel real change, then we were happy. And there *was* real change, not only in terms of public perception but also with the passing of laws and tangible mechanisms like the Kimberley Process to stem the flow of conflict diamonds.

The OECD described the oil business as one of the most corrupt on Earth. It still is. But our being alerted to the vast oil revenues being stolen from Angola by the country's own leadership started a chain of events that has forced a level of transparency on both the oil and mining industries that was unimaginable back then. Perhaps more importantly, it exposed the link that connected the shadowy world of theft and corruption with the petrol you put in your tank. The oil companies themselves either turned a blind eye or directly conspired with host governments to loot citizens of their birthright. In order to maintain that blind eye, they needed to make it as hard as possible to be able to detect their corruption; thus they hired former spies, expert at doing their work in the shadows and adept at keeping an eye on the opposition. Meanwhile their lobbyists ceaselessly stride the corridors of power advocating against any legislation or mechanism that might shine too strong a light into the darkness they thrive in.

Former Ukrainian Mafia boss Leonid Minin was the initial channel that enabled one of Africa's most brutal warlords to sell the luxury hardwoods from Liberia's rainforests to Europe and China, but he was quickly followed by 'respectable' established international timber importers across the world, eager to snap up this rare harvest. Like Minin, these regular businessmen had no compunctions about what Charles Taylor would spend their money on. Even as their executives rushed to fill the waiting ships with the last cargoes of illegally felled timber, they presented a façade that what they were doing was completely legal. I should feel impartial, but I am filled with disgust for them – and it demonstrated almost better than anything else something that we come up against time after time. To paraphrase Winston Churchill's quip about Americans: companies *can always be trusted to do the right thing, once all other possibilities have been exhausted. This is true of most governments and companies*. It is why campaigning organizations like Global Witness and investigative journalists must exist.

Corrupt and usually dictatorial ruling families like the Obiangs or the Nazarbayevs use the secrecy jurisdictions of the Caribbean, the Channel Islands and elsewhere to mask the looting of the nations they rule. Their dirty money is washed clean as it's laundered through anonymously owned shell companies and then ploughed into real estate in the world's most exclusive streets or squandered on the clichéd trappings of the super-rich. Their only saving grace is their comical denials of corruption, like a child with his pockets on fire denying he's been smoking.

But in many countries this level of sophistication isn't required. If the resources you're after are hidden away in some of the remotest regions of the planet, then it's often cheaper and simpler to resort to brutality to get what you want. Land is the most valuable natural resource of all, and we have seen that companies and governments will even murder to get hold of it. The 200 or so people killed each year defending their territory and way of life against land-grabbing by corporations are a testament to that.

A combination of ideas, coincidence and happenstance had drawn us into the conflicts in Cambodia and Angola, and unwittingly we became pioneers in tackling what became known as the Resource Curse or the Paradox of Plenty, as Terri Lynn Karl called it in her book of the same name. At the same time, and often ahead of these leading academics like Karl, Columbia University's Jeffrey Sachs and Paul Collier at Oxford, who were putting this issue under the economic microscope, we were on the frontlines uncovering devastating real-life examples, identifying both the perpetrators and the victims. While analysts could better work out the global economic impact of the Resource Curse, we identified which crooks and corporations were doing it and how and where they spent their money.

One of our most important discoveries was a simple one: make it personal. The perpetrators of these grand thefts – whether conventional criminals or the pinstripe army of company executives – like to keep their activities in the shadows. Kleptomaniac politicians, the architects of corrupt deals and the traders in conflict resources like to keep their names out of the public eye. Their lawyers liberally splatter their threatening letters to us with 'Confidential – not for Publication'. They don't want their names in the papers either. Why?

It's easy to be a pillar of society if you live at the right address, drive an expensive car, belong to the best clubs, are seen in the most fashionable places and support some worthy charities. But if your wealth has stemmed from corruption, theft or war and this fact becomes public, then not only do you find that you're a less desirable party guest, but you could also be at risk of prosecution – or, perhaps even more dangerous, you become a liability to your peers.

This is why, in addition to highlighting the facts, we have always made it personal. We name names not because we're gratuitous, but because we know it drives the point home, directly into the surprisingly thin hides of the architects and enablers of the crimes we document. It's not just about banks laundering money; it's which bank and which officials within it. It's not just about a corrupt oil deal, but exactly how it was done, and which company executive inked the deal. We want the corrupt dictator's son sipping champagne on his superyacht in the marina at Capri or Monaco to know that his neighbours know he's a sleazy crook, presuming they're not sleazy crooks too. And we want those parasitic lawyers and PR people who usually lurk in the background to be held accountable for helping protect the predators.

Now, a fifth of the way through the 21st century, it has become far harder for oil and mining companies to get away with corrupt deals: the banking sector's role in channelling stolen money into the secret accounts of politicians, laundering cash for corrupt business-people and organized crime, is under a brighter spotlight than ever before. The UK, Europe and the US have imposed laws to ensure that the identity of the real owners of companies is known, and one of the most famous advertising slogans of all time – 'A diamond is forever' – was eclipsed by a new term: 'Blood diamonds'.

Has the Resource Curse ended? Far from it – the scramble for the world's resources is greater than ever. Have we destroyed the shadow network? No. But it's not quite as obscured by shadows as it was, and we have learned many valuable lessons. It's just as well, because it turns out that everything we have done so far has just been a rehearsal.

In 1992, the representatives of 180 countries, including over 100 heads of state, descended on Rio de Janeiro for the first interna-tional Earth Summit. 'No place on the planet could remain an island of affluence in a sea of misery. We are either going to save the whole world or no one will be saved,' said the summit's secretary-general, Maurice Strong. 'One part of the world cannot live in an orgy of unrestrained consumption while the rest destroys its environment just to survive. No one is immune from the effects of the other.'

In a dizzying whirl of collective enthusiasm to save the planet, these leaders signed the UN Framework Convention on Climate Change and the Convention on Biological Diversity, endorsed the Rio Declaration and the Forest Principles, and adopted Agenda 21, a 300-page plan for achieving sustainable development in the 21st century. So what the fuck happened?

Well, one problem was exemplified before US president George H W Bush had even got back into Air Force One for the trip home. 'The American way of life is not up for negotiation. Period.' It was a shocking statement, but it turned out that Bush was just being more honest than his peers. No Western government, so it seems, had been prepared to negotiate their country's way of life – while their counterparts in the Global South never had much to negotiate with in the first place.

And what is that way of life they're so scared of losing? It is one based on self-interest, deregulation and inequality and the common denominator – the one key thing that has screwed up those lofty aspirations expressed at Rio more than anything else – has been the shadow network and its main weapon: corruption. Our understanding of corruption has evolved since Global Witness started out. The handing over of envelopes or even suitcases of cash to get a contract is its most obvious form, but it's not one of the most dangerous ones. It is that pinstripe army of lobbyists patrolling the corridors of power, cajoling lawmakers and politicians to legislate their way, or preferably deregulate altogether, all the while oiling the wheels with political donations. It's the lawyers smothering deals in layers of opacity, through the use of secrecy jurisdictions or legal threats. The sheer amount of money available to corporations means the interests of ordinary citizens and even of entire governments are mired in an often hopelessly unequal struggle. When Mittal Steel made a truly terrible mining deal with the government of Liberia, a deal so bad for the country's citizens that the new government later demanded its renegotiation, the personal wealth of the company's owner, Lakshmi Mittal, was 295 times greater than Liberia's national budget.

If those pledges to achieve a sustainable and equitable world were to be achieved, it would require a mind-bogglingly radical overhaul of the entire global economic model, which is based on GDP growth. In turn this is based on the infinite extraction of the Earth's resources, but infinite growth in a finite world is physically impossible. It doesn't take a rocket scientist to work out that it's not *if* we run out of oil, minerals and everything else we want to consume, or *if* we exhaust our planet's ability to sustain life. It's when. The science and economics were clear about all of this long before Rio and now we're seeing the impacts begin to play out in real time. So how is it that we have failed so badly?

The principles adopted at Rio posed the biggest threat imaginable to the capitalist system and to anyone else who wanted to make as much money as possible regardless of consequence, and that was something that simply couldn't be allowed to happen. Like a mycorrhizal fungus, the shadow network had already spread throughout the roots of the political system. One of its most powerful sectors is the oil industry. It had the resources, the political heft, the raw power and the creativity to undermine the whole process. Money began to flow into pseudo-scientific research to debunk the reality of climate change, and into shadowy think tanks like the Cato Institute and the Heritage Foundation.

Perhaps the scariest of these was the Project for the New American Century (PNAC), which exemplified the raw power of the shadow network. Formed in 1997, its goal was to 'shape a new century favorable to American principles and interests'. When George W Bush swept to power in 2001, several members of his Cabinet were founding signatories to PNAC's principles, including Vice President Dick Cheney and the hawkish Secretary of Defense Donald Rumsfeld. It took them just a couple more years to fulfil one of PNAC's founding goals: regime change in Iraq. The 9/11 terror attacks were used as the excuse, even though it was clear to many at the time – and later proved beyond doubt – that albeit evil, Saddam Hussein's regime had nothing to do with 9/11. It's possible, of course, that US Intelligence had got its facts badly wrong, but the more likely explanation was that this had always been part of the plan; after all, Iraq is conveniently rich in oil. This was the shadow network at its most powerful.

In both Copenhagen and Paris, world leaders signed up to strict reductions in carbon emissions in order to keep the post-Industrial Revolution temperature rise below 2 degrees Celsius. This equates to keeping 80 per cent of known oil and gas reserves under the ground. Another way of looking at this is that the oil and mining companies are worth just 20 per cent of their book value. So how is it that these companies, with the blessing of governments across the world who want a slice of the action, keep looking for new reserves? Perhaps you don't need to look much further than the political donations made by the fossil-fuel industry. In 2020, of the US$110 million of oil-industry donations that flowed to the candidates fighting for seats in Congress or for the presidency itself, just over US$3 million went to Donald Trump, but Biden's US$1.5 million was not insignificant. The shadow network knows no political boundaries as it leads humanity into a mass greed-fuelled suicide.

The power, reach and dogged determination of the shadow network's army hit painfully home to us when, in February 2017, the newly installed President Trump picked Rex Tillerson to be his new Secretary of State, the second-most powerful office in the most powerful country in the world. Tillerson was the CEO of the oil major Exxon, at that time the 6th-largest company in the world, and one that stands accused of misleading the public about what it knew decades ago of the threat from climate change, for which it's now under investigation by the New York attorney general.

Tillerson was also a former chair of the American Petroleum Institute. He was the same 'red-faced angry' Rex Tillerson I wrote about in Chapter 6, who flew to Washington to tell Senator Richard Lugar that Section 1504 of the Dodd–Frank Act – the section that required every oil and mining company listed in the US to disclose all payments they make to the governments of countries they operate in, on a project-by-project basis – would damage the oil industry and put it at a competitive disadvantage. What he really meant was that it would seriously hamper companies' ability to bribe their way into getting hold of valuable new reserves. Because Section 1504 captured most of the world's major oil and mining companies, it was a truly groundbreaking anti-corruption law that would have made deals like the corrupt acquisition of OPL 245 virtually impossible to disguise.

Tillerson's elevation to high office coincided with Section 1504 being neutralized by the US Congress, one of the first of many progressive laws that Trump dumped. The oil industry had got what it wanted and what it had paid for with its hundreds of millions of dollars of political donations. Early indications are that the Biden administration will seek to give Section 1504 back its teeth, but it might be slow in coming given that Biden came to power at a time of domestic and global crisis.

By late 2020, Global Witness was home to over 100 investigators, campaigners, IT and communications experts, fundraisers, finance managers and administrators, with an annual budget of around £10 million. This was a far cry from our beginnings, but we were still a close-knit team, passionate about what we did and totally inter-dependent on each other. In addition to our London HQ, we had offices in Washington and Brussels and a representative in Beijing. We had always tried to avoid growth, but despite the manifest dis-advantages of it, growth is simply a reflection of the amount of work that needs to be done. Having started out with just the three of us and absolutely no money at all, it is humbling to see what Global Witness has become and is a testament to the amazingly talented and dedicated people I've had the privilege of working alongside. It's a cliché, but all Global Witness is is its people.

Fit, square-jawed and steady, Mike Davis has been with us for 20 years. He joined in 2002 and ran our small office in Phnom Penh until he was forced to close it three years later because of the mounting physical threats to our Khmer staff. Since then, he has worked on almost every campaign we have had, rising to become our director of campaigns in 2016 and then CEO in 2020. Under his leadership, Global Witness paused for reflection and examined the state of the world. It was a very different one than the one we started working on 25 years before. To try and tackle the terrible problems we faced required a new approach. 'It's the natural evolution from where Global Witness started – the nexus between corruption and environmental abuses and human-rights abuses,' Mike reflected.

All the campaigns we've worked on and the skills we've learned over the past quarter century have been a rehearsal for one of the biggest challenges we have taken on. The biggest challenge there is: the climate crisis. We have seen the shadow network grow and adapt to maintain the status quo. Much of our work going forward will be the same, uncovering abuses of power, the kind of opaque deal-making where the public interest is sacrificed to the private interests of people who are profiting from destruction. But now the stakes simply couldn't be higher. As Mike said, 'We need to get to the heart of the destructive economic model which has been baked in for decades – supported by powerful lobby groups and exploited by criminals.'

Our opening salvo wasn't long in coming.

Our first forays as investigators had taken us into remote and dangerous places to gather the information that we hoped would end a war. We were carried along the tortuous forest tracks of Ratanakiri in northeast Cambodia on the backs of motos; we got bogged down in mud-filled holes deeper than the 4x4 we were travelling in was high; and we clambered up malarial scrub-covered hillsides in the searing tropical heat to gaze down on remote logging camps through our binoculars. We still do carry out investigations like that – although drones now give a better view – but there's more than one way to skin a cat.

When Gavin Hayman was our executive director, he brought in a young computer expert called Sam Leon, a man possessed of the know-how to use computing power as an innovative investigative tool as well as a shrewd and mischievous campaigning nous to go with it. In turn, Sam brought in a data adviser called Louis Goddard, and it was Louis' work that made possible our December 2020 report, *Beef, Banks and the Brazilian Amazon.*

The Amazon rainforest is the largest tropical rainforest in the world. It absorbs an estimated 5 per cent of global CO_2 emissions. This rainforest spans nine countries, but 60 per cent of it lies in Brazil. Campaigners, men like Chico Mendes, indigenous leaders like Sonia Guajajara and an array of national and international NGOs, have for decades been fighting and dying to save the Amazon. Between 2005 and 2015, successive Brazilian governments managed to reduce the deforestation rate by 80 per cent; impressive in itself but still not enough. The pressures on the forest are immense and the most serious one comes from the beef industry, responsible for around 70 per cent of deforestation in the Amazon. The ranchers – the Ruralistas, as they're known – form a powerful political lobby and in 2018 their champion, Jair Bolsonaro, became Brazil's president. A far-right former paratrooper and unabashed fan of the brutal military dictatorship that ruled Brazil from the 1960s to the 1980s, Bolsonaro declared war on the country's forests and the indigenous peoples that have lived in them since the dawn of time and who are its best protectors.

The clearing of the rainforest has rocketed. A none-too-intelligent populist with gangster connections, Bolsonaro diluted laws that protected indigenous lands and human rights. Violence against these peoples was encouraged and law enforcement protecting the forest weakened. Brazil, already the most dangerous country in the world to be a land defender, rapidly got worse.

According to Brazilian scientist Carlos Nobre, if the Amazon forest loses around 40 per cent of its original extent, it will pass a tipping point and become dry savannah. At the current rates of deforestation this tipping point is just 20 to 30 years away: after that we cannot win the battle against climate change. But the ranchers are cutting increasing swathes of forest to satisfy their insatiable demand for more land, to satisfy in turn the increasing global demand for beef. But how to tackle a vastly powerful and violent industry backed by a racist and ideological government? It was a matter of deduction.

We knew there was little point in targeting the Brazilian government because we had no influence with them. Bolsonaro's predecessor President Temer had already dismissed our work as 'fake news', and he was a pussycat compared to Bolsonaro.

Following the trailblazing work by the local investigative-reporting organization Repórter Brasil, we turned our sights towards the beef industry and those that bankroll it, the banks and financiers of the US and Europe: our home territory. To do that we needed to rely on what we had always relied on: solid evidence. The Covid pandemic that had grounded our campaign teams did not impact the sophisticated data investigation carried out by Louis Goddard. We teamed up with Brazilian environmental group Imazon and got to work. Focusing on Pará, Brazil's second-largest state, which covers an area greater than France, Spain and Portugal put together, Louis began tapping away on his keyboard.

Louis combined three data sources: date-stamped satellite imagery obtained from the Brazilian Federal Space Agency, showing areas of deforestation; the state and federal land registries mapping farm boundaries; and then the best bit. 'To map the supply chain for beef in Pará, we used a technique called web scraping,' Louis told me. He developed a software program and downloaded more than 3 million documents on cattle movements, from birth to slaughter, from the state-government's website. 'It wasn't easy – we had to rent 20 different servers in a São Paulo data centre to get around restrictions preventing access to the site from outside Brazil – but we ended up with a complete picture of the cows' convoluted journey from farm to slaughterhouse.'

He fed this immense amount of data into a database which in turn was analysed to identify where deforestation overlapped with a farm boundary. The next job was to determine exactly when the deforestation occurred, and then to compare that to the sales made to beef companies. This would enable us to see whether those farms had violated their anti-deforestation commitments by sourcing beef from that ranch. 'The larger a company's pool of suppliers, the more deforestation risk is introduced into its supply chain,' Louis said. 'Developing a complex network of suppliers is a business decision and there's no excuse for failing to properly monitor it,' he continued. 'But Brazil's big beef companies continue to claim that using freely available cattle-sale documents to track their own purchases is impossible. This position keeps them in the good graces of major global financial institutions, which have underwritten billions of dollars in bonds to bankroll the firms' expansion.

'Our report showed that combining public data on deforestation, farms and cattle sales creates a powerful lens through which to inspect cattle supply chains in Pará, which could be extended to other Amazon states and to other commodities associated with deforestation, such as soy,' Louis continued. 'If we can do it, so can multinational companies with billions of pounds in revenue each year.'

The results of the investigation were shocking. In Pará alone, Brazil's three largest beef companies, JBS, Marfrig and Minerva, all of whom have a chequered history of corruption, between them directly and indirectly purchased cattle from over 4,000 ranches responsible for the destruction of around 100,000 hectares of forest, an area equivalent to 140,000 soccer pitches.

Auditors DNV-GL and Grant Thornton dutifully certified the companies' compliance with their pledges, despite their divergence from the facts. Meanwhile the companies' financial backers include household names like Deutsche Bank, Santander, Barclays, BNP Paribas, ING and HSBC. In fact, a 2019 Global Witness investigation exposed that over 300 banks had provided US$44 billion to just six of the world's most destructive agribusinesses. A glance at the record of any of these companies should have given the banks pause for thought.

From small beginnings and awash with government handouts, JBS, Marfrig and Minerva have become global giants. Together they slaughtered over 18 million cattle in 2017, and in 2018 their gross profit was over US$8 billion. JBS is the largest processor of beef and pork in the world, and one of its biggest food companies.

Like many companies in Brazil, in 2017 JBS and Marfrig were sucked into 'Lava Jato', the massive 'car-wash' corruption scandal that ripped through the top echelons of the country's political and business elite. One JBS executive admitted paying US$100 million in bribes to 1,829 politicians; it's hard to imagine how he found the time. The owner of Marfrig was forced to pay US$19 million in compensation for his company's bribery. Not wishing to miss the party, a Minerva slaughterhouse was investigated for bribing Ministry of Agriculture inspectors. The shadow network in action.

On the day of the report's release, Chris Moye was interviewed on BBC TV's flagship current-affairs programme, *Newsnight*. The first impact was immediate. Confronted with the role of British banks in deforesting the Amazon, Tory MP Neil Parish, chair of the House of Commons' Environment, Food and Rural Affairs Committee, said he would introduce an amendment to the new UK Environment Bill to include the role of financial institutions in deforestation. On 6 January 2021, he made good on his promise with an amendment that, if enacted, requires that financial institutions 'must not provide financial services for commercial enterprises engaging in the production, trade, transport or use of a forest risk commodity unless relevant local laws are complied with in relation to that commodity'.

It was a start.

These data-based investigations are now a critical part of Global Witness's arsenal, and in addition to the tech-based sleuthing by Sam and Louis, in 2020 we formed a new campaign team to tackle a rising new challenge, one of the most insidious forms of corruption: digital threats against democracy.

The role of the abuse of social media in manipulating elections became big news with both the Brexit referendum in the UK and Donald Trump's presidential campaign in 2016. An unholy alliance between Facebook and a shadowy UK company called Cambridge Analytica was immortalized in the documentary film *The Great Hack*. Cambridge Analytica had been involved in numerous election campaigns, including in India and Kenya, but the real scandal broke when a whistleblower exposed that, funded by both the pro-Trump and Brexit campaigns, they had harvested the personal information of around 87 million Facebook users in a massive data breach. They profiled these users and targeted the information to influence the outcome of both these elections, which together have arguably changed the face of politics. Brexit alone is one of the biggest geopolitical events since the Second World War.

The tactic used is known as political micro-targeting (PMT). Corruption has always been a threat to democracy, but here it was being targeted at the heart of the democratic process – and it doesn't get more dangerous than that. Social-media platforms like Facebook and Google trawl their users for information, scraping the digital seabed clean of every useful scrap. From the moment you enter a site, you are being watched. The site tracks how long you spend looking at different things as you scroll down a newsfeed; the more clicks navigating you through a site, the more 'likes' and 'dislikes' you flag, the more ads that you open, the more information is sent back to the vast and hungry databases of the tech giants and, inexorably, they build up a picture of what you're interested in, what you buy, where you live and, critically, what makes you angry. Divisions in society are reaching new levels and social media has proved to be a willing partner to those who seek to exacerbate that division; it has become a key tool of the shadow network. Anger spreads faster on social media than anything else, and the more traffic there is, the more advertising revenue the companies generate. It seems that this insatiable lust for this money trumps any other consideration. It really pays.

Global Witness's digital-threats team consists of Ava Lee, Rosie Sharpe, Naomi Hirst and Nienke Palstra. In one of their first projects, they decided to find out just how easy – or not – it is to use the shadow network's new super-weapon to sow the seeds of division. The goal was to obtain evidence to support our advocacy around the European Union's proposed Digital Services Act (DSA), which has the potential to govern how information can spread on social media, opening up tech companies' secretive algorithms and ad targeting for scrutiny. This would help crack down on political microtargeting and the spread of ads promoting hate speech and violence.

'The question we asked ourselves was, what was the most dangerous ad Facebook would accept? We wanted something that was so outrageous that we actually hoped it wouldn't work,' Rosie explained as the team embarked on their first investigation – the tech version of Ralph Kayser's exploits in New York and Karl's in Hamburg. The team settled on a subject painfully close to home.

One of the most dangerous aspects of Brexit was the future status of Northern Ireland. The Good Friday Agreement in 1998 had brought an end to almost 30 years of the Troubles, which had seen over 3,500 people killed by a combination of UK forces and both Protestant and Catholic paramilitary groups; the border between the Republic of Ireland and the North had become a militarized zone. Sectarian divisions in Northern Ireland are still raw and the rumps of the old terrorist groups, long immersed in organized crime as a lucrative sideline, are still dangerous. As Brexit neared, old wounds reopened, rhetoric flew and tensions rose around the possibility of a renewed hard border between north and south; whether or not Northern Ireland would be part of the EU Customs Union; perhaps even whether a United Ireland was finally on the cards, which would be anathema to die-hard Unionists.

'If you're looking to foment violence, then targeting to small numbers of people likely to be sympathetic to your ideas is key,' Rosie said. 'If you have to broadcast those ideas to everyone – as political parties had to do in the past via TV, radio and billboard ads – then you can't hope to push such messages as the majority of people have no time for such extremism.'

Just what would happen, the team thought, if during the tortuous Brexit negotiations between the UK and the EU, we posted a really inflammatory ad on Facebook, targeted at some of the most politicized people in Europe, split along this febrile sectarian divide?

The team set up two separate Facebook accounts as the vehicles for the deception they were about to carry out and began to navigate Facebook Ads Manager, the online interface that allows advertisers to select the audience they want to target according to their interests and, if you want, where they live. Facebook ads can zero in on a 1-km radius from a particular point, effectively a UK postcode minus the last two digits. In Belfast that could be BT13 3xx – the Shankill Road area.

Our main goal was to check Facebook's adherence to their own 'Community Standards', one of which is to prevent its platform being used to promote 'Violence and Incitement'. So how do Facebook's systems ensure this?

'Ads are subject to Facebook's ad review system,' their website states. It goes on to say that this system 'relies primarily on automated review' to check ads against Facebook's advertising policies: 'We use human reviewers both to improve and train our automated systems and, in some cases, to review specific ads. This review happens before ads start running.' Could an ad inciting violence and promoting hate speech make it through this verification process? If it does, then all the advertiser has to do is to pay the money, which can be as little as a dollar a day.

Working with an external design company we created a simple ad, a photograph of a burned-out car on an urban street. Emblazoned across the top of the photo was a simple message: 'Voting hasn't worked, take to the streets.' Its intent couldn't have been clearer. The next thing to do was to target the ad to the sections of society most likely to get inflamed.

'If you type, for example, Manchester, the Ad Manager auto-suggests relevant interest categories, like Manchester United or Manchester Metropolitan University,' Naomi explained. Based out of their homes during the Covid lockdown, Rosie, Naomi and Nienke shared their screens as they planned their strategy, much like real-life promoters of violence might do in the locked-down digital age. They decided to begin with a location. Around two-thirds of the killings during the Troubles had taken place near the graffiti-strewn 'Peace Walls' that divide many of the Republican and Loyalist areas in cities like Belfast: names like the Falls Road and the Shankill Road are indelibly stamped in the memory of those who lived through the Troubles.

'You can use postcodes to understand which areas are going to be predominantly faith-based communities,' Naomi continued. 'I was theoretically targeting messages to Protestants in certain locations, by postcode. Similarly, messages to Catholics would be skewed against Protestants in those same locations.' Sitting at her dining table, Rosie typed in 'Catholic' and a bunch of sub-categories popped up. Then she typed 'Pope' and up came a few more. Nienke tried 'Protestant'. Quite quickly the team arrived at what looked like the most inflammatory segmentation they could envisage. Combined with the nature of the ad, it could prove to be an explosive mix.

The team knew they were playing with fire. 'We got a bit giddy about it,' Naomi said. They were trying to put themselves into the mindset of someone who would do this; it was like trying to inhabit the mind of someone like Steve Bannon. It felt a bit dirty.

It also felt very serious and very scary to have those potentially destructive tools so easily at their fingertips. The team double-checked, triple-checked and sense-checked their methodology to make sure that these ads wouldn't actually go up. 'We made sure we had multiple eyes on all of this when we were taking things up and down, which speaks to our nervousness about what we were doing,' Nienke said.

The team also steered a neutral course through this potentially dangerous political minefield. 'We were trying not to be too glib about it. We can't demonize groups of people because we disagree with them,' Naomi said. 'Everyone's got a right to their political views and free speech.'

And so the team had to navigate a fine line. 'We needed to balance people's rights with the need to help clean up the internet from being a facilitator for discrimination and hate speech. We had to ensure we were not being calculating about people's different political opinions,' Naomi said. 'But at the same time, that's exactly what the Facebook ads allow.'

The time had come when the team was ready to submit the ad. They were proud of their creativity and their handiwork, but they also felt a little sick that they could have dreamed up an idea so obscene. If we carried through the project to its logical conclusion, then theoretically some of the most susceptible people on both sides of the sectarian divide in some of the most dangerous parts of Northern Ireland would soon be reading an ad exhorting them to violence. Some of them could share the ad with their networks, and some of those networks could well include members of the paramilitaries. There would be rising levels of anger and fear – emotions that travel further and faster than any other traffic on social media. Surely such an ad wouldn't make it through Facebook's verification process?

In January 2021, their preparations complete, Rosie, Naomi and Nienke signed into their computers and shared their screens. From their separate homes, they looked at each other and then back to the Facebook Ads Manager, the online application form fully completed with the inflammatory photo attached. If such an ad were published, would it help stoke the already simmering anger, adding to the risk of rekindling the violence, to nudge people over the edge? Donald Trump's calls to storm the Capitol in Washington, DC certainly showed the potential.

Rosie looked at the others questioningly and they nodded. She pressed send.

When Simon, Charmian and I founded Global Witness all those years ago we were driven by anger, but we weren't very righteous. Our anger was directed at the perpetrators and enablers of corrupt and destructive deals that impacted literally millions of people, yet who were able to amass enormous wealth and whose 'achievements' and position meant they were revered by our perverse society, their greed and lust for power amply rewarded. Well sod that.

Our strategy was always to try to reach these people – these individuals – to expose them, shame them, hopefully to right a few wrongs, and we fully intended to enjoy doing it. One of the things that has always given me a warm feeling inside is that many of the subjects of our investigations simply don't understand what drives us. Is it our politics? Have we been funded by some national or corporate rival? Are we the tool of the intelligence services of the UK, France or elsewhere? Or, as we're most often accused of being, are we just part of a George Soros-inspired plot? We've been accused of them all. The fact that these people don't understand why we do what we do is one of their greatest weaknesses, and one of our greatest strengths. I don't mind putting it here, because they won't believe me anyway.

We wanted to do the right thing, and we wanted to wind up the bad guys on the way. For a quarter of a century, we have fought against the odds and thoroughly enjoyed giving the corrupt a really hard time.

And we're not about to stop now.

Now I really had better get back to work.

ACKNOWLEDGEMENTS

Without meeting Simon Taylor and Charmian Gooch, my partners in crime and best friends for the past thirty years, there would have been no Global Witness and no story to tell.

One of the greatest privileges about Global Witness has been working alongside some of the most brilliant people imaginable. The list would be too long to name them all here, but I want to thank everyone who worked for and with Global Witness over the years, and those who have so generously funded us, for helping to make the dream come true, for helping to change the world a little for the better, and for bringing light into what could be a grim job, given the subject matter. It's been a gas!

I owe a massive debt of gratitude to all those who agreed to be interviewed for this book, and for being part of the story. Some remain in sensitive environments and wish to remain anonymous, but those I can thank include:

Johnny Miller, for his memories of 1995 Phnom Penh and his enthusiasm for our work then and this book now. Without Tim Rieser's incisive support on Capitol Hill, our campaign to bring down the Khmer Rouge may have fallen at the first hurdle. We, and almost everyone working on human rights, owe him a massive debt of gratitude.

Allan Thornton, for his recall of those pre-Global Witness days when he provided moral and financial support, not to mention the germ of the idea of what became the campaign on blood diamonds. Aidan McQuade, whose experience of the civil war in Angola has been so enlightening; Charmian's fellow campaigners on the trail of blood diamonds, Alex Yearsley and Corinna Gilfillan; Dianna Melrose, the FCO insider with a fantastically helpful photographic memory; Martin Rapaport of the Rapaport Group and Andrew Coxon of De Beers, for their candid recollections of the dark days of the blood diamond trade, and Ed Zwick for his illuminating insights.

Silas Siakor, who relived his brilliant and horribly risky investigations in Charles Taylor's Liberia; Alice Blondel, for reminding me about the finer details of our detective work across the Mano River region and her amazing advocacy at the United Nations; the late Walter Mapelli, who enthralled me with his memories as a young local prosecutor interrogating Ukrainian Mafia kingpin and arms trafficker Leonid Minin; and Filip Verbelen at Greenpeace International, who told me the inside story of how he helped divert the *Rainbow Warrior* to intercept 'blood timber' imports to France.

Gavin Hayman, Anthea Lawson and Rob Palmer for their (often hilarious) recollections of meetings with bankers and international law enforcement agencies; Maud Sarlième of Sherpa for filling in the gaps about the French investigations into Teodorin Obiang; Woo Lee of the US Department of Justice's Kleptocray Initiative, who gave me valuable insights from the time of Obiang's trial; and Tom Mayne, whose anecdotes from the numerous investigations we talked about litter this book.

Dan Balint-Kurti and Leigh Baldwin, two of our star sleuths who did so much to expose BSGR's 'Deal of the Century', for filling the gaps in my knowledge and for reminding me of the roller-coaster investigation that it was.

Diarmid O'Sullivan, the truffle hunter, and Barnaby Pace who, along with our compatriots Nick Hildyard of The Corner House, Lanre Suraju of HEDA and Antonio Tricarico of Re:Common, explained the enormous complexity of the OPL 245 case to me, and to former Detective Superintendent Jonathan Benton of the Metropolitan Police, who was able to tell me a little of his probes into the deal.

Ellie Nichol, who told me about how she arrived at the idea of the No Safe Havens campaign; Chido Dunn and Ava Lee for their anecdotes; Rachel Davies of Transparency International UK; old Global Witness hand Rosie Sharpe, and to Ralph Kayser and Karl, who recalled their surreal undercover investigations charming unwitting lawyers into telling them how to launder a corrupt politician's money, and luxury yacht builders into telling them what they could spend it on.

Olesia Plokhii, who recounted her horrific experience when she witnessed the murder of our former colleague Chut Wutty; Billy Kyte and Ben Leather, who talked me through their investigations in Honduras; Chris Moye and Alex Soros for recapturing our journey to Saweto in the Peruvian Amazon; Sonia Guajajara for her insights into the threats against indigenous defenders in Brazil, and to Felipe Milanez for his reflections on the dire situation there.

Louis Goddard, Sam Leon, Nienke Palstra and Naomi Hirst all helped explain to my technologically befuddled brain the evolution and amazing impacts of our data investigations work.

I owe a special debt of thanks to Aryeh Neier, who told me why he took the decision to support us all those years ago, and to George Soros for his reflections, his immense support over the years and for writing the foreword to this book. I especially want to thank Pilar Palaciá and her wonderful staff at the Rockefeller Foundation's Bellagio Center for providing me with the space and the peace to begin this book.

I'm indebted to all those who read various drafts and who expressed invaluable enthusiasm for the project, and their subtle and sometimes not so subtle insights into how I could do it better, in particular Jane Brennan, Mike Davis, Caroline Digby and Philippe Le Billon. Philippe also introduced me to two of his students at the University of British Columbia, Isabella Pepe and Nico Jimenez, who volunteered to become my (unpaid) research assistants and helped dig up various hard-to-find facts and figures to help refresh my dim memories of times before they were born. I'm also very grateful for the wise advice of Global Witness's in-house lawyer Nicola Namdjou, who helped with the legal read.

I can't thank my agent Eugenie Furniss enough, not just for having faith in a rookie writer, but for having the idea about exactly how to tell this story, and to her colleague Alexandra Kordas for working so hard on my behalf; to the team at Monoray: my publisher Jake Lingwood, for being persuaded by Eugenie to take me on, and for his guidance, editing suggestions and patience throughout the writing of this book, to Alex Stetter for her skilful editing, Monica Hope for her insightful copy-edit and Simon Heilbron for the legal read.

I owe most to my darling wife Breda, who has stuck by me through both the good and the challenging times at Global Witness, and who has been my inspiration and rock since I embarked on this book, and not least for her patience as I added being an author to my day job. Without her insights and innumerable read-throughs, suggestions, edits, creative ideas, unshakable support and her love, I simply couldn't have written it.

Finally, I want to thank all those people around the world who've worked with us and to whom this book is dedicated. It is their knowledge, courage and inspiration that has made Global Witness's work possible, and is really the only reason to have started the thing in the first place.

INDEX

How to Help Global Witness's Investigations

By reading this book, you're already helping Global Witness to investigate and expose the activities of Very Bad People.

Global Witness is now directly confronting the global economic systems – and the Very Bad People behind them – that are profiting from and consequently perpetuating the climate crisis, including the fossil-fuel companies whose rampant corruption and unceasing search for more oil, gas and coal are threatening us all, and those whose greed is deforesting the last great tropical rainforests and threatening the lives of anyone that gets in the way. Our goal is a more sustainable, just and equal planet.

If you would like to support our work, you can do so at:

www.globalwitness.org/en/donate/

development@globalwitness.org

Or you can contact me directly at: palley@globalwitness.org